P9-EJJ-564

THE OLD TESTAMENT
SINCE
THE REFORMATION

EMIL G. KRAELING

SCHOCKEN BOOKS · NEW YORK

First published in 1955

First SCHOCKEN edition 1969

Copyright © 1955 by Emil G. Kraeling

Library of Congress Catalog Card No. 70–83671

Manufactured in the United States of America

Published by arrangement with Harper & Row, Publishers

CONTENTS

PREFACE

THE studies included here were undertaken in the desire of garnering the fruits of modern theological history for our subject. Only passing attention can be given to the history of Old Testament scholarship, for we seek something more fundamental: the thought concerning the authority and meaning of the Old Testament for the Christian. Matters of purely antiquarian interest must, therefore, fall by the wayside. The views of many who have dealt in some way with our theme are rehearsed in detail. Our desire has been to make the full weight and range of the standpoints reported discernible. That of course necessitated selectivity. But the information here assembled should give the reader an adequate picture of the more recent phases of what may well be called "the greatest inner-Christian debate"

INTRODUCTION

THE first book on the Old Testament to arouse my curiosity was that of James Orr,[1] which stood on the shelves of the library in the manse in which I grew up. I was attracted by the bright red colour and gold lettering to finger this volume and dip into its contents from which, though they were far above my head, I gathered this much, that there were some people in the world who chopped up the books of Moses and the prophets and considered much of Old Testament history as composed of myth and legend. It was evident that Dr. Orr was worried about the truth of such critical theories and recoiled from the consequences they had for the Christian faith. He sought to discredit them by showing how they cancelled each other, and he held that archaeology was providing wonderful confirmation for a more conservative view. The subject troubled me enough, however, to wish to get to the bottom of it.

A vast change has come over the world since Orr's book was written. There no longer is any great excitement about the "higher criticism". The barriers he and others sought to raise up against it have been abandoned. Universally it is conceded that Old Testament scholarship has given us a new, realistic and dependable picture of the way in which the literary materials of the Old Testament arose and of what they mean historically.[2] While the future may bring many corrections, nothing that could be adduced along critical lines could change the situation very much in principle. The passing of the debate over the higher criticism still leaves us with the real problem of the Old Testament: *should it have any authority in the Christian Church and if so how is that authority to be defined?*

Once one has awakened to commanding importance of this question one will be able to see that it runs through the whole of Christian history with a scarlet thread.[3] Yea, more: one can see that much of the difference in theologies springs from the extent to which they build Old Testament ideas or impulses into the primitive Christian patterns. And the latter, one may discover, differ in themselves already because of the degree of Old Testament influence received. The Old Testament problem, therefore, is not just one of many. It is the master problem of theology. And even for those who regard the first half of the question, as formulated above, beyond debate, the second half still remains in force. All theology that operates in any way with biblical heritage hangs in the air until it is settled.

Informed discussion of the Old Testament problem requires some insight into its history. A particular importance attaches to the genesis of the problem in early Christianity and to the diversity of attitudes and viewpoints concerning it that are revealed there. The relation of the Testaments is commonly studied from the angle: "the Old Testament in the New". The question is not: does early Christianity have strong links with the Old Testament? It is rather: do these links with the Old Testament merely represent the egg-shell out of which Christianity emerged, and which therefore may be discounted? Or, if one refuses to accept that question, then it is this: what part of the Old Testament heritage received by the early Christians is permanently binding for Christianity? We hope to deal with the beginnings of the problem in another volume [4] and can only stress their importance in passing here.

Our concern in the present book is with the thought on the subject of Christianity and the Old Testament since the Reformation. At that juncture attention became centered on the Scriptures. The humanists had paved the way for a better understanding of these writings than was possible through the Latin translation. Reuchlin had advocated the study of Greek and Hebrew at the universities and had even published the first grammar of Hebrew in 1506. Erasmus had brought out the first Greek New Testament in 1516, and the first Rabbinic Bible appeared in 1516/17. The tools for more precise Biblical study and translations into modern languages were thus at hand when the Reformation began in 1517. How the Reformers reacted to the Old Testament heritage must thus be of great interest. They had to take positions with respect to it, and their thought remains valuable to this day.

Chapter One

LUTHER AND THE OLD TESTAMENT

IN Roman Catholic Europe of the Middle Ages Scripture had not enjoyed as influential a role as it had in the Church of the first six centuries. Theoretically, the Bible was the supreme authority (especially for Duns Scotus and Occam), but in practice it did not function as such. Even the guardianship of the Canon was not exercised very rigorously,[1] for apocryphal pieces like the Epistle to the Laodiceans and Fourth Ezra could be carried along in the Latin New Testament without compunction, and the Old Testament contained materials later rejected by Catholicism at Trent. The Church, furthermore, had come to set up an accumulating "tradition" as a second principle of authority, and by means of it neutralized Scripture authority wherever it chose. As a devout son of the Catholic Church, Luther did not at first deny the authority of tradition. As late as the Leipzig disputation with Eck in 1519, he still held fast to it. But soon afterwards he took the fatal step and set aside a tradition that put to nought the Word of God (Mark 7: 13 f.). The Protestant Church now became a necessity and a reality, and this Church apparently had the principle of the Bible as sole authority put right into its cradle.

Influenced as he was in his early years by the scholastic belief in a fourfold sense of Scripture,[2] Luther did not at first see the problem of the unity of the contents of Scripture, which would at once have raised the Old Testament problem. At the time when he gave his first exegetical course at the University of Wittenberg, he had already devoted much effort to biblical study. In his grasp of the Bible as a whole, as revealed in his early lectures on the Psalms, he had, according to Holl,[3] only been equalled by men like Tertullian or Origen. But he had never doubted that the Bible in all its parts has the same meaning, for the Holy Spirit, who, as Catholic doctrine that he did not question taught, stands behind the Bible, naturally must

be consistent in the intention of making known God's redemptive purpose. Hence, Luther in those days could read Paul's
doctrine of justification and Christological interpretations into
the Psalms without observing that he was doing violence to
their plain meaning.

The assumption of a definite, clear and consistent meaning of
Scripture as a whole then becomes for Luther a cardinal point
when he begins to teach that the Bible is the sole authority.[4]
If there were any doubt as to what the Bible meant to teach,
how could faith have a firm foundation, and how could man
turn to the Bible?[5] In the disputation with Eck, Luther pointed
out that it was not enough to have the immediate context of
a biblical passage in mind in interpreting it; one must have the
totality of the Bible before one's eyes to appraise properly the
sense and bearing of a given passage. He once advised Spalatin
to read the whole Bible from beginning to end—then only, he
asserts, can one interpret with success.[6] "If one pauses at some
individual passage and seeks help for its interpretation in the
patristic books, one has nothing but sorry patchwork in one's
hands." In the controversy over indulgences Luther was forced
to maintain the right of individual Scripture interpretation over
against the collective authority of the Church. He did this not
by affirming his personal qualifications, but rather by teaching
the clarity of Scripture; "no clearer book has ever been
written." By that he did not mean that it was devoid of obscurities. He himself had often enough spoken of its profundity
and of the need of gradually growing in the understanding of it.
What he meant was that in the things that mattered for man's
salvation the Bible was absolutely clear. The principle of using
clear passages to explain obscure ones (which he followed, e.g.,
in his dispute with Zwingli over the words "This is My body",
giving heed to I Cor. 10: 16f.) naturally flowed from this.

But after Luther had emancipated himself from the scholastic
doctrine of the fourfold sense of Scripture and had begun to
apply his principle of literal interpretation more consistently,
he became increasingly conscious of the diversity of the contents of the Bible.[7] He saw that even within the New Testament there was not the full unanimity that, in view of the
doctrine of inspiration, really ought to be there. Catholic
theologians were not slow in pointing out the passages that dis-

agreed with his understanding of the message of Paul and which, in the light of the principle that the Bible cannot contradict itself, had somehow to be harmonized with Paul's statements. But Luther was unable to accept such sophistries. When pressed, he chose the alternative of differentiating between elements of the Bible having greater and lesser authority, or such having an importance for all time, and such having an importance only for a time that is past.[8] "The question is," he once says—

"What is the Word of God for me?" One must deal carefully with Scripture. The Word of God came about in diverse ways from the beginning and one must not only see whether it is God's Word and whether God spoke it, but, much more, to whom it is spoken and whether it is intended for thee or for another. Then there is a partition as between summer and winter. God spoke a great deal to David and told him to do this and that. But it is no concern of mine. Nor is it spoken to me. He can speak to me if He wishes to have it so. You must look at the Word that concerns you, that is spoken to you and does not concern another. There are two kinds of "Word" in the Scripture. One does not concern me or have aught to do with me. The other has to do with me, and following that which has to do with me I may boldly go forward and rely on it as on a strong rock. If it does not deal with me, I must stand still. The false prophets rush in and say, dear people, this is God's Word. It is true, we cannot deny it, but we are not the people to whom He speaks.

It is apparent, then, that Luther, in his own spontaneous and original thinking, shies away from unilateral biblicism. Not "the letter that killeth" is supreme, but the message of salvation through Jesus Christ that Paul preached is his principle of authority. The Bible as a whole is only the Word of God when and to the extent that he can view it as in harmony with or expressive of that message. At the time of the writing of his prefaces to his translations of the biblical books he seems to have realized more clearly than before that the gospel is not originally a book but an oral message. The writing down of it was already an ailing in the spirit of the early Church; it became necessary because of the perversions of it that were being spread abroad at that time. The Bible as a whole is not an end in itself—it is merely the vehicle of a certain content. And the thing with which the Bible is concerned is to make evident "the great fire of God's love for us".[9] This love, of course, is expressed in the gospel of Jesus Christ. He once refutes an opponent who harps on Scripture: "You base your claim on the slave, i.e., Scripture, and not on the whole of it or its most excellent portion. I leave this slave to you. I invoke the Lord who is the King of Scripture." Yea, Luther would undertake to draw on the Psalms, Isaiah, and the same Holy Spirit and fashion as good a New Testament as the apostles have written.[10]

He finds that all the proper sacred books agree in this respect, "that they all preach and treat of Christ (*Christum treiben*). Furthermore, this is the right yardstick wherewith to criticize all books—whether they treat of Christ or not. For all Scripture exhibits Christ (Rom. 3: 21), and Paul will know nothing but Christ (I Cor. 2: 2)."[11] This emphasis on the contents makes Luther supremely indifferent with respect to formal matters such as the authorship of the biblical books. "That which does not treat of Christ is not yet apostolic though Peter or Paul taught it. And again, that which preaches Christ would be apostolic though Judas, Annas, Pilate or Herod taught it. Christ alone and nothing but the Crucified and none other do we recognize for our Master. Paul would not have us believe him or believe an angel (Gal. 1: 8, 12), unless Christ dwell in him."[12]

It is important to discern that Luther is forced to discriminate between more and less authoritative areas even in the New Testament. From the immutably fixed centre of the gospel as preached by Paul (who, it must not be forgotten, affirms the unity of his faith with that of the Jerusalem Church), he came to evaluate the various writings in a surprisingly free manner. His observations were so shocking to subsequent Lutheran orthodoxy that they were consigned to oblivion until Semler (following Wetstein) again called attention to them in 1764.[13]

In effect, Luther puts certain New Testament writings into a primary and others into a secondary position. Paul, with his Epistles to the Romans, Galatians, and Ephesians, naturally stands in the foreground. The Gospel of John and I John, I Peter and Acts also meet with his favour. In the latter book

he overlooks the "Catholic" leaven and finds a demonstration
of the manner in which the Holy Spirit came to men through
the hearing of the gospel and not of the law. He did not
esteem the Synoptic Gospels so highly because he finds them
dealing more with Christ's miracles and with the works and
fruits of faith than with the real Christian message. His
strictures against the Epistle of James[14] are well known—he
regards it as late owing to its dependence on Pauline and
Petrine sayings. Jude he considers secondary and based on
II Peter; the author of Hebrews, too, speaks like a later disciple
of the apostles (2: 3), and was not Paul, as the ecclesiastical
tradition claimed. Revelation seemed to him rather close to
II Esdras (where the Vulgate, indeed, puts it), and not truly
apostolic or even prophetic. In his Bible translation he even
puts Hebrews, James and Jude at the end of the Epistles and
before Revelation, thus in effect establishing a group of books
of secondary authority. We can therefore see that Luther not
only disregards the doctrine of Scripture-inspiration (at least
for a portion of the New Testament), but is in effect, though not
in method, verging rather close to one of the positions of
Marcion, who had set up ten Epistles of Paul and Luke's
Gospel as authoritative.

It seemed essential to us to set forth Luther's general attitude
on Scripture before entering upon the problem that is our particular concern. We may now turn to the latter and ask, Where
does this leave the Old Testament?

We have seen that Luther, at the very beginning of his career
and so long as he still held to the scholastic idea of the fourfold
sense of Scripture, was full of the thought that the gospel was
to be found in the Old Testament. Under the influence of his
new principle of exclusively literal interpretation, he later modified that as evidenced by the preface to the Psalms in his Bible
translation. Nevertheless, the problem of how to relate the Old
Testament to the gospel and thus give the Old Testament a
value for the Christian occupied him. Following the New
Testament writers and the Church Fathers from Justin Martyr
on, he believed that the Old Testament contained individual
utterances or sections in which there is anticipation of the
Christian message. How could this be otherwise when the same
Holy Ghost who had given the New Testament had also given

the Old Testament? One could not, of course, expect the Holy
Ghost to impart the full truth to men on the Old Testament
stage of existence; pedagogical considerations made it possible
or even necessary for Him to give teachings not yet up to the
evangelical level. But here and there the evangelical element
breaks forth like the sun through the clouds. These passages of
the Old Testament have a high importance. Luther can, on
occasion, demand that the whole Old Testament is to be interpreted in the light of the gospel; he can compare it to a testa-
mentary letter of Christ that is only to be understood properly
from the standpoint attained after the death of Christ. In
speaking of Matthew 22: 40, he says:

> The Lord therewith shows us the right technique to interpret
> Moses and the prophets and gives us to understand that Moses
> with all his stories and parables points to him, pertains to Christ
> and means him—namely, Christ is the point in the circle about
> which the whole circle is drawn, and whoever faces toward him
> belongs in it. For he is the point in the middle of the circle and
> all the stories of Holy Writ, if they are rightly regarded, refer to
> Christ.[14]

From a psychological angle, one feels that Luther is really
setting up a defence-mechanism. Behind this reasoning stands
the fear that the Old Testament interpreted alone—without
regard to the gospel—has a natural drift leading in another
direction. Since he cannot emancipate himself from the New
Testament Scripture proof, he is forced to emulate early
Christian example in resolutely seizing the Old Testament and
subjecting it to Christian purpose. But it is one thing to set up
such a principle and another thing to carry it out in detailed
exegesis. In his early study of the Psalms he could do it on the
basis of a sincere false assumption and with the help of the
scholastic doctrine of interpretation. Can it be done on the
theory of an alone legitimate literal interpretation?

Since Luther was entirely dominated by Paul's understanding
of the difference between the way of the law and the gospel of
grace,[15] he naturally looked at the Old Testament by and large
as representing the way of the law. The late Jewish view of the
Old Testament, it must be recalled, had put the emphasis on

Moses and the law, and Paul had imbibed and shared that view. In thinking about the law Luther yields to highly enlightened viewpoints. The early Church had emphasized the moral law of the Old Testament as distinct from the bygone ceremonial law also found in that work. Luther found it difficult to disengage the moral from the ceremonial element in Old Testament law. Even in the Decalogue there is a ceremonial ordinance—the Sabbath commandment, and a commandment that is no longer important in Christian countries: the prohibition of graven images. It becomes clear to him that the entire Mosaic law is an indivisible whole, intended for a definite nation of a definite time. He conceives of it as essentially parallel to other bodies of national law, such as the *Sachsenspiegel* (a collection of laws in vogue among the Saxons, made about A.D. 1200 and widely quoted in Luther's time). Hence, Moses is the *"Sachsenspiegel* of the Jews"*. Non-Jewish people can simply substitute their own laws for the Mosaic law.

He makes an interesting distinction, however, between what he calls "natural laws" that forbid sins we understand as such and the "Levitic laws" that are without a discernible moral basis. As the designation "natural" shows, he does not consider this moral law as requiring supernatural revelation, but rather looks upon it as "written in everybody's heart". The significance of the Decalogue he finds in this—that these "natural laws are nowhere so finely and properly stated". But even this moral law has lost its importance as a way of salvation (cf. Romans 3: 28). It can, however, serve the useful purpose of a yardstick with which one may gratefully determine "how far the Holy Spirit has brought us with his sanctification, and in how far we are still deficient, so that we do not become too self-confident and think that we now have done everything, and that we may thus continually grow in sanctification and increasingly become a new creature in Christ".[16] The office of Moses, he argues, was to make the Jewish people conscious of sin and thereby to pave the way for redemption. Essentially he looks at the remainder of the Old Testament as merely continuing that function.

What now are the other books of the prophets and the narratives? Answer: nothing else than what Moses is. For they all carry on Moses' office and ward off the false prophets so that they don't lead the people to (rely on) works(!) but let them stay in the right office of Moses and knowledge of the law. And hold fast to this, that by the right meaning of the law they keep the people in (the consciousness of) their own unworthiness and drive toward Christ as Moses does. And they exhibit a twofold example, of those who have Moses right and who don't have him right, and the reward and punishment of both. Thus the prophets are nothing else than handlers and witnesses of Moses and his office that through the law they may bring everyone to Christ.[17]

We likewise find Luther affirming his rejection of the applicability of the Mosaic law as a whole over against the enthusiasts who claimed that Christians must obey the Old Testament also.

Therefore say to these same enthusiasts: Leave Moses and his people together. They are a thing of the past and none of my business. I hear the word that concerns me. We have the gospel. Christ says: "Go ye and preach the gospel, not only to the Jews . . . but to all creatures" . . . These words include me . . . for I am one of all creatures. If Christ had not added: "preach to all creatures", I would not bother about it and would take the same attitude toward it I now take toward Moses. I pay no attention to him, he does not concern me.[18]

It is quite obvious, if one views the Old Testament primarily as preaching the law and views its law as being primarily a Jewish national concern, or an illustration of what reason can produce without the aid of revelation, that one is very close to robbing it of most of its value for the Christian.[19] While Luther in the Antinomian controversy shrank back from the consequences of his earlier position, this was due more to practical considerations than to better theological insight, and both he and his opponent Agricola may well be accused of veering away from the true evangelical idea of faith in this debate.[20]

If Luther felt free to evaluate the New Testament canon on the basis of his central principle, it is to be expected that he would feel even more free to express independent opinions on the Old Testament writings. He valued Genesis highly and, because it praised faith and because of the use Paul makes of it,

he considered it an almost evangelical book.[21] The rest of the
Pentateuch is, of course, so much concerned with the law that
it could not have much appeal for him. He makes little use of
the historical books. In Judges he finds excellent heroes and
deliverers portrayed. He once refers to the Books of the Kings
as the Gazetteer of the Jews, in which the Jews are well described,
and places its credibility above that of Chronicles. Essentially,
therefore, he looks upon this as patriotic historiography rather
than as sacred literature. Esther is offensive to him as a
Judaizing document, and of Ezra-Nehemiah he says that it
"Estherizes and Mordecaizes" in like manner.

He valued the prophets chiefly for their Messianic prophecy,
but in the latter he saw primarily the special activity of the
Holy Ghost. Isaiah 53 is a witness of Christ that stands so
bright that even in the New Testament, apart from Paul, there
is hardly a passage to equal it. He puts Daniel among the
prophets and considers him the most excellent one next to
Isaiah because of his supposed prophecies of the death of Christ.
But otherwise he does not have much use for the prophets.
Their prophesying of future things he considers of no benefit to
faith; indeed, such prophesying "is almost one of the least of
gifts; yea, occasionally it comes from the devil". He finds them
prophesying concerning kings and worldly events, wherein, he
says, they often erred. He recognized the fact of literary
dependence when he says the earlier prophets studied Moses,
and the later prophets previous ones, and implies that occasionally hay, straw and wood got into their teachings along with
silver and gold. This amounts to saying that there is a great deal
of material in the prophets which is of no value for us. Concerning the prophetic books he was willing to assume redactional
activity by other hands in arrangement of material—expressly
so in the case of Hosea, Isaiah and Jeremiah.

Luther had a particular fondness for the Psalter.[22] He had
given his first exegetical course on that book, and its phraseology (notably Psalm 31: 2) had helped him to discover the true
meaning of the New Testament gospel as expressed in Romans
1: 17.[23] He gave utterance to his affection for it in classic
fashion in his preface to his translation of it in the edition of
1531 (partially quoted below). But it is to be noted how far he
has progressed in his understanding of that book since his early

grappling with it. There is little left of the "Christological" interpretation or of any supernaturalism. His view of it seems to be entirely human, for he now looks upon the Psalms as expressing the living reactions of the Old Testament saints in the concrete situations of life. Over against the Catholic fondness for hagiography, he points out that the Psalter does not tell of the works of the saints but reports their *words*—how they spoke with God and prayed to God. "Yea, it enables us to look into their hearts and see what thoughts they had and how their hearts reacted to all the happenings, exigencies and necessities of existence." He compares the human heart to a ship at sea driven by winds blowing at different times from all four directions:

Fear and worry over that which is to come, sorrow and sadness over present evil, hope and pride of future happiness, assurance and joy of things presently enjoyed—such are the winds that blow and teach the tongue to speak and open the heart to pour out its contents. In the Psalms the chief thing is such a speaking in all manner of stormy winds. Where does one find a finer word of gladness than the psalms of praise and thanksgiving have? There you look into the heart of all the saints as into lovely, blessed gardens, yea as into heaven; you perceive fine, lovely flowers grow therein in the shape of all manner of beautiful happy thoughts toward God and His kindness. Again, where do you find more profound, more sorrowful, more miserable words of sadness, than in the psalms of lamentation? There you again look into the heart of all saints, as into death, yea as into hell. How black and dark it is there from all manner of sorrowful seeing of the wrath of God. And so also where they speak of fear and hope they use such words that no artist could paint the fear and hope, and no Cicero or other orator form them in such a way. And as already said the best thing is that they speak such words to God and with God, which has the result that a twofold seriousness and life are in the words. For where one merely speaks to men of such things, it does not come out of the heart so deeply, does not burn, live and penetrate to such an extent. Hence it comes about that the Psalter is the booklet of all saints and everybody in whatsoever situation he may be finds Psalms and sayings in it that rhyme with his affairs, and seem to him as though they were thus formulated just for his sake. So that he himself could not formulate them better or find them or wish for them.

This is almost a modern psychological understanding of the Psalter, though coupled with a belief in the validity and authority of its words which does not accord well with such a point of view.

The Book of Job is linked by Luther with those Psalms which deal with the trials of the pious.[24] The pious sufferer is an example of that trial which Christ later was to endure—that of extreme forsakenness of God. He does not consider it strictly historical, but rather a poetic creation. The three books ascribed to Solomon stand apart from the main stream. Proverbs is chiefly concerned with the individual and his private existence and is a *liber oeconomicus*. Ecclesiastes, whose direct authorship by Solomon he doubts, (in one instance even conceding the possibility of its being edited and assembled by Sirach), Luther first viewed as inculcating the lesson of Matthew 6: 34 (take no thought for the morrow, learn the uselessness of all human undertaking and leave everything to God). Later he looked upon it as chiefly addressed to those in authority, counselling them to fear God and endure bravely amid the trials of their position; it is a sort of *liber politicus*. In Song of Songs, which he also derives from Solomon only in a secondary way, he allegorizes the bride as referring to Solomon's kingdom. Where there is obedience and good government God dwells and kisses His beloved bride with the kiss of His mouth, viz., His Word. A poem of Luther's own time by the poet Theuerdank, in which a bride symbolizing his kingdom is brought to the Emperor Maximilian, seems to have influenced his interpretation here.

In his arrangement of the Old Testament books in his Bible translation, Luther, as in the case of the New Testament, follows a literary classification. He has three divisions: (1) historical books, under which heading he put "the law" and the "former prophets" (with Ruth after Judges), the Chronicler's work (I and II Chronicles, Ezra, Nehemiah), and Esther; (2) the didactic books (Job, Psalms and the three Solomonic books); (3) the prophetic books (i.e., the "latter Prophets" of the Hebrew arrangement, but with each of the twelve "Minor" Prophets counted separately, and with Lamentations put after Jeremiah, and Daniel put after Ezekiel). Luther heeded the Jewish tradition, however, in eliminating those books which were not found in the collection of the synagogue. Since in the

Vulgate I and II Maccabees stand after Malachi, he put the other rejected books (except I and II Esdras which he discarded entirely) with them, thus setting up a whole division which, taking a cue from Jerome, he called The Apocrypha.

That the arrangement of books in the Protestant Old Testament translations thus inaugurated (for the Authorized Version followed suit) possesses certain advantages is undeniable. But one might wish that Luther had accepted Carlstadt's suggestion and had gone back to the Palestinian Jewish arrangement which graded the books in three groups of decreasing authority.[25] This would have put troublesome books like Daniel, Chronicles, Ezra, Nehemiah, Esther, Song of Songs and Ecclesiastes in the third division and hence on a distinctly lower level than others.

Luther is a whole cosmos of thought and impulses. Ecclesiastical responsibility, combat with extremists, reluctance to depart very far from the common ground established in the early Christian creeds, the impossibility of thinking through all Christian problems, prevented him from following up his many original insights and personal leanings. Indeed, many statements can be adduced from his works in which he emphasizes Scripture authority in a manner that seems inconsistent with the knowledge he had attained. One definitely feels that if it were not for the use of the Old Testament made in the New Testament Luther might have veered farther in the Marcionitic direction.[26] If he had realized as clearly as we are able to do to-day that the Messianic prophecy of the Old Testament does not actually predict the life of Christ or the redemption brought by Him in as clear and direct a manner as the New Testament writers and the early Fathers believed, the revelation of the Old Testament would probably have shrunk to purely historical significance in his eyes. Human values of a spiritual or moral sort alone would have remained. The epochal thing about Luther and the Scriptures is really that he subordinated them to what he conceived to be the Christian gospel.[27]

Chapter Two

ZWINGLI AND CALVIN AND THE OLD TESTAMENT

UNLIKE Luther, who was concerned with the individual's certainty of salvation, the Reformed theologians placed their emphasis on the Christian life flowing forth from such certainty. They appreciated the importance of creating a social and political environment favourable for Christian nurture. A Christian state run according to Christian principles was to them an objective worth striving for. The New Testament did not provide a sufficient background for their ecclesiastical and political practice,[1] for the early Christians had been a minority group in a hostile world. One had to go back to the Old Testament to find a community run on such a basis as they envisioned, and hence the Reformed leaders had a particular interest in stressing the authority of the older portion of the Canon.

This already becomes vivid in the work and thought of Zwingli. For the Swiss Reformer, the Holy Spirit is the overriding factor in religion. He looks on Scripture not as teaching us what God did in the past to redeem man, but rather as teaching what He now does and what we must do to serve Him.[2] Christ is not so much the heart and centre of Scripture, as He is one of a series of biblical personages revealing the will of God to man. Zwingli's humanistic background, which had given him a rich appreciation of Greek and Roman thought, led him to broaden the concept of revelation and to esteem noble sayings of a Plato or Seneca as manifestations of the working of the same Holy Spirit who inspired the biblical writers. The difference is that Scripture is inspired throughout. In interpreting Scripture Zwingli shows a most remarkable ability to discount the local and temporal elements; only after that is properly done is it authoritative. The Old Testament to him has the same dignity as the New, and where the latter does not prescribe afresh the Old Testament regulation is still in force. The external revelation of Scripture must, however, be brought to appreciation and understanding by the Holy Spirit working in us. Interpretation of Scripture must be free from any curbs or restraints. The only limitations he recognizes are a few simple hermeneutic rules: (1) Every passage has a plain meaning.   (2) Allegorical interpretation is without validity, but, especially in the Old Testament, is permissible. (3) Scripture is fully consistent in itself. In case of doubt as to how to interpret, that meaning which is most in line with God's glory is to be preferred.

In building a Protestant political as well as religious community the Swiss Reformer was faced by the fact that the Anabaptists, who were seeking to translate the ideals of the Sermon on the Mount into local group life, were an obstacle. Since the Old Testament alone provided the justification for a national religious ideal the Anabaptists were driven to reject that book as given only to the Jews and no longer authoritative for the Christian. Other arguments against it were also adduced by them, notably that the Old Testament did not have a belief in individual immortality and thus was not on the level of Christian faith; but they were of secondary importance. In his *Refutation of the Wiles of the Anabaptists*, 1527, Zwingli dealt with their claims in the following manner. He insisted that there was only one covenant and one people of God (thereby affirming the relevance of the Old Testament for the Christian), but went so far as to concede the following differences between the two parts of the Canon: (1) Christ was given to the Christians and only promised to the Jews. (2) Christians go to heaven after death while the Jews go to Abraham's bosom. (3) For Christians, the Old Testament types and shadows are done away with. (4) The understanding of religion in the New Testament is clearer than in the Old Testament, because in the latter religion is impaired by ceremonialism. (5) The universalism of the New Testament religion stands on a higher plane than that of the Old Testament.[3]

Zwingli's position on this matter was followed at first by Bucer, but the latter subsequently made a sharp about-face in his commentary on the Gospels, and particularly in his commentary on Romans. Here he denied that there was any dif-

ference between the Old Testament and the New Testament and
read the whole Christology and doctrine of the Atonement
back into the former. This seemingly cut the very ground
away from under the feet of the Anabaptists.

Bucer's line of thought was taken up and developed further
by John Calvin in his *Institutes* of 1536, a work which was
expanded and improved in subsequent editions.[4] Since Calvin
became the dominant teacher of a great segment of Protestantism, it is worth while to take up his views in some detail.

Unlike Zwingli, whose humanistic and philosophic bent
inclined him to so broad ideas, Calvin was purely a Biblicist.
He had little use for secular wisdom, but looked exclusively to
the Bible as the source of all religious insight. But a basis
had to be found for the belief that the Bible is the Word of
God. The Catholic believed it on the authority of the Church.
In a book on the *Central Doctrines of St. Paul*, (1539) Calvin
attempts to controvert that position on the basis of Eph. 2: 20,
according to which the Church rests on the foundation of the
prophets and apostles (erroneously taking this to mean the
prophetic and apostolic writings!). But he then adduces arguments to buttress the revealed character of Scripture—first,
the consideration that Scripture provokes our reverence by its
power, and second, that the witness of the Holy Spirit convinces us of its divine origin. In the latter particular he had
been anticipated by Luther, though Luther did not raise
the thought to such high prominence.[5] In the *Institutes* of
1550 Calvin not only added these reflections but increased his
emphasis on the authority of the Bible.[6] The famous saying of
Augustine, "I would not believe the gospel if the authority of
the Catholic Church had not impressed me", is controverted by
him on the basis of Augustine's own words, for he finds that
Augustine actually has other and better reasons for believing,
viz., the inner illumination by the Spirit, and that the Church
has only a preparatory role in connection with the origin of
faith. In the final edition of 1559 Calvin first discusses the
witness of the Spirit, which he now regards as principal proof
for the authority of Scripture, and then adds other auxiliary
proofs, viz., the dignity of the subjects treated, the diction of the
prophets, the antiquity of the writings, the attending miracles,
the miraculous preservation through the ages, the obedience

Scripture has received through many generations, and the witness of the martyrs who died for its truth.

Calvin did not follow Luther in the point of feeling free to evaluate and even criticize the canon. He viewed the Bible as the book in which God had set forth His will officially and definitely for all time. The biblical authors were to him only the amanuenses of the Holy Spirit and their writings were therefore oracles from on high. Every part of Scripture is equal to the other in authority. Supremely logical, he drew every consequence from this doctrine of inspiration, which he presupposes, though he does not develop it. Presumably his legal training influenced him in the direction of imagining the Bible as a sort of ideal *corpus juris*.

Without realizing it, Calvin, while elevating the Bible to the rank of sole principle, was actually governed by a second principle—a doctrinal slant that grew out of a subjective choice of biblical materials which suited his type of mind and his interest. With the help of this slant and these materials he mastered everything else in the Bible that stood in his way. The thing in Scripture that appealed most to Calvin was the idea of a God bent on his own "glory". We have seen that Zwingli had made that thought central for biblical interpretation, though not for doctrine, as Calvin now proceeded to do. "What is man that thou art mindful of him and the son of man that thou visitest him?" These words of Psalm 8 have been aptly said to describe the spirit of Calvin's theology. Whatever happens in the world may serve some useful purpose, but that is not the ultimate reason why it happens: God has primarily His own glory in mind and founded the whole world to the end that it might be the scene of that glory. Thus Calvin takes man out of the centre of the stage—an achievement in itself—and puts God there instead. The idea of the glory of God is raised to the nth degree by being combined with an absolute determinism.[7] The corollary to that is that certain people, the "elect", are predestined to be saved and all the others predestined to be lost. The Church is the society of the elect. Some may, indeed, have got into this society who are not of the really "elect", but the Church has an obligation to exercise strict discipline and to expel such persons as soon as it becomes certain of their status. The idea of the chosen people is thus reconstituted, though on non-national lines, in the spirit of certain Old Testament writings like Deuteronomy.

It is quite surprising in view of such presuppositions to find Calvin as an exegete showing a far-reaching insight into the historical conditioning of Scripture.[8] He interprets Scripture literally with a lawyer's precision and usually resists the temptation to impute to the author of an Old Testament passage a deeper meaning than the words themselves warrant. Even the New Testament interpretation of Old Testament passages does not deter him from first taking the latter in the plain meaning which the context in his opinion demands. But since, for him, one and the same Holy Ghost is the author of Scripture, there is a tendency on his part to view ideas and thoughts of Scripture that are on a distinctly lower level as an accommodation of the Holy Ghost to the plane of the time when such utterances were made, and to look for elements tending toward a nobler insight such as is attained in passages that are on a higher level. The particular biblical passage thus is to be interpreted in the light of the great connection of the whole process of scriptural revelation. Calvin's biblically-derived philosophy of revelation, which views all history as under the aegis of an eschatological promise, with Christ's appearance on earth as the pledge of a final fulfilment, gives him an opportunity to put everything in its proper place. Interestingly enough, he is able to view that philosophy of revelation itself as one that emerges gradually and thus to appraise its earlier and cruder forms of expression as only preparatory.

Turning now to the problem of the "law", let us see how Calvin dealt with it in the successive editions of his great work. In his treatment of it in the first part of the *Institutes* of 1536[9] his purpose is the strictly evangelical one to show that the law, by revealing the will of God, makes us conscious of our inability to fulfil it and thus prepares us for the message of the gospel of grace. But in carrying it out, Calvin Christianizes the Old Testament law to an extent that we would not consider historically permissible. In fact, he practically closes his eyes to the new moral values in the preaching of Jesus and reduces Him to the level of a correct interpreter of Moses; for Jesus, he holds, did not add anything to the law—He merely did away with Pharisaic misinterpretation of it. If the Catholic Church asserted that Jesus had added "special counsels" to the law, but that these were only applicable to monks, Calvin insists that these special counsels are already implied in the eternal law of the Old Testament. He denies the double moral standard of Catholicism and asserts that everything in the law is too difficult for us to fulfil unless God gives us the strength to do so. The *pièce de résistance* of his whole section on the law is an interpretation of the Ten Commandments, after the manner of Luther's catechism. But Calvin's strict biblicism does not permit him to accept Luther's arbitrary elimination of the second commandment and his partition of the tenth commandment into two commandments; the former gives Calvin a welcome weapon against Catholic "idolatry". Interesting is his partial spiritualization of the Sabbath ordinance in this early phase of his thinking; its "ceremonial" aspect, he holds, is merely a shadow of things to come, and is no longer binding. The commandment now signifies that we should desist from our evil works and find rest in God. Since there is no qualitative difference between one day and another, the Christian Sunday serves just as well as Saturday as a day of rest from labour and for the assembly of Christian congregations.

In the *Institutes* of 1539, Calvin made significant revisions and alterations in the direction of Christianizing the Old Testament law still further and of watering down Christian principles with Old Testament ideas. In his revised interpretation of the Decalogue he now is bent on showing that it is a perfect code of morals. He assumes that each commandment contains a great deal more than the mere words express, and his way of discovering its full range is to inquire into the Lawgiver's intent. After Christianizing the Decalogue all along the line, he can affirm that the law is by no means abrogated, but is in full force for the Christian. In contrast to his earlier exposition of the first commandment, in which, like Luther, he had emphasized faith combined with love and hope as of cardinal importance, he now placed these things in a cultic framework, making them subsidiary, as it were, to divine *worship*.[10] This cultic orientation of religion affords an easy transition to the discussion of images, of the hallowing of the name of God, of the Sabbath and of the

oath. With respect to the Sabbath he now—after three years!—
acknowledges the divine institution of a special rest day,
though arbitrarily substituting the first day for the seventh,
and thus takes a first step in the direction of later Calvinistic
Sabbatarianism that played such a great role in England and
America. In his discussion of the oath, his "watering down" of
the New Testament ethic becomes particularly apparent. If the
Anabaptists based their refusal to swear on Matt. 5: 34, Calvin
rejects that because the oath is commanded in the Old Testament (Deut. 6: 13). To interpret the words of Jesus as the
Anabaptists do, he asserts, is to make Christ contradict the
Father. The intention of Jesus, he argues, was merely to curb
the misuse of the oath. So he proceeds to justify the oath and
set forth its permissible varieties, interpreting Jesus on the basis
of Moses, the New Testament on the basis of the Old Testament.

In the second edition of the *Institutes* Calvin added an appendix of a general character to this discussion and exposition of
the law.[11] It was evidently provoked by the attacks of the
Anabaptists on the Old Testament. He accuses them of thinking of the Hebrew people much as one might think of a herd of
swine that was being fattened on earth by God without any
hope of eternal life. Calvin asserts that "all persons from the
beginning of the world, whom God has adopted into the society
of His people, have been federally connected with Him by the
same law and the same doctrine which are in force among us".
He thus emphasizes the point that there was only one covenant,
so that those of the days before Christ and ourselves are in an
uninterrupted religious sequence. It should be noted, too, that
he sets up a concept of a "society of God's people" into which
men are "adopted". He thus substitutes the Church for the
Jewish racial and national community. Having prepared the
ground in this manner he states that he is now going to show the
similarity and the differences between the Old and the New
Testaments. He narrows the discussion down unduly, however,
by confining himself to setting forth what kind of a covenant the
Lord made with the Israelites before Christ and what it is that
He has entered into (note avoidance of the word covenant here!)
since Christ. He finds the one and the same covenant enduring;[12] that of the Christian period varies only in administration.
He maintains (1) that the Jews of the Old Testament were

adopted into the hope of immortality; (2) that their covenant
was not founded on their merits, but purely on the mercy of the
God who had called them; (3) that they possessed and knew
Christ as the Mediator, through whom they were united to God,
and so became partakers of His promises. We and they thus are
one in the hope of immortality, in the character of the covenant
as covenant of grace and in the knowledge of the Mediator Jesus
Christ.

In undertaking to substantiate these claims in detail Calvin
had his difficulties. The first point, in particular, that the hope
of immortality was the same in the Old Testament as in the
New Testament, posed a considerable hurdle. His starting-
point was the Christianizing and spiritualizing interpretation of
the Old Testament found in the New Testament. Paul's line in
I Corinthians 10, stressing the essential identity of the Hebrew
and Christian religions, and finding the Christian sacraments
present with Moses in the desert, provides the key. If in
John 6: 49 Christ establishes a contrast between the manna of
the desert that could not keep the fathers from dying and
Christ's own flesh that gives eternal life, Calvin explains this as a
concession to the low mentality of His listeners, who could not
penetrate to the deeper mystery that Paul had in view. But
Calvin also seeks to demonstrate the actual presence of a hope
of immortality in the Old Testament itself. He adduces some
rather subtle arguments to the effect that this is implied in
God's communicating Himself to the saints in His Word of life—
notably in the covenant formula, "I will be your God and ye
shall be my people", and connects herewith also the argument
of Jesus over against the Sadducees (Matt. 22: 32). But he also
seeks to demonstrate more directly that some pious Israelites
had received the assurance of immortality. Does not the
eleventh chapter of the Epistle to the Hebrews suggest that it
was only this hope that gave the fathers, from Adam on,
strength to endure in the midst of this miserable existence?[13]

Various subsidiary thoughts support the position. Why the
struggle for the right of the first-born in the patriarchal history,
if a higher blessing is not implied? What but eternal life can be
meant when Jacob, dying, anticipates the salvation of God
(Gen. 49: 18)? Without lingering further in the Law, Calvin
then turns to the Psalms. The utterances dealing with the

transitory nature of our earthly pilgrimage, such as Ps. 39: 13 and 103: 15, he claims, must be seen against the background of the hope of everlasting life. Psalms 49 and 73 are naturally stressed also. From here he passes to Job 19: 25, in which he at least finds this hope reflected, even though he concedes that Job is primarily referring to the day when God will show His grace to him here on earth.

Proceeding to the prophets, he finds that all the descriptions of future blessedness, with their earthly colours, are but suggestions of supernal realities. Thus, while he concedes that Ezek. 37 applies primarily to the national restoration of the Hebrew people, he thinks it simultaneously has the purpose of teaching the Jews the resurrection of the flesh as such. A comparison with Isa. 26: 19 is employed to make this reasonable. Isa. 66: 22 and Dan. 12: 1 f. are naturally also utilized by Calvin to re-enforce his thesis. In reality, this is meagre proof for his sweeping assertion that the hope of eternal life is found *throughout* the prophets. In the light of our modern critical insight these intimations of immortality appear on the scene only in very late Old Testament passages, and are not characteristic of the Old Testament religion.

In developing the second point that the Old Testament and New Testament are one in the character of the covenant of grace, i.e., that there was only one covenant and one people of God, Calvin, like Zwingli, is willing to grant that some differences between the Old and New Testaments do exist.[14] He devotes a special section to these differences. In the New Testament the hope of immortality appears with much greater clarity. While establishing this fact he concedes, what he had not admitted previously, that the Old Testament saints valued the life this side of the grave much more than is befitting for Christians, who should meditate on the future life.[15] But he sees a process of purification and clarification going on within the Old Testament itself. A second difference is suggested by the Epistle to the Hebrews, with its typology of the Old Testament cult and priesthood as prophetic of Christ and the Atonement. The proof of the correspondence between particular prophetic passages and their fulfilment, as attempted in the Gospels, is not prominently taken up by Calvin at all. In dealing with Jesus' saying on the new covenant (Matt. 26: 28), Calvin twists it to fit his theory of only one covenant; the old covenant, he argues, became new and eternal in its truth through the blood of Christ. In the third place, Calvin, proceeding from Jer. 31: 31 and its interpretation in II Cor. 3: 6, grants a difference between the law of the letter and the gospel of the spirit. He finds Paul speaking with more hatred of the law than Jeremiah, but he excuses this on the ground of his opposition to the Judaizers (a point Melanchthon had also made). In the central position that the law can tell man what to do but that man is powerless to do it, Calvin maintains Paul's standpoint, though in concluding the discussion he obscures Paul's position by again contrasting the gospel and the *ceremonies* of the law. In the fourth place, Calvin contrasts Old Testament and New Testament as bondage and freedom, in accord with Paul's teachings in Galatians and Romans. Even so, he finds traces of the spirit of faith and its freedom already present among the Old Testament saints. Finally, Calvin contrasts the universalism of the New Testament with the particularism of the Old. But Christian universalism, prophesied by the prophets, is fulfilled in Christ only gradually—primarily after His resurrection. Such sayings as Matt. 10: 5, 15: 24 (which modern scholars by and large incline to regard as Judaizing) suggest the idea of a development.

In his edition of 1543, Calvin was moved to append a paragraph defending the idea of the immutability of God against doubts arising from the impression that God had changed His own original arrangements. For it could be argued that in the New Testament God rejects what He had previously commanded, and even abhors that which He had previously delighted in—e.g. the animal sacrifices and all the arrangements of the Levitic priesthood. Can God take back what He has said? Here Paul's idea of a divine pedagogy is utilized by Calvin as a means of escape from the difficulty.

The third point that the Old Testament and the New Testament are one in the knowledge of the Mediator Jesus Christ is also taken up in the second edition of the *Institutes*, but finds its most elaborate development in Book II, chapter 6, in the final edition of 1559, to which we shall here confine ourselves. Genesis 1–3 and speculations based thereon now loom large. Calvin put the Christian ideal of religion in the pre-lapsarian state. The Fall made redemption necessary. The whole history of Israel, including the Mosaic legislation, is viewed as a revelation of the redeeming God through the pre-existent Mediator, Christ. Wherever God showed His grace to Israel, everything depended on Christ. In justifying this position, Calvin stresses Messianic prophecy. These predictions, he holds, were intended to draw men's eyes toward the Redeemer. After such a Christianization of the Old Testament and its history, he subordinates the whole Old Testament legislation to Christology in chapter 7. The law was given to nourish the hope of salvation in Christ until He should come. All the seemingly absurd sacrifices and rites had a spiritual sense that becomes revealed in Christ. The Davidic kingship and the priesthood, too, pointed to Christ. As for the moral law of the Old Testament, Calvin stresses its perfection and the utter impossibility of fulfilling it; its purpose is to awaken the longing for forgiveness through the Mediator Christ. All this spelled such a Christianization of the Old Testament, and notably of the law, that the newness of the gospel was almost lost sight of. The latter is merely the fuller revelation of the mystery of Christ. The difference between the two revelations is only one of degree of clarity. And so in the ninth chapter of Book II Calvin really abandons Paul's (and Luther's) antithesis of law and gospel. This is largely due to his yielding to the influence of the Epistle to the Hebrews and its Christianizing allegorical use of Old Testament law and institutions. In connection with Christology Calvin affirms that Christ came as priest to effect atonement made necessary by the Fall and its consequences, but he also stresses His prophetic and regal office. It is significant that this whole Christological pattern of the *munus triplex*, the threefold office of Christ as Prophet, Priest and King, that still survives in numerous works on Christian doctrine, is based on the Old Testament!

Here a strong-willed, sober and clear-headed man set forth the characteristic Reformed position in a thorough and powerful way. Providence willed that Calvin should become the most influential teacher for a large segment of Protestantism. Thus a form of Christianity that was full of Old Testament spirit moulded the ideas and ideals of generations—just at the time when a new promised land had opened up to receive another chosen people.

The question is: can that which Calvin taught about the relation of the Testaments be regarded as valid? In recent years some have turned to him for light, as others have turned to Luther. Thus, even such a critic as Albertz can remark that "theology and the Church would have been spared the following of many erroneous paths if with respect to the unity of and the differences between the Old Testament and the New Testament they had borne in mind what Calvin is able to say on that question in so careful and circumspect a manner in his *Institutes*."[16] It will have become obvious, however, from our critical account of what Calvin himself has to say that many of his positions are untenable.

The plain fact is that Calvin has Christianized the Old Testament and Judaized the New Testament in his efforts to make the two appear as one. He was able to Christianize the Old Testament largely because he viewed it through the coloured glasses of the author of the Epistle to the Hebrews. We, however, must view the Old Testament through the clear lenses of realistic observation and interpretation. The philosophy of history offered in the Epistle to the Hebrews is an interesting attempt from the time of the early Church to cope with the problem of the relation of the earlier dispensation to the Christian order, but it was intended for Hellenistic Jews and is highly speculative in character. The history of the New Testament canon shows, furthermore, that the Epistle to the Hebrews is among the New Testament writings carrying the least weight for Christian doctrine.[17] The really crucial question then is: can one, discounting its support, in fact maintain Calvin's position that there is only one covenant and one people of God? Other early Christian thinkers, notably Paul, saw contrast rather than continuity in the relation of the two orders, and the early Church in calling the two Testaments "Old" and "New" clearly differentiated them. It may be, however, that Paul's view is too one-sided and due to his involvement in sharp controversy with Judaism. There is a real problem here which cannot be settled in an external manner by appeal to authority, but which requires a fundamental approach in the full freedom of Christian reflection.

Chapter Three

THE OLD TESTAMENT FROM THE REFORMATION TO THE MIDDLE OF THE SEVENTEENTH CENTURY

IN the great creative period of the Reformation the opportunity existed to place a new construction upon the Bible as a whole and the Old Testament in particular. But great decisions had to be made and stands had to be taken before there was a sufficient development of unfettered biblical scholarship. Essentially the Catholic doctrine of inspiration remained in force. There was no attempt to develop further the liberal insights of Luther or the thoughts of Carlstadt. Nevertheless, the extreme restraint shown in the Augsburg Confession of 1531 with respect to the Scriptures (there are only passing allusions in prologue and epilogue that the teaching is being set forth "out of the Holy Scriptures and the pure Word of God") may largely be due to a realization on Luther's part of the complexity of the problem. The Lutherans subsequently clung to one element of their founder's heritage: the overriding importance of the doctrine of justification by faith. They made the latter the "material principle" which was to stand side by side with the "formal principle" (Scripture authority).[1] Scripture was to be interpreted after the analogy of faith, i.e., the material principle (justification) was to govern the interpretation of Scripture. Thus biblical statements were, if necessary, brought forcibly into line with the basic Pauline gospel and a seeming harmony of Scripture established. The Reformed theologians, on the other hand, held fast to the formal principle without any qualification. They thus could strive to use the whole biblical heritage more freely. Since they, too, regarded Scripture as inspired by the Holy Ghost and then argued that the Holy Ghost could not have contradicted Himself, their interpretation likewise became harmonistic.

It is interesting to see how the Roman Church reacted to Protestant biblicism. On April 8, 1546, in its fourth session, the Council of Trent declared:[2] (1) That the Church accepted all the writings of both Testaments *and* the unwritten traditions going back to Christ and the apostles with equal reverence. (2) The Council set up a list of the authoritative books. In it not only the books acknowledged by the Palestinian Synagogue, but the so-called Apocrypha of the Old Testament, were accepted as canonical. In the New Testament the Epistle of the Hebrews was declared Pauline and that of James apostolic, but II Esdras, which the Vulgate puts after Revelation, was quietly omitted, following Luther's example. (3) An anathema was pronounced upon all who did not consider these books in all their parts as found in the Latin Vulgate sacred and canonical. (4) The Vulgate was declared authoritative for all public lectures, disputes, sermons and interpretations. (5) Since the text of the Vulgate was often carelessly or arbitrarily given in manuscripts and printed books, it was moved that an official edition of the Vulgate be made (this edition appeared forty-six years later in Rome under Pope Clement VIII). (6) All biblical books, it was asserted, have equal authority, for they are all divinely inspired. (7) The Church is the final, because infallible, judge of the true sense of the Sacred Scriptures. The last mentioned point is not taken to mean that scholarly research in the sphere of Scripture interpretation is forbidden, but rather that the interpreter must not contradict the consensus of the Fathers, or an exegesis officially accepted by the Church in the past, and must be ready to retract a new interpretation if the Church condemns it. Such individualism as that shown by Luther was thus declared out of order.

The repercussions of the western debate over the Scriptures were not felt until much later in the Eastern Catholic Church. By way of rounding out our picture of the attitude of Christendom toward the Bible and notably toward the Old Testament, we may, however, make brief reference to it here. In the eastern area the authority of the articles of faith set up by the ancient ecumenical councils was regarded as resting partly on Scripture and partly on oral tradition. The latter proceeded from the apostles, was handed down in the Church, and was fixed by the councils and the holy Fathers. Scripture is inspired throughout and the Church is the guardian of its integrity and interpretation. In the Confession of the Synod convoked at Jerusalem in 1672 the Old Testament was declared to include also the Apocrypha.[3] Since Scripture is clear in its meaning as to central dogmas, but not readily understandable in all its parts, it is not meet that all people should have the privilege of reading the Bible, but only those with the proper understanding. Notably, some books of the Old Testament are to be kept from the layman. A certain fear of the consequences of reading the Old Testament is evident in this attitude of the eastern Church, and this is comprehensible since it did not have an infallible tribunal to govern biblical interpretation, as Rome did.

Reverting again to sixteenth-century Europe we note that Trent left its impress on Protestantism, too. The Reformed theologians were induced by Roman example to enter in more detail into the matter of the Scripture doctrine than the Lutherans had done. Two basic thoughts about Holy Writ reappear with ever-increasing sharpness in their Confessions:[4] (1) that the Scripture canon is forever definitely fixed; (2) that its authority is not from man, nor from the Church, but from God. The Second Helvetic Confession[5] of 1566 interprets Deuteronomy 4: 2 ("ye shall not add unto the word which I command you") and Revelation 22: 18 f. ("if any man shall add unto these things") as commandments of God with reference to the canonical writings of both Testaments. It also declares its loathing of all the heretics of former times who either did not recognize the inspiration of these writings, or rejected some and changed others with interpolations. With respect to the Apocrypha, the view of the early Church that they are not to be used for Scripture proof, and hence not to be regarded as canonical, but that they may be read in the churches, is upheld. On the second point, viz., that Scripture has received its authority from God rather than from the Church, the clash is more sharp. The Second Helvetic Confession insists that Scripture has this authority inherently, in so far as God himself spoke to the prophets and apostles and continues to speak to Christendom through their writings. The question how we know that this is so and whence we derive the right to declare these particular writings inspired and authoritative in contrast to others, is answered in this Confession by a collection of biblical quotations which really relate partly to Old Testament writings (under the presupposition of their inspiration), partly to the oral preaching of the gospel by the apostles, and partly to the ecclesiastical arrangements made by the apostles.

Other Reformed Confessions, however, go so far as to make declarations of the extent of the canon—the 39 Articles of 1562, the Confession of the Anglican Church, designate those books of the Old Testament and of the New Testament as canonical whose authority has never been doubted in the Church (a statement rather interesting in the light of the debates in the history of the canon). More explicit still are the French Confession of 1559, the Belgian (based on the French) of 1566, and ultimately the Westminster of 1648, all of which list the writings considered canonical. These Confessions declare, "We recognize these Scriptures as canonical and as the absolutely certain rule of our faith, not so much because of the agreement and assent of the Church as because of the testimony and inner persuasion of the Holy Spirit who teaches us to differentiate them from other ecclesiastical writings."[6] Some influence is thus conceded to the tradition of the Church, in the matter of canonicity, but the decisive thing is the witness of the Holy Spirit, in accordance with the doctrine put forth so forcefully by Calvin.

In claiming that the Holy Spirit testified to them that all these books were inspired and canonical, the Reformed theologians ignored the fact that other men and groups of men likewise claiming the Holy Spirit for their guide had arrived at other judgments. The prelates at Trent in the introduction to their decree on the Scriptures declare themselves as a "synod lawfully assembled in the Holy Spirit", and yet were induced to recognize the Apocrypha as canonical. Luther evidently did not hear the witness of the Holy Spirit for quite a number of writings; the Church Father Irenaeus uses *The Shepherd of Hermas* as canonical; Athanasius does not count the Book of Esther as canonical, but includes Baruch and the Epistle of Jeremiah in the Book of Jeremiah. Did the Holy Spirit not testify to these leaders? The Calvinistic theory really ignores the fact that the canon has evolved gradually and in a process of compromise. In the light of the knowledge that was even then available to those who had patristic learning, Zahn declares, the theory that God had fixed the canon was "as much a fiction as any fable of the Papal Church".[7] And equally fictitious, he asserts, is the idea that the witness of the Spirit could enlighten one to know that exactly the twenty-seven New Testament books accepted by the Church in the fourth century and exactly the twenty-four Old Testament books accepted by the Jews were inspired and authoritative. One may safely say that what these men took to be the witness of the Spirit is no new revelation at all but only an echo of that which is traditional in the Church. It is difficult to see what prompting of the Holy Spirit could have convinced a seventeenth-century Protestant that the Books of Ecclesiastes, Esther, or Jude's Epistle are canonical, but that Sirach, I Maccabees and the Epistle to the Laodiceans are not worthy of that esteem. Calvin himself could adduce no other ground for the canonicity of the Epistle of James in the Preface to his Commentary on it than that he sees no reason for rejecting it and feels able to harmonize its teachings with Paul's. The witness of the Spirit in this case amounts to nothing but an acceptance of the traditional canonicity of the Epistle, without any real investigation into the question of how well it was attested and how it came to be received.

With respect to the relation of the Old Testament to the New the 39 Articles of the Church of England were more liberal than other Reformed Confessions. The Seventh Article states:

> The Old Testament is not contrary to the New: for both in the Old and New Testament everlasting life is offered to mankind by Christ, who is the only mediator between God and man, being both God and Man. Wherefore they are not to be heard, which feign that the Old Fathers did look only for transitory promises. Although the law given from God by Moses, as touching ceremonies and rites, do not bind Christian men, nor the civil precepts thereof ought of necessity to be received in any commonwealth; yet notwithstanding, no Christian man whatsoever is free from the obedience of the commandments which are called moral.[8]

The belief that Christ speaks in the Old Testament and that the Old Testament saints hoped for eternal life is expressed in the first part of this statement. This is evidently the Calvinistic line, whereas the emphasis on the non-binding character of the ceremonial and civil law that follows suggests the influence of Zwingli or Luther.

With Confessions sprouting up on all sides the Lutherans, too, felt the need of going beyond their Augsburg Confession. True, the latter was regarded as possessing symbolical authority by considerable sections of the Reformed group; no less a man than Calvin had subscribed to it (in 1541). But in the *Formula of Concord* of 1580 there now was set forth a fresh and more comprehensive statement of the Lutheran position.[9] So far as the Scriptures are concerned, its restraint is remarkable. It simply states, in its opening paragraph, "We believe, teach and confess that the only rule and norm according to which all teachings and teachers are to be judged and appraised are alone the prophetic and apostolic writings of the Old and New Testaments." The primary point here is the elimination of the Catholic principle of tradition. No reasons are given for the normative significance of the Bible, no doctrine of inspiration is taught, and the prophetic and apostolic writings are not identified in detail. There is not even an attempt to insist on the authority of the Hebrew and Greek texts over against the Vulgate. The extremely reticent position taken by this the most elaborate Lutheran Confession suggests that Luther's insights and the lessons of Carlstadt's treatise were not yet forgotten. This paragraph gave a considerable advantage to modern German and Scandinavian theology, because of its very general terms. The rise of biblical criticism was much more difficult in the Reformed Churches, because their Confessions were more specific in the matter of the Scripture doctrine.

Looking at the Lutheran theological rather than the purely ecclesiastical and confessional scene, it is of interest to note how Martin Chemnitz (one of the authors of the *Formula of Concord*) dealt with the Catholic doctrine of Scripture.[10] The great problem at issue for a Protestant theologian, of course, was how to escape the logic of the Catholic claim that the Church is the source of the canonical authority of Scripture. Chemnitz asserts that the present Church is bound by the testimony of the early Church, but even the early Church had no other function in this respect than to declare authority that is inherent in the biblical writings: i.e., they merely recognized the reality that existed but did not create it, as already taught by Zwingli and others.

But he then goes so far as to differentiate between proto-canonical and deutero-canonical writings in the New Testament. Only those can be regarded as proto-canonical and be authoritative for doctrine which (1) are derived from the authors from whom they claim to come and (2) are recommended by the sure and unanimous testimony of the ancient Church. This position is astonishingly liberal. If the first rule were applied to-day to the New Testament in the light of modern historical insight only eight or nine Pauline Epistles could be regarded as proto-canonical. For the Old Testament the consequences would be even more serious. In Chemnitz's day, of course, the authenticity of most biblical writings was still taken for granted. It is not surprising that subsequent Lutheran theologians did not maintain the distinction of proto- and deutero-canonical.[11]

The emphasis on the inspiration of the whole received Bible, making its supposed supernatural origin the self-sufficient basis of its authority, remained characteristic of the Reformed approach. The Westminster Confession of 1647 states that the "authority of Holy Scripture for which it ought to be believed and obeyed dependeth not upon the testimony of any man or Church but wholly upon God (who is truth itself) the author thereof; and therefore it is to be received because it is the word of God". The sacred books are "given by inspiration of God to be the rule of faith".[12] But in introducing the discussion of the Scripture doctrine this Confession betrays some qualms over the emphasis on biblicism, when it concedes that God had originally given His revelation to men in other ways, but that He had then decided "for the more sure establishment and comfort of the Church against the corruption of the flesh and the malice of Satan and the world to commit the same wholly unto writing, which maketh the Holy Scripture to be most necessary; these former ways of God's revealing His will unto His people now being ceased".

Other Reformed Confessions put the emphasis on Scripture even more sharply. Thus the Helvetic Consensus of 1675, which was accepted by most of the Swiss Churches, claims in its first article that God watched over His written word in so fatherly a manner that no jot or tittle ever was or ever could be lost. From this it was inferred that even the vocalization and accentuation of the Hebrew text of the Old Testament was inspired and that all attempts to set up a purer text with the help of Greek and Latin translations or the Samaritan Pentateuch were an undermining of religion.[13]

The unanimity and resoluteness with which the Reformed Churches emphasized their Scripture doctrine impressed the Lutherans to such a degree that they yielded to an increasing extent to its influence. The doctrine of the witness of the Holy Spirit gained practically unanimous consent among them. Hollazius, for example, in objecting to such a position as that of Chemnitz, taught that external witness could only produce human convictions, not true faith in Scripture—such faith rested in the last instance on the internal testimony of the Holy Spirit. But there was some disposition to doubt that such witness could support the canonicity of all received books. Thus Quenstedt (c. 1685) denies that this can be an article of faith, and concedes that there are true believers who do not accept a number of the books of the traditional Canon.[14]

With respect to the relation of the Old Testament to the New Testament Calvin's ideas also had a powerful influence upon the Lutherans. In the debates with Catholics on the one hand and Protestant sectarians on the other hand they were constantly invoked. Thus Gerhard[15] in his polemic against the Catholic Bellarmin rejects the latter's claim that the Old Testament doctrine is "inchoate" while that of the New Testament is "perfect", and that the Old Testament only teaches obscurely and imperfectly such mysteries of the faith as the Trinity; he asserts to the contrary that the Old Testament too, is perfect, since it teaches the same fundamental articles of faith which Christ and the apostles state in the New Testament.

The Socinians, who were banished from their main centre in Poland in 1658 but whose émigrés in Holland and England exercised a considerable activity, soon became an object of orthodox polemic, in part because of their stand on the Old Testament. These Protestants, though conceding the divine character of the Old Testament, claimed that it now had only a historical interest and was not essential for Christian doctrine. True, both Testaments had certain mandates—the moral ones— in common, but otherwise there was a great difference between the perfect mandates and promises of the New Testament and the imperfect ones of the Old; and the latter book, furthermore, taught such inadequate doctrines as that of retribution. The orthodox theologians countered by asserting that both Testaments were one in the covenant of grace and insisted that the belief in eternal life was already found in the Old Testament. The doctrine of the single covenant is espoused by the Lutheran Carpzov so wholeheartedly that he would even do away with the terms Old and New Testament and replace them with Old and New Instrument,[16] thus Christianizing the Old Testament and making a sort of *corpus juris* out of the Bible.   In fine, for orthodoxy, Lutheran as well as Reformed, the Bible became a single book, and passages of both parts were used indiscriminately in scholastic fashion to supply proof-texts for doctrines.

Nowhere in the Christian world did the Old Testament receive such a warm reception or penetrate so deeply into the lives of men as in England.[17] This cannot be attributed entirely to the fact that the Anglican Church from about 1550 on became increasingly influenced by Calvinism. For one would then expect the Old Testament emphasis to have been even greater at Geneva, where Calvinism was to be found in undiluted purity. The amazing phenomenon of the permeation of English life by Old Testament ideas is due rather to the dissenters.

The free Churches, established in the seventeenth century in opposition to the state Church, found in the Old Testament, in which prophets denounce and oppose kings and priests, a marvellous weapon for their own cause of freedom. A curious symptom of this love of the Old Testament is the use among the dissenters of Old Testament names as baptismal names in a degree not found elsewhere. Another symptom is the way in which the Sabbath legislation was foisted on England and the reluctant Anglican Church after long agitation and pressure by the dissenters. We need not speak here of the extremes of a "lunatic fringe" which demanded adherence to Jewish dietary laws and the acceptance of circumcision, or of British Israelitism which regarded the Anglo-Saxons (or some other group in the British Isles) as descendants of the Lost Tribes.[18] Even apart from such extremes, the Old Testament character of English life became ever stronger. Nowhere else, not even in Switzerland or Holland, with their Calvinistic populations, was there any such surrender to Old Testament influence. Doubtless the almost complete absence of Jews in the English scene, from their expulsion in 1291 to their re-admission in 1655, made it much easier than elsewhere for Christian people to consider "Israel" a synonym for "people of God", rather than a national designation, and then, with complete *naïveté*, the membership of one's own sect. The Old Testament influence that got into the very bones of the English people through the dissenters and was carried to America by the Puritans and others was a leaven that helped to' make the Anglo-Saxon mentality different from any other Western European mentality.

One may well accuse Protestant orthodoxy of having placed a heavy yoke on men's shoulders with its biblicism in place of the light yoke that Jesus Christ proclaimed. Harnack points out that modern conservatives who still insert such items as inspiration, infallibility, clarity and sufficiency of Scripture into doctrinal systems in a few spots, but ignore them in a hundred other places, have no idea how terribly realistically these things were taken at one time. But even the generations that still knew and understood the implications of this terminology, he says, were not consistent. They allowed themselves to dilute the meaning of Scripture, or in innumerable instances simply did not draw the consequences that the doctrine really required. "A sacred document, a thousand pages long, written by the finger of God," he observes wrily, "is an intolerable burden for the weak human race, whether one reads it or not." The orthodox dogma of the Scriptures, he thinks, has only been taken seriously in books on Doctrine, or generally speaking, "on paper".[19] But it must not be forgotten that where scientific thought endangered the Scripture doctrine at any point the latter was quickly invoked. Above all it was the insistence on the authority of the Old Testament that blocked progress in almost every sphere of knowledge. The story of that struggle makes melancholy reading.[20]

Chapter Four

THE REACTION AGAINST THE ORTHODOX VIEW
OF THE OLD TESTAMENT

A NUMBER of factors, however, were tending to break down orthodox biblicism. The first and most important was the rise of philological and historical scholarship of a new order. One presupposition of orthodoxy had been the conviction that the words of Scripture were very words of the Holy Ghost. That implied the perfect dependability of the received text of Scripture, for it was held that the Holy Ghost had been active in its preservation as well as in its creation. But the new art of the critical evaluation of ancient texts, evolved in the study of the Greek and Roman classics, showed that the text of Scripture was by no means as certain as had been believed. The French Protestant Capellus demonstrated that the vocalization of the Hebrew consonant text—which at the same time is an interpretation, without which other translations were possible in obscure connections—was of relatively recent origin, and that even the consonant text itself was by no means perfectly preserved.[1] The French Catholic Morinus next discerned that the old Greek translation, the Septuagint, often had readings better than those of the Hebrew text, and therewith laid the basis for what we call "textual criticism".[2] A Protestant who had reverted to Catholicism, Richard Simon, advocated the right to deal with the Old Testament according to principles of historical investigation, thereby inaugurating what we call "higher criticism".[3] In the same year Spencer in England sought to link the cult of the Mosaic law with other ancient Oriental cults, thus prophetically paving the way for the application of a comparative religious method to the religion found in the Old Testament.[4]

At the end of the century an *émigré* from Geneva to Holland, Clericus, produced a great work of critical scholarship, in which, among other things, he pointed out that the Old Testament

43

canon was by no means produced according to a blue print from heaven, but had had a historical growth and development[5]—a thought that was to become important in the following century through the labours of Semler.

A second factor tending to disrupt orthodox biblicism with its unilateral treatment of the Bible as Word of God from cover to cover, was the federal theology[6] that was inaugurated in the Reformed Church in the era of the Thirty Years' War by J. Cocceius of Bremen, who subsequently went to the Netherlands (1669). He held that there was a twofold covenant of God—one of nature and good works, concluded with man before the fall, and the second of grace and faith concluded after the fall. The latter has three stages—before the law, under the law, and under the gospel. This thought suggested a development in revelation, thus making relative the earlier stages of the record, and was antecedent to the "progressive revelation" philosophy that came up in the conservative theology of the nineteenth century.[7] Cocceius recognized the defects and limitations of Old Testament piety in comparison with the New Testament, though this led to violent attacks on him since it was contrary to the Reformed idea of the identity of the Testaments. A distinctive feature of his approach was his fondness for typological interpretation, which found much following. He regarded it as permissible to put as much mystical meaning into biblical verbiage as seemed possible. If it had not been for this defect his thinking might have carried much farther in the modern direction.

But a third factor working against Biblicism was secular thinking, now beginning to emancipate itself from ecclesiastical control. A man like Hugo Grotius, famed as the founder of International Law, espoused a Christian tolerance in an age of intolerance and favoured a single Christian Church for all confessions. As biblical exegete he showed an objective, matter-of-fact approach and an ability to interpret ancient texts out of their own time.[8] Hobbes, in his *Leviathan*, brought extremely radical ideas to the fore in England.[9] He sought a secular state, emancipated from all ecclesiastical influence, and held that whatever the state sanctions is good. Religion, he taught, is fear of invisible powers whose existence is invented, or just accepted on the basis of tradition. In biblical criticism he advocated the principle that the time of origin of biblical books must be inferred from the books themselves, rather than from traditions about them, and put forward critical views of his own concerning the Pentateuch and Daniel.

But even more significant of this trend was the reliance on reason that came up through the philosophy of Descartes. Its application to the biblical problem appeared on the scene in Spinoza's famous Theologico-political Tract.[10] Such was the terrorism practised by Protestant orthodoxy that he found it wise to publish it anonymously and with a false place of publication on the title page (Hamburg, rather than Amsterdam). Spinoza desired a non-dogmatic kind of religion, focused on practical conduct. Over against the orthodox claim that the Bible is the revealed book, absolutely reliable and consistent in every respect and the proper yardstick by which all truth is to be judged, Spinoza set forth that the Bible is no such system of revealed truth, and urged that its stranglehold on philosophy and on the state be abolished.[11] He denies the doctrine of inspiration which provided the basis for this view. The biblical books, he says, must be understood as historical documents of their own time and place, and not as a set of supernaturally given, timeless teachings. He distinguishes, too, between the sphere of knowledge and that of obedience. The latter is the proper sphere of the sacred writings, which then were not intended to convey theoretical truth, but must be interpreted as providing what is for our moral improvement. Consequently, they have their authority and meaning in the realm of morality alone. He then proceeds to develop a historico-critical view of the origin and character of these writings, which, though it cannot satisfy us to-day and hence need not detain us, was far in advance of his time. He even asserted that the Pentateuch was not written by Moses and thus is the precursor of the great critical movement that was to come long afterward. But greater than any single insight on the Old Testament that he contributed is the fact that he built into the whole future development the belief that religion must not contradict reason, and that where they clash the representatives of religion should not have the power of suppression of reason that they were claiming as a matter of divine right. It was a century or more, however, before this principle was to prevail.

There is one further element in Spinoza's discussion which deserves special mention, as fraught with future significance. Observing that the supposed Mosaic revelation rests on the idea of the election of Israel, he subjects the latter tenet to criticism. The belief of having been elected, or shown favouritism, he asserts, is basically not religious. The advantages of one are the disadvantages of another. He who rejoices in his advantages really finds a satisfaction in the fact that others do not have them. Thus the proud and self-satisfied feeling of "election" belongs to the sphere of a self-love, envy, and wickedness that have nothing in common with piety and the love of God. The Hebrew belief of having been elected among all peoples as the people of God, therefore, is not religious but selfish in its roots. To what end did the Jews believe themselves elected by God? Obviously only to obtain something that human nature could not achieve without His help. This desired end was not true knowledge, or virtue, or piety, for these things are attained only by the help of God within us. There is thus no election with respect to them. The object of election for Israel was the attainment of external things "that thy days may be prolonged and that it may go well with thee". This is the goal of the Jewish faith—to be blessed and rich and powerful! Obedience to the law was a means to that end, because it was supposedly the condition for God's granting their desires, while disobedience meant punishment, misfortune. This Jewish belief in election and in the law, he insists, is not religious but political. Thus the Jew Spinoza challenges the religion of his own people at its very foundations, and in this respect also throws a searchlight far into the future. For this materialistic and nationalistic philosophy of the Old Testament to which he opened men's eyes has in recent times become a great source of offence. From Spinoza the line leads via Kant to Schopenhauer.

There now came into existence a peculiarly divided situation —a continued, entrenched orthodoxy, and opposed to it an enlightenment, prevailing primarily among intellectuals. In France, Bayle proclaimed the rule of reason in morality and denied religion's right of interference; Church and state were to be separated, atheism to be tolerated.[12] In England, conditions were particularly favourable for the reign of reason, for here as nowhere else religion was ruled out of philosophy. On the other hand the unsatisfactory religious situation led to a movement aspiring to set up a purer and more enlightened form of Christianity. Deism, beginning in that spirit, soon got involved more and more in polemic against existing Christianity and, favouring a natural theology, assailed the theology based on revelation.

The Old Testament provided a convenient object for such attack. In the third decade of the eighteenth century we find Morgan publishing an imaginary dialogue between a Christian and a Jew.[13] He has some sound principles of biblical criticism and makes intelligent observations on the authorship and antiquity of various biblical writings. To some extent he is led astray by inferring from St. Paul's use of the Old Testament that that work contains things incomprehensible to its contemporaries because of their blindness and obduracy but capable of being understood by those who have good sense and reason. This is exegetical backsliding, when viewed in the light of such principles as those of Luther and Calvin, and tends toward theosophy. In other respects Morgan wants to subject Scripture to the judgment of "sense and reason", to see whether it be coherent with all other reasonable knowledge. It is no wonder that one who wants everything to be reasonable should dislike the Old Testament and the people whose life it reflects. Miracles and revelation, of course, had to be denied. The immoralities of the Old Testament were another thing at which he took offence.

Morgan's work elicited much theological discussion, but since Deism in England was about to pass into general decline it did not exert any widespread popular influence. Methodism was now coming to the fore in that country and influencing people's minds. On the apologetic side, Warburton defended the Old Testament against deistic attacks.[14] He conceded the absence of a doctrine of immortality in the Old Testament, but held that this did not detract from the weight of the Mosaic law, for which, therein influenced by John Locke, he had a high esteem. He even ventured to take the position that God had so ordered things in individual as well as collective life in the time from Moses to Christ that the doctrine of retribution was actually operative during that period!

Stimulated by Voltaire and the English Deists, a German,

Reimarus (really an Oriental philologist), author of some popular books of a philosophical nature, wrote a voluminous work of sceptical character about the year 1747. Desiring to avoid persecution by the heresy hunters, he wrote this treatise only for private circulation. Portions of it were published thirty years later by Lessing, without revealing the author's identity.[15] To shield the family from opprobrium Lessing called the excerpts the *Wolfenbüttel Fragments*. Actually he had been shown the manuscript in the author's house at Hamburg. In these "fragments" the reality of the biblical revelation was denied; the revelation of God in nature was regarded as the only true revelation.

It cannot be said that the published "fragments" added much to what the other Deists had already said about the Old Testament, though for the New Testament they did put forth original ideas that subsequently were to have an influence on Strauss' *Life of Christ*. The significance of the publication lies primarily in the fact that it involved Lessing in a discussion with the champions of orthodoxy, in which he expressed significant ideas of his own, and that this debate had an effect on the moulding of his famous drama *Nathan der Weise*. In a brief paper of 1777 Lessing, while not denying that Christ had performed miracles or had risen from the dead, emphasized the fact that no historical certainty was obtainable on these matters and that therefore beliefs could not be built on them.[16] He noted that an Origen saw in present evidences of the activity of the Spirit and in contemporary miracles done by holy men a proof more powerful than any that dialectics could provide; but he complains that nowadays we no longer see such evidences, and that the proof for that sort of thing has sunk to the level of mere human testimonies about such phenomena in the remote past. If it is asserted that such testimonies are guaranteed by the inspiration of the sacred writers, that claim, too, unfortunately is historically uncertain. Lessing finds the only support for Christian belief in the teachings of Christ, which carry conviction by their own weight.

Lessing was now attacked by Goeze, a Hamburg divine,[17] and replied to that attack in his *Anti-Goeze* (1778), which has been described as "the most important polemical writing in the struggle between Philosophy and Theology".[18] The chief issue between the contestants is that of the relation of Christianity to the Bible. According to Lessing, the author of the *Wolfenbüttel Fragments* (Reimarus) and Goeze have one thing in common: both say the Christian religion depends on the credibility of the Bible—for the former that book is incredible, while for Goeze it is infallible. Lessing, in contrast to both, tries to differentiate the Bible and religion. Religion was there prior to the Bible, he asserts. It consists of eternal truths (therein showing himself to be a true son of the age of enlightenment), that can never be demonstrated by particular facts. He asserts that the set of truths that existed before the New Testament and that form the basis of Christian belief, the rock on which the Church was founded, was the *regula fidei*, the confession of fundamental tenets exemplified by the Apostles' Creed. The value of the apostolic writings lies not in their being the source but only the oldest expression of this rule of faith.

In his discussion of this controversy Harnack declares Lessing to have done more than anyone else in breaking the terrible stranglehold which the dogma of the authority of the Bible had upon Protestantism. While some of the theses Lessing put forward in his *Anti-Goeze* are not tenable and were undermined by the learned Walch, his main contention was unshakeable and forever robbed of intellectual respectability a biblicism operating with the idea of an infallible, authoritative book.[19]

In the essay (1780), of which Lessing claimed to be merely the editor (perhaps to escape being held accountable by the heresy hunters), he views the revelation of God as the "upbringing" of the human race. The divine pedagogy accounts for the vicissitudes of history—notably of that of the chosen Hebrew people—and for the gradual progress in this people's religious and moral insight as reflected in the books of the Old Testament. The comparison is even employed at a point where a side-glance is directed at other nations. While God was leading Israel through the various stages of training, other nations went their way by the light of reason with which the Creator had endowed all mankind. Some of them remained very backward, but a few, such as Greeks and Romans, even advanced beyond Israel. But just as the few who progress by their own initiative do not disprove the value or necessity of education, so the Gentile nations that exceeded Israel in the knowledge of God up to a certain point prove nothing against revelation. The properly trained child eventually catches up with the more fortunately organized child of nature and surpasses him permanently. Lessing then compares the Old Testament to an elementary school book, given to the Jewish people. Its lack of a doctrine of immortality with reward and punishment in a life after death is no proof against the divine origin of this book. An elementary book must be suited to the actual stage of life for which it is intended. It cannot and need not give information unsuited to the age of those it is to instruct. All that can be required of it is that it does not block the road to knowledge temporarily withheld. The doctrine of retribution, he holds, tended to drive men in the direction of a belief in immortality; the latter solves the difficulty raised by the clash between reality and the divine justice experienced in individual life. The Jewish people was sent into Babylonian captivity, as a child is sent to a foreign land. Here they saw that other people knew more than they did, and under Persian ægis attained a nobler idea of God, and the idea of the immortality of the soul. Ashamed of themselves, they turned to their discarded elementary school book, the Old Testament, in order to place the blame on it for their previous backwardness. But they realized that the guilt was their own, not the book's. The latter had all the qualifications of a good elementary book—if they had only heeded it!

But an elementary book is only for a definite age. It is harmful for a child to linger longer over it than he is intended to do. Such a procedure has a bad effect on the mind and character, and this is discernible in the Jewish people. A better pedagogue must come and take this elementary book out of the child's hands and give it a new book. This happened when Christ came. He was the first dependable and practical teacher of the immortality of the soul, and His disciples who handed this truth on to other nations and gave them the new second-book— the New Testament—are thus among the benefactors of mankind. Let us not criticize them too much for mingling other less convincing teachings with this main one, but let us rather investigate whether a new impulse was not thereby given to human reason. Certain it is that the New Testament in comparison to the Old Testament is the more advanced schoolbook. But it is not the final book. As we can now dispense with the

Old Testament for the doctrine of the unity of God, so some of us can even begin to dispense with the New Testament for the doctrine of the immortality of the soul. In some of the more difficult doctrines of the New Testament Lessing finds indications of a higher stage of the divine pedagogy still to come, in which a new, eternal gospel will be given, and thinks the enthusiasts of the thirteenth and fourteenth centuries were not so far wrong when they asserted that the New Covenant must become antiquated just like the Old; they erred chiefly in thinking of being able to make their contemporaries, who were still on the childhood level, worthy of being citizens of that third world age. The ideas thus set forth represent a bold, speculative attempt to set up a popularly understandable philosophy of revelation. Its chief weakness is the rationalistic outlook—the emphasis on "truths" as the essence both of Old Testament and New Testament religion.

But the most important thinker of the time, the man who toppled reason from its pedestal, Immanuel Kant, also put forth weighty thoughts on the matters that concern us. In the *Critique of Pure Reason* (1781) he at one point makes an interesting observation on the idea of Sacred History; speaking of the antinomies he points out that both the statement that the world had no beginning and the opposite that it had a beginning in time can be proved as well as disproved, but that the second finds greater favour with mankind, for man flees the endless and desires a point where he can rest. "Thus there rises amid the miserable huts of men the cathedral with the everlasting peace of God." And then he adds, "So also religion in the endless flood of happenings has a Sacred History, where God works immediately and reveals himself directly to men."[20] While Kant does not state that this idea of a Sacred History is an illusion, a product of wishful thinking, that conclusion could readily be drawn, and doubtless represents Kant's opinion.

In his treatise *Religion within the Boundaries of Pure Reason* (1793), Kant has occasion to speak of biblicism in general and Christianity's relation to the Old Testament in particular. Religious faith, Kant held, was reasonable and exclusively based on the moral law written in the heart. The belief in a special divine revelation is rejected because it assumes the existence of statutory laws which are not based on the law written in the heart and thus are accidental and contrary to the true nature of man. It is our duty to hold fast to the moral religion and to hope that it will eventually prevail over the so-called revealed religion. The latter is of and for the senses and it is conceded that it serves a useful purpose in the present order of things. If the conflict between this illusory revealed religion and moral religion is to be reconciled at some future stage the former must have something in common with the latter. It is to be found, Kant held, in the predisposition to a moral religion which lay hidden in human reason from the outset and was partly operative in the formation of the belief in a special revelation.

This position already contains the nucleus of a philosophy of the history of religion. Religion, Kant taught, originally introduced humanity to moral teachings in the course of a historical process. Reason could have done the job, too, but humanity was not yet on the level where that was feasible. Since the history of the religion of individuals cannot be written, one can speak of religion only in terms of ecclesiastical history—the history of that (Christian) Church which from its beginning possessed the germ and the principles that could lead to true religion (in the Kantian sense; i.e., ethics). At this point Kant denies that the Jewish faith stands in any essential connection (i.e., exhibiting unity with respect to concepts) with Christianity, even though it immediately preceded and gave the physical occasion for the founding of the Church.

In explaining why he thus cuts the cord between Judaism and Christianity, Kant declares that the Hebrew faith is an aggregate of merely statutory laws on which a state constitution was founded. Whatever moral elements were added thereto at first or later do not belong to Judaism as such. The latter is no religion at all, but just a union of people of the same tribal origin for the purpose of attaining a common life under political laws. It was not projected to be a Church, but rather a worldly state, and if it were destroyed by accident there would still survive the political faith in its restoration (at the coming of a Messiah). That this state organization supposedly is theocratically governed (actually this only means a domination by priests or leaders, who claim to have received instructions directly from God), and shows reverence to the name of God (who here is imagined chiefly in terms of a sovereign and does not address himself primarily to the conscience of man) does not make it a religious organization. It is clear from the following reasons that it did not intend to be that at all:

(1) The Old Testament laws are of the sort valued and imposed by a political organization because they only concern external actions. Even the ten commandments, though they might be considered ethical before the forum of reason except for the fact that they were publicly promulgated, are not in that legislation associated with the requirement of a moral attitude in connection with obedience but are only directed to external observance. (2) All consequences of obedience or disobedience are innerworldly, and even these are not in accord with ethical concepts, as when children are to be punished for the sins of the fathers. Since (in the view of that rationalistic age) no religion worthy of the name can be conceived of without belief in eternal life, Judaism is no religion. Whatever genuinely religious ideas the Jews may have had, they were not included in this political programme which has come down in the Old Testament law. (3) Far from being the universal Church, Judaism excluded humanity from its fellowship; declared itself the chosen people, viewing all others with hostility and receiving hostility in return. Its imageless worship is not to be valued too highly, for among most other nations, too, there was a trend in the same direction. A God, furthermore, who only demands external obedience to such commandments as this Hebrew law contains and does not require an improvement in fundamental moral attitude of his devotees is not the truly moral Supreme Being that we need for a religion. Conceivably a polytheism in which people thought of their gods as approving only of him who adhered to virtue with his whole heart would even be preferable to a monotheism of the Jewish sort.

Moral religion, then, according to Kant, began with Christianity. It was an abandonment of Judaism and the introduction of a new principle. If the first teachers strove to connect the two and represented Christianity as a continuation of the old order, which in its types and shadows had contained all that later flowered forth, this must be regarded as an effort on their part to introduce religion to people of Jewish extraction without too much offence to their prejudices. The subsequent abolition of circumcision shows that the new faith was not bound to the statutes of the old, nor to any statutes at all, but was a religion valid not only for one people but for the world.

Much as he dislikes the fact, Kant perceives the religion of Protestantism as existing in his time in the form of faith in a book. Religious and moral instruction must therefore operate with the Bible, and so Kant recommends expounding the biblical writings by moral reason. The method may be arbitrary and unscientific but it is necessary, for a literal interpretation such as is alone admissible for scholars and their students can contribute nothing to the improvement and redemption of men. One must not interpret morals according to the Bible, but the Bible according to morals. If, for example, God is asked by a Psalmist to destroy his people's enemies, this refers actually to the enemies of the Jewish people. But that literal sense is contrary to morals. One should, therefore, re-interpret the passage and give it a moral meaning by making the "enemies" of the Psalmist symbolical of our own evil inclinations. Kant sees that taken literally, in its true meaning, the Old Testament is at many points an intolerable burden. Only allegorization provides an escape from the consequences of the canonical authority of this collection.

Kant's foray into the theological field brought him a letter from the Prussian king, Frederick William II, reprimanding him for having spoken in a derogatory manner concerning some fundamental teachings of Holy Scripture and Christianity. The philosopher preserved a loyal silence until under the next ruler. The official climate then having changed to one of "tolerance" he reverted to the topic in his *War of the Faculties*, wherein he made public the exchange of letters between himself and the new king's father, and restated his position in a fresh and interesting way.[21] A striking example of Kant's Old Testament study is furnished by his discussion of the theodicy problem which leads him to speak in detail of the Book of Job.[22]

The Old Testament question also attracted the attention of the two men who were to attain great influence in philosophy after Kant. The young Fichte, in his first philosophical treatise, attempted to show that revelation, too, was a postulate of practical reason.[23] Assuming that the moral law which had been revealed to men before the Flood had lost its earlier influence on mankind, he held it conceivable that God should have inaugurated anew a revelatory process imparting moral impulses to men by way of the senses. He could well have chosen to manifest Himself to them as lawgiver by some such visible and audible arrangement as tradition presupposes. Since the doctrines of God, liberty and immortality are all we need to know about the world of the Divine, these teachings must have formed the contents of such a revelation. All in all a naïve acceptance of Old Testament history undergirded by a parallel speculation! The young Schelling, on the other hand, in the course of his theological studies had attained the important insight that it was not enough to have grammatical interpretation, such as had been advocated; it was necessary to understand the biblical writings and their ideas historically-genetically. He rejected, too, the belief of Kant and others that "philosophical" interpretation of Scripture was legitimate; that, he rightly held, could only result in perversion of the real sense of those writings and was damaging to true philosophy.[24] In his dissertation on *The Third Chapter of Genesis* and a related paper on ancient myths Schelling set forth the theory that religious ideas initially had to take on mythological form. The story of the fall of man was utilized by him in the former production to apply this theory. In this tale, as in all myths, there is an underlying philosophy, and he ably sets forth its deeply pessimistic view. Schelling thus became the precursor of those who were later to use comparative mythology for the illumination of Scripture in a more external, historical manner than that which he here demonstrated.

Meanwhile biblical studies had been receiving impulses to progress. In 1753 the French physician, Jean Astruc,[25] rediscovered the key to Pentateuchal criticism that a German cleric, Witter, had found in 1711.[26] Astruc's views would probably have been forgotten like Witter's, the more since the leading Old Testament scholar of the day, Michaelis, found them unacceptable. It was their espousal by Eichhorn a generation later which gave them an epochal significance for Old Testament criticism. Of more immediate importance for late eighteenth century thought was Ernesti's introduction into German theology of the grammatical-historical exegesis[27] which had been pioneered by Dutch scholars like Grotius, and Semler's great work on the canon.[28]

Semler insisted that the early Church did not consider Scripture a fixed norm of doctrine for all time but rather a list of the books publicly read in Christian gatherings, and that purely external reasons had governed the selection. The idea of a canon is virtually abandoned or hollowed out, and the New Testament is viewed simply as a collection of early Christian documents. He claimed full freedom on the Christian's part to criticize them. Under the influence of Spinoza's thought he set up the principle that only those biblical books which serve man's moral improvement can be considered authoritative. On the basis of this rule he rejects Song of Songs, Ezra-Nehemiah-Chronicles, and less emphatically, Joshua, Judges, Samuel. In the case of the Gospels, he concedes some interpolations and claims that they were written for Jewish Christians and were permeated by Jewish phraseology and ideology which the Christian must first of all discount. The Book of Revelation he condemned as the product of an enthusiast. The line begun by Semler leads straight over to modern historical criticism.

Since Semler and in consequence of his work the idea came up with increasing force that ecclesiastical doctrine and Biblical teaching were at variance, and this brought about a more methodical analysis of Biblical teaching. Rationalists as well as some supernaturalists shared in this undertaking, though with very different results. Zachariae's work was written from the supernaturalist standpoint.[29] The rationalistic attitude, on the other hand, underlies that of Bauer.[30] The rationalists held that one must make allowances for local and temporal "disguises" of scriptural truth; this done, they tried to get at the pure underlying truth of the scriptural documents. At that point, however, their exegesis often passed into absurdity, for the truths they found were those of the "common sense" mind of their day. That limitation was soon to pass with the changing spirit of the times. Gabler's discourse of 1787[31] is regarded as the starting-point for the critical differentiation of the "theologies" of the various biblical writers, a subject thereafter called Biblical theology. With a sound higher criticism developing under the pioneering leadership of Eichhorn[32] and de Wette,[33] Biblical theology, utilizing criticism's results, was able to become truly historical in character.

Over against all this array of intellectual forces on the one hand and a stubborn orthodoxy on the other hand there stood that movement commonly called Pietism in the continental scene, and akin to Methodism in the English scene. In addition to nurturing a deeply religious spirit and showing great missionary zeal, Pietism produced theologians[34] and exercised a great influence on some who cannot be labelled as of that class. A theosophic current ran through this pietist theology and appears notably in men like Bengel, Oetinger and Crusius, whose thought was to affect the standpoints of various conservative scholars in the nineteenth century as well.[35] With these men we may mention one whose place is rather in the philosophical current, Hamann, an opponent of rationalism and exponent of the importance of emotion.[36] For all of those referred to, Old Testament prophecy had a great authority and attraction.

The days of the "reign of reason" were about over. Symptomatic of the changing outlook was the interest in nature and in the life of unspoiled children of nature that arose through Jean Jacques Rousseau. Attention was now also directed to folkways, folktales, folk-poetry and folk-song. In Germany Herder for the first time studied some of the materials of the Old Testament in the light of folk-literature, and found it a rich repository of that sort of thing, on which the educated taste may dwell with infinite delight.[37]

Influenced by Herder's example, the most versatile mind of the time, Goethe, also gave attention to the Old Testament from a secular angle and even contributed to biblical criticism.[38] Instructive as revealing his general position are several little papers in which he took the role of a country parson. In one he writes that when he was a student the Bible was explained too universally, as though everything said in it was for the whole world and for all time. His son, the Master of Arts, has the opposite foolish notion of twisting all passages that do not fit into his system of ideas into "local bagatelles". He thinks he has struck a middle of the road-course, and sets up a sign post showing the direction. This is done in the form of an allegory, reminding one of that of Lessing (p. 49 f.). The Jewish people was a wild unfruitful trunk in a circle of similarly wild, unfruitful trees. But on this trunk the celestial gardener grafted that noble branch Jesus Christ, that it might improve the nature of the tree and that from it new scions might be obtained for the grafting and ennobling of all the other trees. The history and teachings of this people, from the first germ to the time of grafting, was particularistic, and the little of universalism that may have occurred in it, in view of the impending divine intervention, is difficult and perhaps unnecessary to seek out. After the grafting, however, the whole thing took a different turn. Teaching and development now become universalistic. Although each tree that was grafted from that one source has its special history and its special teachings, according to circumstances, it is nevertheless the parson's opinion that there is as little that is particularistic here as there is universalistic yonder. This line of thought indicates that Goethe, however much he may have loved the Old Testament, saw the centre of things in the new order that began with Christ.

But through Herder a rich stimulus was also given toward appreciating other religions. If Spencer a century before had discerned the affinity existing between Hebrew ritual laws and the laws of other peoples, this was now carried further into the field of mythological ideas and theological concepts and perspectives of a universal history of religions arose before the mind. Biblical theology was bound to become enriched with comparative religious observation—a process that was destined to assume rising importance once the recovery of ancient Oriental civilizations provided first-hand testimony about the beliefs of Israel's contemporaries. This whole literary-historical and comparative-religious approach was, in spite of Herder's own theological slant, destined to become purely secular, and, purified of the romantic idealizations of Herder's time, is still bearing rich fruit in Old Testament research.[39]

Chapter Five

SCHLEIERMACHER AND THE OLD TESTAMENT

THE orthodox doctrine of Scripture had been toppled from its pedestal in the eyes of all those amenable to reason. It might take a long time before the Churches were driven to acknowledge the fact, but an unfettered theology could not do otherwise than to concede it. The problem now arose what was the right way to regard Scripture, and implicit in it was also that of the degree of authority to be accorded to the Old Testament. The greatest mind in Protestant theology since the Reformation, Schleiermacher, grappled with this, as with many other things, and set forth views that in retrospect carry forward the problem from the point where the advanced line in Luther's thinking had left it.[1]

For Schleiermacher, revelation does not stand at the centre of theology. He is closely linked with German Idealism, which had occupied itself with the ontological problem of the idea of God.[2] It had realized that God cannot be treated theoretically as a conditioned innerworldly entity, for He is the unconditioned. It posed the question for theology: how can we speak of God's Being in such a way as to do justice to His absoluteness? Idealism, furthermore, had an understanding for the practical nature of religion; it is not a theoretical certainty, but one that bears and governs our lives. Schleiermacher, therefore, sought its true sphere in the feelings and gave his famous religious-philosophical definition of (higher) religion as "feeling of absolute dependence on God".[3] Revelation for him thus could be no communication of knowledge, as for the supernaturalists, but only the rise of a new religious experience. He defines revelation as something new in the sphere of religious feelings that is basic for a certain religious community's life and is not understandable from the historical nexus preceding.[4] He makes no assertion about the new being divinely caused, for that would be dualistic. Thus theology through Schleiermacher, after searching for God in vain in the objective sphere, came to look for him in the subjective.

It is obvious that Schleiermacher has absorbed the lesson of Lessing's researches. In his general doctrine of Scripture[5] he teaches (1) that Holy Scripture cannot provide the basis for faith in Christ and only receives a special distinction where such faith is already present; (2) that the Holy Scriptures of the New Covenant are the first of an ever-since continued series of presentations of Christian faith and that they are normative for all subsequent presentations; (3) that the New Testament writings are "authentic" in their origin, (which term he dilutes to mean productions of the circles influenced by the Holy Spirit that went forth from Jesus, but not necessarily written by the authors to whom tradition attributes them), and that they are sufficient as norm for Christian teaching. The question is, Where does this leave the Old Testament?

Since Schleiermacher is bent on analysing the living Christian consciousness and extracting from it the beliefs that are a real expression of Christian convictions and spirit (for that is his new approach to doctrine), he naturally saw more clearly than those who operated in external fashion with Scripture authority that a gulf exists between the Hebrew and the Christian consciousness. He comes to grips with the matter of the Old Testament already when he discusses the relation of Christianity to Judaism on the one hand and to heathenism on the other.[6] It is not enough to quote his general proposition and then dismiss it as is so often done. The discussion with which he attempts to substantiate his proposition deserves careful attention.

By "Judaism", Schleiermacher says he means "the Mosaic institutions" and anything earlier that influenced the Jewish people in the direction of separatism. He concedes that Christianity has a historical connection with Judaism in so far as Jesus was born a Jew. But one must not imagine this connection as too exclusive, for at the time of Christ this people's manner of thinking was no longer centred entirely on Moses and the prophets, but had been refashioned in many respects by non-Jewish ideas absorbed in the captivity and dispersion.[7] On the other hand, Græco-Roman heathenism had also been prepared for monotheistic developments and was filled with the expectation of a new shape of things to come, while among the Jews the

Messianic promises were partly abandoned and partly misunderstood. If one views the entire historical situation comprehensively the differences between the two areas—Jewish and Græco-Roman—are less than would appear at the first glance. And the Jewish origin of Jesus is counterbalanced by two facts: first, that many more Gentiles than Jews went over to Christianity, and second, that Christianity would not have found as much acceptance among Jews as it did if Judaism had not itself been permeated by extraneous Græco-Roman influences.[8]

In so far as Christianity represents a transition from both Judaism and heathenism to another entity, its relation to both is the same. The transition from heathenism to Christianity appears more difficult, since the heathen had first to become monotheistic in order to become Christian; but in reality the two things were not so far apart, for monotheism was now given to the Gentiles in the form of Christianity, as previously in the form of Judaism. By contrast, the requirement made of the Jew not to rely on the law and to interpret the promises to Abraham otherwise than he was in the habit of doing was no less of a hurdle. Since we, therefore, must infer that Christian piety, as it was constituted from the very beginning, cannot simply be derived from the Judaism either of that time or of an earlier time, Christianity cannot in any way be regarded as a mere revised form of Judaism. If Paul in the third chapter of Galatians regards the faith of Abraham as the prototype of Christian faith and represents the Mosaic law as a temporary departure, one might infer that he wants to portray Christianity as a renewal of the original and pure Judaism of Abraham. But his real idea was only that Abraham's *faith* was related to the promise as ours is to the fulfilment, and not that the promise was the same to Abraham as the fulfilment is to us. And where he speaks specifically of the relation of Jews and Gentiles to Christ, he portrays Christ as the same for both, and both as equally far removed from God and therefore in need of Christ.

If Christianity bears the same relation to Judaism as it does to heathenism, it cannot be a continuation of Judaism any more than it is of heathenism. Whether the individual hails from the one area or the other, so far as his piety is concerned, he becomes a new man. The promise to Abraham, in so far as it is fulfilled in Christ, is only portrayed as having a relation to Christ in the divine plan and not in the pious consciousness of Abraham and his people. And since we can only concede the sameness of a pious fellowship where the consciousness is formed in the same way, we cannot recognize an identity of Christianity and the Judaism of Abraham any more than an identity of Christianity and later Judaism or heathenism. Nor can one say that a purer, original Judaism bore the germ of Christianity in itself in such a manner that in a natural progression, without intervention of something new, Christianity would have evolved out of it, or that Christ Himself was so involved in this Jewish progression that a new common life and existence could not have begun with Him.

The widespread belief that there is a single Church of God which has existed from the beginning of the human race and will continue to the end, does not, Schleiermacher urges, contradict his statement as much as would appear. For if the Mosaic law has a place in this unified divine order of salvation, the same is also true of the Greek wisdom of the world, notably that tending toward monotheism, according to acknowledged Christian teachers.[9] One cannot assert, of course, that the teaching of Christianity forms one whole with pagan wisdom without entirely cancelling the distinctiveness of Christianity. But if by this doctrine of the single Church one wishes to express the absolute relevance of Christ to all that is human, and make it extend even to the sphere of the past, then this is a purpose concerning which he cannot as yet express a judgment at this point in his doctrinal system, but with which his statement can well be harmonized. And so in Old Testament prophecy itself there is ascribed a different character to the New Covenant than to the Old (Jer. 31: 31–34). The juxtaposition in terminology already expresses the intrinsic separateness of the two quite definitely. Therefore, the rule is to be set up that for Christian use almost everything else found in the Old Testament is only a container for this particular prophecy, and that whatever is most definitely Jewish in its pages has the least value for the Christian. We can, accordingly, only find those of our Christian sentiments which are of a more general nature and not developed very peculiarly, reproduced with any exactitude in Old Testament passages; for those Christian sentiments that are distinctively developed, however, the Old Testament sayings will not be a suitable expression if we do not mentally subtract something or add something. Taking that into account we shall doubtless find in the utterances of the nobler and purer sort of heathenism many things relatively just as close and conformable to our point of view. Hence, apologists were formerly quite fond of referring to certain prophecies of Gentile origin that they regarded as "Messianic" and so recognized in that quarter a tendency of human nature toward Christianity.[10] The classic proposition in which Schleiermacher sums up this discussion is —"Christianity, it is true, stands in a special historical connection with Judaism, but with respect to its historical existence and its purpose, it has the same relation to Judaism as to heathenism."[11]

After setting forth his doctrine of Scripture as summarized above, Schleiermacher adds an appendix on the Old Testament.[12] This material, he says, stands outside the pale of doctrinal exposition because it is polemical, and thus will be superfluous as soon as the difference between the two groups of writings is recognized. He concedes, however, that the time when this will be the case is still remote. It would be audacious, furthermore, he grants, to set this up as the "Christian" teaching, since, in some quarters so much use is made of Old Testament passages for Christian edification that the New Testament only seems to play a minor role. And this takes place for opposite reasons both at the hands of those who place less value on that which is distinctive in Christianity and those who recognize that distinctive element as all-important for the salvation of man. Schleiermacher addresses himself only to the latter group because with them alone could he reach an understanding.

Turning to the Old Testament writings he distinguishes law and prophets. Concerning the law he says that if Paul is right in saying that the law, though divinely ordained, is something which came in between the promise to Abraham and its fulfilment (Gal. 3: 19), and that it is lacking in the power of the Spirit out of which Christian life proceeds (Rom. 7: 6 f. and 8: 3), then one cannot assert that the law was given by that same Spirit of which the apostle says that He is not communicated through the law and its works (Gai. 3: 2), but that God only sends Him into the heart in view of our connection with Christ.

Nor does Christ represent the Spirit that is sent (and with whose testimony He associates that of the disciples—John 14: 26, 15: 26, 27) as the return of one that was formerly present and had only disappeared for a time. But all the historical books from the giving of the law on hang together with the law.[13] And if we contrast Messianic prophecy as that most related to Christianity with the law as that most foreign to it, nobody will dare to assert that the Jewish historical books contain more of the history of Messianic prophecy than that of the law. Yes, even in the prophetic writings the bulk of the material refers to the legal constitution and the affairs of the nation as such, and the spirit out of which these things have come is none other than the spirit of the group, and therefore has nothing to do with the Christian Spirit which as the One should remove the wall separating this people from other peoples. Hence Messianic prophecy alone is left which could be due to inspiration in the sense in which we use the term. But if we recall that the prophets only rise to such heights on rare occasions and that only with respect to this is the spirit that animated them called "Holy" (II Peter 1: 21), then we must conclude that such prophesying only occurred infrequently. The spirit of the group combined with the consciousness of a need of redemption expressed itself in the form of intimation of a more spiritual divine sovereignty. This intimation bore in itself the highest receptivity for the Holy Spirit, and was also able to kindle and maintain it outside of itself.

Next Schleiermacher inquires into the matter of the authority of the Old Testament. It cannot be denied on the whole, he thinks, that pious Christians recognize that a considerable difference exists between the two portions of Holy Scripture. Even the noblest psalms always contain something that Christian piety cannot regard as a pure expression of itself, so that one must first deceive oneself by unconscious addition and subtraction if one thinks that one can set up a Christian doctrine of God out of prophets and psalms. On the other hand, he finds that the great fondness of Christians for availing themselves of individual Old Testament sayings as expressions of piety is almost always combined with a legalistic mode of thinking or a bondage to the letter of Scripture.

Turning to the use of the Old Testament for theological purposes, he grants that there are few Christian doctrines for which one has not attempted to adduce Old Testament passages as proof. But how, he asks, should it be possible that anything belonging to the doctrine of redemption through Christ should have been presented so clearly in the period of mere divinatory anticipation that it could still be usefully employed alongside of that which Christ Himself said, and that which His disciples said after His completion of the work of redemption?[14] Or, if one wishes to imagine this as possible through inspiration, would not an entirely different recognition have had to be accorded the Redeemer and the manner in which He announced the Kingdom of God by that part of the Jewish people that was learned in the Scriptures, so that the effect would in no way be commensurate with the cause to which one would ascribe it? Furthermore, the history of Christian theology shows plainly how this effort to find our Christian faith in the Old Testament has partly had a baneful influence on our application of the art of interpretation, and partly heaped upon the development of doctrine and the debate concerning its more exact definitions a lot of useless complications; so that an improvement is only to be expected when one entirely abandons the Old Testament Scripture proof for Christian teaching and leaves aside supposed doctrines that are primarily based upon it.

But if something that has long been in vogue in the Church is to be reformed, it is necessary to show how this practice arose. There are two grounds upon which the external co-ordination of the two collections rest. First, that not only Christ and the apostles based teachings on Old Testament Scripture lessons but that this was continued in the early Church before the New Testament canon was formed. But it is impossible to conclude from this that a similar homiletic use of the Old Testament should even now continue, or that we would have to reckon it a disaster for the Church if the Old Testament were no longer as well known to Christians as the New. Indeed, the gradual recession of the Old Testament, in so far as its ecclesiastical validity stems from this historical connection, is in the nature of the case, and least of all can that historical connection guarantee the normativeness or the inspiration of these books. The Pauline passages which testify to the usefulness of the Old Testament writings primarily relate to this customary homi-

letical mode of using them, and the free manner in which the
apostle himself employs them agrees entirely with that which
we have said, so that he would testify for us that we have no
further need of these proofs.

The second reason is that Christ and the apostles themselves
refer to the Old Testament writings as to divine authorities
favourable to Christianity. But from this it does not by any
means follow that we shall have need of these adumbrations for
our faith, since we have the experience—and the New Testament Scripture (John 4: 42) approves of it—that one ceases to
believe for the sake of such testimonies once one has more
direct and immediate certainty. He concedes, however, that it
belongs to historical fidelity and completeness that that to
which Christ and His first witnesses appealed as authority
should be preserved. This applies almost exclusively to the
prophetic writings and the Psalms; on this basis the practice of
appending the Psalms to the New Testament seems justified.
But since these writings had no separate existence at the time
of Christ but only existed as parts of the holy collection, and
are often only cited in this manner; and since, furthermore,
occasional quotations from other books occur, one cannot
object to it that the Old Testament (even though it cannot
possibly form an indivisible whole for us in the same sense as
for the Jewish people) be linked with the New Testament. Only
the true state of affairs would be better expressed if the Old
Testament were put after the New as an appendix, since the
present order seemingly sets up the requirement that one must
first go through the whole Old Testament in order to get to the
New in the right way.

The greatest theologian of nineteenth-century Protestantism
was thus in favour of putting the Old Testament in an extremely
subordinate position. But he hesitates to draw the full consequences of his standpoint by joining the Marcionitic group.
Elsewhere he asserts that from the arguments against conceding
equal authority to the Old Testament it does not follow that
the Bible should be cut in two. The latter is a resultant historical
entity. That the Church has put the two parts together is a fact
of such antiquity that no cause exists to change this, for the
disadvantageous consequences that can arise from this circumstance can be obviated by other means.

This is all religious thinking of a high order. It should, perhaps, be mentioned that modern Old Testament scholarship cannot concede to Messianic Prophecy the weight that Schleiermacher gave it. But it is true historically, at least, that Jewish Christianity arose out of the sphere of Jewish Messianism, and so his point can stand with some modification. More controversial is his thesis that Christianity is as much a continuation of "heathenism" (in the sense noted above) as of Judaism. I have encountered no endorsement of it, unless it be the somewhat related, yet different view of De Lagarde (p. 93f.). But there is more to be said for Schleiermacher's view than is commonly realized.[15] In the light of to-day's insight the Greek element in early Christianity was a very important factor in its survival and success. A mere Jewish messianic movement had no prospect of becoming a world religion. It was its metamorphosis into a religion of redemption, its employment of Greek mysticism and thought forms that set it aloft among the nations and permitted the properly denationalized Semitic element in it to become operative.[16] Schleiermacher could not yet have seen this as clearly as we can. But apart from these historical considerations, a mere appraisal of the Hebraic and Greek heritage in Christianity, when properly carried out, will show that the latter is both considerable and essential. It seems to me that Schleiermacher's position in this matter deserves consideration.

Chapter Six

THE OLD TESTAMENT IN NINETEENTH-CENTURY
THEOLOGICAL THOUGHT BEFORE RITSCHL

DOMINANT though the influence of Schleiermacher was on the subsequent theological development in so many respects, his views on the Old Testament were soon discounted. Even those who were his most immediate followers accorded them no defence. The unilateral treatment of both Testaments as the source of authority in the age of orthodoxy had impressed itself so deeply on the Christian mind that men were disposed to speak with regret about Schleiermacher's limitations in this matter and were quick to restore the Old Testament to a more exalted place.[1] We therefore need not linger over the successors of that master.

Some attention should, however, be bestowed on De Wette, who in certain respects continues the enlightenment, while in others he belongs to the new era. As biblical scholar he ranks with Eichhorn—above him, in fact, in originality of contribution. At this point, however, we are concerned with his theological views.[2] He was greatly influenced by the philosophy of Fries, who over against the scepticism of Kant in metaphysical matters held that the human mind could apprehend transcendent reality through feeling or intuition.[3] De Wette viewed all dogmas from the angle of discovering their underlying religious content, after abstracting their thought-forms as antiquated shell. Everything in the Bible which is not capable of appealing to this intuitive feeling is thus of no significance for us. The Old Testament is to be sharply differentiated from the New, but at the same time they are to be diligently compared. The process of life and thought in the Old Testament, he thinks, is strange to us in great measure; he sees it as "a great, wide territory of the unconscious or immediate in which the Spirit of God is operative in a mysterious way, filling the hearts of the

enthusiastic and the pious with intimations which they themselves cannot control or express clearly and purely, but which
His creative breath constantly fashions according to archetypes
unknown to them; using men as the unconscious agents of his
activity and as exhibitions of a divine-human life that develops
in the conflict with the world in stage after stage until it reaches
its consummation with Christ." De Wette defines the Unconscious as something general and indefinite, which lies at the
bottom of the particular; it is partly the universally human and
partly that which links the Old Testament with the New and
composes the life element in which the former moves on toward
the latter. It cannot be circumscribed intellectually, but only
apprehended by the feelings.

De Wette seeks to present the Christian faith in terms of
Biblical Dogmatics (therein a representative of an earlier age).
In handling the Old Testament materials he differentiates
between Hebraism and Judaism, with the Babylonian exile as
the dividing line.

In one of his later works[4] De Wette describes the Old Testament as containing the history of the founding and development
of that distinctive life of the Hebrew people which is commonly
called "theocracy". He distinguishes between the original
revelation of the Mosaic era and the further development of that
revelation, and finds a similar situation in the Christian order;
for there, too, the original revelation in Jesus Christ had a
further development after His time. The significance of the Old
Testament books for the Christian rests on the relation of the
new order to the old. The latter was imperfect and preparatory.
He finds that the Old Testament is only canonical in a certain
sense. The canon lies in the New Testament and only that which
accords with it in the Old is canonical.

In speaking of Christian use of the Old Testament De Wette
demands strict historical interpretation in complete independence of the New Testament. He finds intelligent handling of
some Old Testament teachings, such as those on retribution,
necessary and asserts that the layman cannot penetrate the
darkness and dusk of the Old Testament unless a teacher who is
filled with Christian truth carries the light ahead for him. He
would avoid preaching from Old Testament texts and finds the
Old Testament useful chiefly for such teachings as are not

covered, but only presupposed, in the New Testament, or for the purpose of projecting oneself back into the pre-Christian situation—a thing that he believes may be edifying.

But a reactionary current, continuing the line of eighteenth-century supernaturalism, now came to the fore and busied itself with battling against the dying enlightenment. It had the support of conservative political forces in Prussia and its chief leader was Hengstenberg, who began editing an influential Christian journal in 1827 and was forced upon the faculty of Berlin in 1828, thereby becoming the colleague of celebrities like Schleiermacher and Neander, the church historian. This current, being primarily ecclesiastical, did not at first affect the whole realm of scientific theology to any marked extent. Only in the field of Old Testament scholarship "in which the difficulty of language and the remoteness of the times with which it deals particularly favoured arbitrary play of fancy, where rabbinic theology and the allegorizing method of the church fathers and of the scholastic theologians had done advance service, was this influence immediately felt". Hengstenberg himself,[5] and kindred minds, carried on an orthodox interpretation of the Old Testament, condemning the higher critical views that had come up through Eichhorn and De Wette. "The Old Testament remained the favourite science of this new Judaism, even after its influence had spread to other fields and had captured important theological faculties." But Old Testament research of this stamp was not "to the taste of the times, which regarded such pettifogging, rabbinical interpretation of the Messianic passages of the Old Testament, such proofs for the Mosaicity of the Pentateuch, etc., with astonishment and amusement."[6]

Vast stimulation on the further development of all theological thinking, including that on the biblical problem, went forth from German philosophical Idealism. If the criticism of Kant trained the mind to operate more cautiously the teachings of Fichte, Hegel, Schelling gave it new goals and powerful inspiration. All the great German philosophers, beginning with Kant, branched out from the study of theology and in their writings show an understanding of its problems and a desire to deal with them. Schelling in the course of his development reaches a point where he views the religious question as paramount for philosophy.[7] The Hebraic heritage as well as the mystical-pantheistic are both strong in him and it is fascinating to observe their relative influence.[8] We shall confine ourselves here, however, to those thoughts which he developed in the final phase of his reflections, in which he dwelt on the philosophy of revelation. A preview of his thought on the matter appeared as early as 1815 and he lectured on it in Berlin in 1844–46.[9]

He brought forward the stone which the Rationalists had rejected—the idea of the eternal Incarnation of God and of His revelation—and made it the corner-stone of his final philosophical system. Lessing had described revelation as a progressive divine pedagogy and the Old Testament and New Testament as successive schoolbooks suited to the different stages. In so doing he had viewed the divine pedagogy rationalistically as consisting in the communication of important salutary truths. Schelling asserts that something can only be "revealed" which we could never know without revelation—something which transcends reason. The revelation that constitutes the content of Christianity is a *fact*—an act of the divine will which we can only understand and become convinced of by experiencing it. The fact of revelation consists in this: that a humanity fallen away from God is brought back to Him and reconciled with Him. This reconciliation was through Christ and therefore the person of Christ is the content of Christianity. He is not only the end and goal but the beginning and sole cause of revelation, and hence revelation in its full scope is embraced in Him. But this revelation which is completed in Christianity also passed through earlier pagan and Jewish stages; mythology, which is the essence of paganism and also is inherent in Judaism, forms the necessary presupposition of Christianity and is related to it as the abrogated is to the abrogator. It is apparent that for the biblical problem Schelling's position here is similar in its effect to that of Schleiermacher: emphasis on the Christian order; the Old Testament abrogated and on a par with pagan mythology.

The philosophical current reached its climax in Hegel. He touches on the theme that concerns us in his posthumously published *Philosophy of Religion*, when he surveys the religions of mankind.[10] We need not linger over his general theory except to note that he puts the Jewish, Greek and Roman religions together in one group as the three "religions of spiritual individuality"; the first is the religion of Exaltedness (*Erhabenheit*), the second that of Beauty (*Schönheit*). the third that of Purposefulness (*Zweckmässigheit*). Christianity then is discussed in a final section and labelled "the absolute religion". Hegel—like Schleiermacher—does not view Christianity as an offshoot of the Hebrew religion. Its immediate predecessor, he holds, is the Roman state religion, which prepared the soil for Christianity by the destruction and levelling down of all independent religious life. Hegel, furthermore, disapproves of representing Christianity as a "revealed religion" (*geoffenbarte Religion*), which looks for proof to miracles, signs, outward testimonies, documents and biblical quotations. He considers it rather "the manifest religion" (*offenbare Religion*), and would have the power of its own inherent truth as apprehended by the mind be its sole demonstration.[11] Obviously his position leaves little room for the authority of a sacred book, and must have extremely negative consequences for the Old Testament in particular, owing to his views on the Jewish religion that we have already referred to.

The close link with theology found in Hegel is snapped asunder in his follower Feuerbach.[12] For him religion is an illusion, and theology nothing but anthropology. The Old Testament religion, he held (therein an apt pupil of the British and French Deists of an earlier day), is entirely immoral; even the highest idea produced by "Hebraism", that of the love of God, is merely a form of human selfishness that puts the self in the place of God. In the doctrine of Creation the human will projects itself into ultimate power. The God of the Old Testament is one who satisfies all the wishes and desires of the human heart. Thus man has created God in his own image. Feuerbach believes Græco-Roman paganism was superior to the religion of the Old Testament; it is rooted in nature and that for him is the only reality.

While speaking of the philosophical development we may mention at this point also the thought of Schopenhauer[13] which was destined to attain a great importance in its effect on the German masses in the succeeding decades. He is a Kantian, but develops Kant's position further by making the will antecedent to reason instead of leaving the two side by side; thought, he held, must serve the will. Therein a change in the view of man and the world was indicated more fundamental than any since the days of the Greeks, for Descartes, Spinoza, Kant all basically continued Greek rationalism. Schopenhauer's basic starting-point could have led to an association with the Christian religious heritage. But his pessimism led him to deny the will to live and therewith to anti-Christian tendencies. Viewing Christianity as derived from Judaism, Schopenhauer made the latter an especial object of his hate, and indeed it may well be said that he paved the way for the anti-Semitic crisis of our century by the publicity he gave to his viewpoint.

The theistic idea of God, he thinks, was made impossible by the Copernican astronomy. He explains the rise of theism with a psychological theory somewhat after the manner of Feuerbach: monotheism arose out of polytheism in a process of reduction of many gods to one, while polytheism arose out of the human desire for agencies able to aid men to get what they want or to ward off what they fear. True philosophical religion for Schopenhauer has two criteria—the belief in the moral significance of human actions and the belief in life after death. The moral significance of our actions consists in self-denial and a virtuous state of mind that excludes all selfish motives. The Old Testament religion is destructive of morality because it awakens selfish motives, making the desire to obtain rewards or to escape punishment fundamental. That religion, furthermore, knows no immortality; where the belief appears on the periphery, as in the twelfth chapter of Daniel, it is of foreign origin. Ecclesiastes 3: 19–21 expresses the real Hebrew view.

In the theological development, however, Hegelianism was the order of the day. Notably the evolutionistic approach that Hegel had applied was having its effect on all historical thinking. Biblical studies now took on a fresh hue, and particularly all efforts to deal with the story of the religious development of Israel and early Christianity. Utilizing the results of the criticism pioneered by Eichhorn and De Wette but proceeding evolutionistically in the spirit of Hegel, Vatke now gave a brilliant presentation of the development of the Old Testament religion,[14] on which a Wellhausen fifty years later still bestowed the praise that it was the most important contribution ever made to the historical understanding of ancient Israel. Fully Hegelian was Bauer's book on the Old Testament revelation.[15] He paves the way for his study by a whole philosophy of religion rooted in Hegelian idealism. Religion is the self-consciousness of the absolute mind (God). This self-consciousness is in the process of evolution and is confronted by limitations which it must overcome in order to attain its full growth. That process constitutes the history of revelation. The contents of revelation are apprehended by the subjective mind (man) in the thought of a divine purpose. Their recording leads to the origin of Scripture. While the initiative in revelation is entirely that of the absolute mind, the subjective mind takes the initiative in the recording (Scripture), but moving the while within the growing self-consciousness of the absolute mind. Limitations and errors of the subjective mind unavoidably creep into the Scripture record, but are corrected and outgrown in the general process.

In describing the history of revelation Bauer sets forth how the true idea of religion is gradually realized in it. Being historical, religion passes through various stages which by themselves are in antithesis to the very concept of religion on its highest plane. The presentation of its history is thus necessarily critical, and involves discernment of the degree of antithesis in which a particular stage stands in relation to the ultimate goal, as well as of the way in which this situation sets up a drive toward attaining a higher synthesis. There is thus an upward progression in the Old Testament revelation. So far as the authority of the Old Testament is concerned little could be left of it under such a view.

In the wake of Hegel, however, the theological interest soon shifted to a more crucial area than the Old Testament—to that of the New Testament revelation. Here Strauss' book on Jesus, in which he dissolved the gospel story into mythology, was a blazing beacon casting its rays far into the future.[16] And then came the great criticism of the New Testament literature and the study of the evolution of Christian dogma by the Tübingen school, shaking all Christendom. What Schleiermacher was to Systematic theology, F. C. Baur was to Historical theology.[17] Generations have laboured at the problems he posed and some of the answers he gave are more nearly right than many were willing to believe.

But theological conservatism, too, produced its important

figures whose positions were to sway many. Out of German Pietism and its fidelity to a biblical study coupled with mysticism, which had flowered so markedly in the work of a Bengel a century earlier, there now arose Beck.[18] He stressed the idea that the Bible is the source of all religious truth, and urged that one must go back to it directly—disregarding all the confessions of the Churches. He viewed the Bible as an organic whole in which nothing is accidental, but each part is planned to serve a function, like the pieces of a picture puzzle. The theologian must extract the essential things from the Bible and restate them in reflective thinking. The Bible contains, as it were, a whole system of truth. Beck does not consider the inspiration of the Bible as verbal, but rather thinks of the persons behind the Bible as inspired men of God. Hence to understand the Bible properly one must have personal religious experience. For Beck, Love is the basis and goal of all revelation. In interpreting Scripture he believes one must first determine the individual physiognomy of a given document and then take the further step of seeking the traits of a Messianic theological character that lie hidden in it (considering the totality of the Scriptural revelation), and in this way discover the significance such a document has in the plan of the Holy Spirit. Apocalypticism, as it lives on in part of the New Testament, had a great attraction for Beck. The coming Kingdom of God as preached by Jesus (and having nothing to do with any ecclesiastical organization) was a vivid reality to him. Since this is really Old Testament heritage in the New Testament it is apparent that an important strand of Old Testament belief exercised a strong effect on him.

Within the current of Hengstenberg which had come to the fore at the University of Erlangen a scholar arose who, next to Calvin, provided the most useful viewpoints for the defence and proper utilization of the Old Testament on a conservative basis: J. C. K. von Hofmann. He realized that mere dogmatic assertion of biblical authority and inspiration was not enough; it was his ambition to justify them by historical means. While his major efforts were devoted to the New Testament, he also gave considerable attention to the Old Testament. His work in the latter field[19] was of basic importance for the development of his whole theological position. He sees the Old Testament against the background of a "history of redemption" or

Heilsgeschichte—a word that he hammered into the more conservative strain of German theology. He imagines this as a real historical development (albeit of a stained-glass window variety) with progressive stages. In this development, he holds, Messianic prophecy played a considerable role. The true significance of any particular prophecy was not discernible at the time it was given, but only becomes clear in the light of the standpoint of redemption, which reached a preliminary completion in the work of Christ and will not be entirely completed until history shall have ended. The full import of some prophecies, therefore, cannot be understood even now. Holding Christ to be pre-existent, he finds his redemptive influence operative in the area of Old Testament thought and experience. He even believes that this pre-existent Christ influenced Gentile trends toward a hope of redemption.

In a second major work[20] von Hofmann then attempted to determine the significance of the biblical materials for Systematic theology. The important point to him is that we Christians are in a relation with God that is a part of a great divine-human relationship extending through history. This larger history is reflected in the Bible in such a way that the divine-human relationship is mediated through Christ. This is the case throughout the entire Bible; at each point, however, we see it in a different stage of its development. A system of theology is demonstrated when all of its tenets are in accord with Scripture, every part of the latter having been studied in such a way that it is seen in its correct position and integral relation to the whole of that development.

To undertake the task of examining all Scripture—at least that of the New Testament—in such a manner in detail was the tremendous project to which von Hofmann next addressed himself.[21] Starting with the Epistle to the Galatians, he hoped to show how the individual stages of the development of the literature of the New Testament fit into the historical process of the earliest history of the Church, and what their relation is to the whole. The growth of the New Testament canon as such was also to be viewed in teleological terms. The final step was to be the investigation of the relation of the Old Testament Scripture to New Testament Scripture in order to determine by what right the Church considers the former a part of its Holy Writ. By striving to show that every part of Scripture served an end and had a necessary place in the scheme of the whole, he hoped to prove its divine origin and inspiration—at least to the satisfaction of the Christian believer. This approach, he thought, would render it unimportant whether any particular New Testament document was really "apostolic" in authorship or not.

Hofmann's project remained incomplete for the New Testament, with its continuation for the Old Testament not even in sight. But his ideas had a powerfully stimulating and enduring effect in conservative quarters. Various scholars of more recent times have called for a resumption of Hofmann's approach in more modern form (e.g., Procksch). His influence survives also in the work of Vischer. Consonant to some extent with Hofmann's *Heilsgeschichte* was the emphasis that A. Vilmar placed on the theology of God's saving acts in history (*Heilstatsachen*),[22] over against rationalistic emphasis on truths or Schleiermacher's emphasis on feeling.

In the continuation of the theological current that stemmed from Schleiermacher various shades of opinion, liberal and conservative, had their share. In connection with the problem of the Bible, Rothe deserves particular mention,[23] for his doctrine on this matter powerfully influenced all subsequent conservative theology. He follows Schleiermacher in differentiating sharply between revelation and Scripture. Since he was more of a believer in the supernatural than Schleiermacher, he placed a much stronger emphasis on revelation than his great predecessor. There are two sides to revelation according to Rothe: manifestation and inspiration. God manifests Himself by His actions in the historical process. Sinful man, however, would not be able to interpret God's action aright if it were not for the fact that God had inspired certain men to do this for Him by their spoken word. As authoritative interpreters these individuals had an active part in the historical process of revelation. But in order that this process of revelation might become a factor in subsequent history, when the living voices of these interpreters were hushed, it had to be reliably recorded. This recording was achieved through the execution and preservation of a series of writings in which the facts of the sacred history and their authoritative interpretations were made available for future generations. These writings have the character of "records" or

official documents and this gives them a permanent authority—
they too have become a part of the extension of the process of
revelation. But they are not inspired as such. They are not
infallible in the sphere of that which does not pertain to revelation, but only in that which does pertain thereto. They form an
instrument that suffices for the necessary knowledge of the
divine revelation because it contains within itself the means to
correct errors contained in any of its parts taken by themselves.
Rothe finds that it was a great weakness of the orthodox period
that it could not differentiate between religion and theology.[24]
The Protestant Scripture-principle must be understood as meaning that one should use the Bible not as a source of doctrines
but of daily companionship, inhaling its sacred atmosphere, as
it were, seeking a living view of its revelation. But important as
the Bible is for the individual Christian, it must be remembered
that it is primarily the book of Christendom as a whole, not of
one day, but of all ages, lands and peoples. This reminder was
particularly important and cannot be stressed too often.

In this connection we may cite the views of another speculative theologian, who, however, belongs to the ecclesiastical
current: Frank.[25] He inaugurated the approach of investigating the grounds of Christian certainty (1870) as a form of
Christian apologetics. On what grounds, he inquires, is the
Christian convinced of the truth of the Christian religion? This
is something very different from attempting to persuade non-
believers. According to Frank, all certainty is based on experience, and the experience of regeneration gives one certainty as
to a considerable number of "objects of faith". He divides these
into three classes: immanent, transcendent and transeunt. In
the last mentioned category belongs "the Word of God". The
latter, he argues, is by no means identical with Scripture, but
since it is laid down in Scripture in its initial and documentary
form, a certainty concerning the Word of God includes also a
certainty concerning Scripture. This certainty in no wise proceeds from our becoming convinced first that various portions of
Scripture are Word of God and then proceeding to embrace the
whole, nor does it exclude doubts as to the divine character or
relevance of some of its parts. Nevertheless, Scripture is a sort
of living organism of many members in which any particular
member is only understood or appropriated in relation to the

whole and receives its vital force from the centre. In regeneration the individual may only have experienced the Word of God as it came to him in the living oral message of the Church. If he turns to the Scriptures and finds portions of them bearing no discernible relation to salvation, he will set them aside, but will all the more firmly embrace those portions which confirm his possession of that salvation and open his eyes as to their content and origin. But in this case the individual really can only be arbitrarily differentiated from the Church, for the Bible (notably the New Testament) is the book of the Church, having arisen out of its own life, and being the expression of its faith in the very days of its crystallization. The faith thus expressed has continued to nourish the life of the Church ever since. Historical criticism has its place and must deal with the matter of the integrity and authenticity of the individual writings. While faith must believe that those who first proclaimed the Word had a special authority owing to the position given them by Christ, this does not preclude the possibility of doubting that every one of those whose writings the Church accepted into its canon really was one of those possessing such authority. However, it is difficult for the individual to isolate himself from the Church or set up his judgment against that of the Church. Furthermore, the spiritual experience which the Church has had with these writings is even more important than such critical considerations of the individual. The original words, handed down in writing and spoken in relation to definite historical situations and concrete problems and experienced as saving Word of God either at the time or subsequently in retrospect, are experienced ever anew by the Church in similar or divergent situations and perhaps with a much richer and fuller understanding.

While certainty as to the Word of the New Testament is the first thing to be embraced as one proceeds backward from the present living Word of God in the Church, Frank holds that the Word of the Old Testament also has a claim upon the Christian because it is the preparation for and the presupposition of the Word of the New Testament. But certainty of the pre-Christian Word is not to be had for the Christian except as mediated through the Christian Church. Our situation was fixed by the early Church when it took Old Testament Scripture to its bosom and read it in the light of Christian fulfilment. And with the Church of that time and all ages, we can discern how God dealt with the people of the Old Covenant in a manner not unlike that with which He dealt with the community under the New Covenant. Born out of the womb of the Old Testament Church, the Church of the New Testament has ever been and still is capable of apprehending the preparatory Word that was given under the earlier Covenant, not indeed without the historical record of the Old Testament, and yet not merely through it, but rather through a spiritual response, confirmed as that is by all the historical threads that tie the two orders together. Naturally the Old Testament Word must recede into the background—not because it was to a lesser degree Word of God, but because it points beyond itself to a fulfilment without which it would lose its significance. There is no Psalm that the Christian can pray without infusing into it elements drawn from the Christian consciousness, and in doing so he does not corrupt the Old Testament Word of God, but takes it to his heart in just the sense in which it is and remains Word of God for him. The preparatory character of the Old Testament order has of necessity antiquated certain of its arrangements which were once in full force and possessed a divine validity for that order. We can discern in them, in spite of human imperfections attending their mediation, the hand of God ordering the life of the Old Testament community with a view to the coming realization of salvation. Even books like Esther or Ecclesiastes can be understood as not entirely unrelated to the Old Testament Word of God in so far as the former testifies to a particular deliverance of the people of God, and the latter to an experience of an Old Testament believer which has points of contact with phases through which Christian experience of life may also pass. Even so, there can be no Christian certainty that must necessarily embrace every book of the Old Testament. The Church itself, as in the case of the New Testament, is in a continuous, never completed process of trying to understand and becoming certain of the Word of the Old Testament.

Careful attention will disclose that this conservative Lutheran thinker has granted (1) that the process of fixing the canon is by no means definitely completed and that doubts concerning individual books are permissible; (2) that the Old Testament belongs primarily to a pre-Christian order; (3) that our acceptance of the Old Testament is chiefly due to its use in the early Church, as reflected in the writings comprising its New Testament. Obviously the liberal views have captured a conservative stronghold, and one may infer that only the feeling for the historical continuity of the Hebrew and Christian orders and loyalty to ecclesiastical tradition make him hold fast to the Old Testament at all. It is not our function here to examine Frank's general theological presuppositions, but we may at least point out this much, that his emphasis on the subjective factor of regeneration *per se* tends to subordinate the idea of the Word of God. This gives his whole theology an anthropocentric tinge and lays it open to criticism at the hands of those who desire a theocentric approach.

We may before terminating this account of the period between Schleiermacher and Ritschl glance at how some leading Old Testament scholars saw the biblical problem. It will suffice to single out Oehler, Diestel, and Ewald.

In his able historical survey of 1845, which was preparatory to his *Theology of the Old Testament* (published after his death), Oehler already sets forth his basic ideas.[26] He rejects all Christianization of the Old Testament, but at the same time views it as preparatory for the New and organically connected with it. Since in every sphere of organic life the earlier stages can be understood only from the final stage, so too the key to the Old Testament is given us by the New. For Oehler the Incarnation and Reconciliation of the world with God are the essence of Christianity. He therefore views the Old Testament as reflecting the movement leading up to the attainment of this reconciliation. The Old Testament presupposes: (1) The differentiation of God and the world—the Holy One versus sinful humanity; (2) The realization that God is for the world and desires to reveal Himself to it and fulfil His purpose in it, and that as the world is of God so it is for God, as place of His revelation and scene of His glory, and especially that man is created unto God. Hence the Old Testament shows on the one hand a progressive manifestation of God to the world and in the world toward the goal of union with man, and on the other hand a striving of man to enter into this fellowship and so become partaker of life. The attempt must then be made to find a meaningfulness in the historical and intellectual developments mirrored in the Old Testament. No thoughts are to be imputed to the ancient writers not warranted by sound historical interpretation, but at the same time that which was in their minds is to be viewed in its nexus with the whole organic development from the Christian standpoint. The ancient writers themselves, he concedes, could not yet have this understanding. In practice this must lead to considerable speculation if one is to discern and explain such connections.

A generation later there appeared Diestel's great study—a vast inventory of our whole subject in all its antiquarian aspects.[27] In a concluding chapter, however, the author discusses what he calls "the solution of the theological problem". The latter, according to him, is that of the "correct discernment of the religious content of the Old Testament". To our present-day way of thinking this would limit him to the purely historical. But Diestel has more than the merely historical in mind. He asserts that the various lines of thought concerning the Old Testament problem that have appeared in the course of time follow diverse principles and main viewpoints which are one-sided and can only do partial justice to the task in hand. He rules out entirely any doctrinal approach (because he regards that as tackling the problem with a ready-made solution in one's pocket), as well as any theosophical viewpoint (because that represents a false fusion of the philosophico-historical and the religious principles), and finds three lines of inquiry hitherto pursued alone legitimate:

(1) The purely historical (Diestel says "national") which stresses the full objective understanding of the Hebrew nation, of its literary remains, and of its religion in the light of its Oriental character and background. He finds this approach unsatisfactory in that it points beyond itself, crying out for an evaluation of Israel—of its place in the world and the relative quality and worth of its literature and religion. Where that task is undertaken at all on this standpoint, it results in what Diestel calls "ethnicism", which he defines as the undue emphasizing of the similarities and the overlooking or slighting of the differences between Israel and the nations. (2) The philosophic-historizing line. By this he means attempts to approach the Old Testament from the angle of a philosophy of religion in such a way as to construe the Hebrew development

in accordance with certain ideas or principles. This approach is
particularly exposed to error when, instead of proceeding from
the standpoint of Christianity, it takes a standpoint in pre-
Christian "ethnic" viewpoints (dualism, deism, pantheism). On
all sides it threatens to fall into a more or less humanistically
fashioned naturalism.   (3) The purely religious line.   This
emphasizes primarily the eternal truths of Israel's religion or
its kinship with Christianity, as well as those historical aspects
of the Old Testament religion that are important from the point
of view of a history of redemption. Presupposing that history is
not merely a work of accident or a product of the human mind,
it sees in these factors the hand of a divinity and thus regards
them as products of revelation. But this view can also become
artificial when it fails to give due heed to realistic knowledge.
The Hebrew records are then looked upon merely as revelations
of God and everything that is not pleasing to ourselves in them
is set aside; as a result the distance existing between this
religion and Christianity at various points is not gauged with
exactitude and the purely human and historical factors operative in the whole Hebrew situation are overlooked. Indeed, the
approach can become so one-sided that it results in a new
Judaism (by neglecting criticism from the Christian angle), or a
sort of Docetism (by denial of the co-operation of any human
factors). Actually the Bible does not content itself with giving
us God's Word, but shows how the latter became the possession
of men, and thus provides us with documents of human piety
as well. Providence, Diestel holds, shows itself most glorious
when it does not put out of action the natural conditions under
which human documents are wont to arise, but when it permits
these to operate undisturbed. If imperfections and errors
necessarily creep into such records, the spirit of Christ, that will
not be lacking in any honest searcher of the Scriptures, will
illuminate the reader so that his eye is not blinded by them, but
rather becomes sharpened and accustomed to proper differentiation.

Diestel then recommends a combination of all three principles,
hitherto used only in a one-sided manner, in their essentially
correct and justified aspects. The really religious approach, he
asserts, must take its standpoint within Christianity and the
Christian idea of God as He revealed Himself in Christ, and thus

must consider the Old Testament phenomena in the light of their approximation to or distance from Christianity. Before Christianity came there could not be any adequate idea of the divine truth. As for the human side of Israel's life, there could be no full understanding or appraisal of its meaning and worth before the coming of Christianity. Just because divinely given possibilities and values work themselves out in that human element, the exact study of the latter must be demanded of Old Testament scholarship in the name of religion itself. To understand the self-revelation of Israel in its religious documents, as they hang together with their ancient environment, must be the object of strenuous effort. Our belief that God is operative in history and that the totality of that ancient history prepared the way for Christianity requires an interest in that history itself. It also justifies our applying the comparative study of religions to the religion of Israel, and gives us the task of discovering and setting forth this religion's exact place among all the others. In such a fusion of three hitherto separate and legitimate approaches, Diestel sees a programme in accordance with which ever new attempts to study the subject must be made. For as long as there is human development and the depths of Christianity remain inexhaustible, our knowledge of it can never be final.

In essence, Diestel here set forth the procedure with which Christian biblical scholarship is now coming to operate. We are inclined to tone down the second principle (though we cannot do without the unifying activity of the mind or evolutionary considerations) because of our modern distrust of all speculative constructions. But the third principle, except for the emphasis on "truths" or on "providence" is now being invoked more fully by Old Testament scholars, in so far as they are Christian churchmen. That the trail thus blazed by Diestel was not followed sooner was partly due to the fact that men's minds became focused on the objective and material side of life, beginning with the 'seventies, and that this spirit, carried over into the field of biblical studies, resulted in their increasing historization and secularization. Graf's great critical work which had already appeared[28] and Kuenen's book now being issued[29] were harbingers of the Old Testament scholarship of the immediate future.

A particularly significant figure is Ewald. He is the first among German scholars to follow the example set in England by Milman's *History of the Jews*, 1829, of treating the history of Israel in secular spirit. His work on that subject is on a large scale[30] and contrasts markedly with the "stained-glass window" presentation (in von Hofmann's vein) given by the noted Church historian Kurtz.[31] Ewald also did yeoman service in awakening literary appreciation for Hebrew prophecy and poetry. The main effect of his labours was thus of a secularizing nature. Nevertheless he wanted to be a theologian, and his theological position on the Bible and the Old Testament in particular was set forth in a Biblico-theological work of 1871.[32]

Ewald recognizes the Bible as only one of three agencies by means of which modern man can come to the knowledge of the true revelation and to the fear of God—the other two being sufficient by themselves to that same end: they are the Christian fellowship which embraces us from cradle to grave with its wealth of impulses, and our own practice and experience of the fear of God whereby we alone attain an actual religious life. But alongside of these two other factors, the Bible nevertheless remains the sole unchangeable mirror of this revelation and fear of God, by means of which we can alone discern for certain whether the other agencies are as pure and undefiled as they should be. Its supreme position for the Church is thus assured, even though it may not be the agency that chiefly touches us as individuals. But high as the Bible stands, it is only a means to an end—a passageway through which we pass. Let us not overestimate this mere passageway and imagine that in this or that word of the Bible we hear the Word of God without considering what the Word of God which we ought to follow really is, and let us not take offence at this or that word and stumble over a book that is meant to elevate and help us.

Ewald differentiates three strata of material pertaining to revelation in the Bible: (1) a stratum of earlier religious ideas no longer fully alive in the days of the authors themselves, e.g., ideas like Cherubim and Seraphim, or of God as Lord of Hosts; (2) the middle stratum lying in the sunlight of full contemporary experience on the part of the people for whom these books were written, e.g., the great truths about God, the Kingdom, and the Messiah, or in the New Testament, Jesus

Christ; (3) a stratum dealing with mysteries such as the secrets of the divine wisdom or purpose of God in the life of individuals and of mankind, and with the remote historical mysteries of the beginnings of the world and of history.—It is our duty to bring these three stages together into a higher unity, taking our starting point *from the middle stage* that lies before us in full clarity, and always following the materials of the other stages in such a way that we ask ourselves whether these things can still have the same significance for us as for the ancients. We must not allow ourselves to be disturbed by former or present errors, no matter how influential they may have become. If the Jews, since the wars of annihilation under Titus and Hadrian, discarded all Hellenistic writings and broke with Christianity as well, how can that obligate us *not* to see the great historical truth? And if many learned Christians would hold only to the New Testament and reject the Old, that is an even graver error and soon leads to the discarding of the New Testament too. Therewith the true and necessary connectedness of the whole great history is overlooked, just as was done by the Jews, and with worse consequences. The Old Testament contains such a host of basic truths, so well and perfectly stated, that they cannot be more profoundly established or more adequately defended in the New Testament, but are simply presupposed there, as standing fixed since of old. If in other respects the Old Testament does not reach the highest perfection, it nevertheless strives toward that goal most valiantly and at least in some of its most advanced areas comes close to it. No greater praise can be accorded the Old Testament than this, Ewald holds, that without it the New Testament with all its fruits which it provides for us would not have been possible.

In this attempt to deal with the problem Ewald practically subordinates the Bible to the Church and individual experience, though theoretically maintaining its supremacy in the long range view. The Scripture problem is thus made less acute than when everything is staked on Scripture. His defence of the Old Testament is less satisfactory. Basically, we are on rationalistic ground when we emphasize ideas or truths. In that respect Ewald's doctrine of revelation is really only a modification of orthodoxy and subject to some of the same criticisms as its progenitor.

A brief glance at the state of affairs in the Anglo-Saxon countries reveals a continuance of orthodoxy on the one hand and the spread of a deep Christian revivalism on the other hand. Theologically speaking the most significant figures in England were Pusey and Newman. The former was a believer in the literal inspiration of the Bible. He reacted strongly against the higher critical movement because he saw in it an underlying "disbelief" in supernatural revelation. This comes to the surface, e.g., in the polemical preface to his commentary on Daniel,[33] where he discerns the uselessness of argument with those imbued with the prejudice that there cannot be such a thing as supernatural prophecy. Newman had less reason than the biblical scholar Pusey to concern himself with nineteenth-century criticism. He stands committed to the inspiration and literal truth of the Bible. This does not prevent him from speaking disparagingly on occasion of the "Jewish Scriptures" as delivering to us only those attributes of God already known to "natural religion",[34] or of acknowledging that some writings like Esther, Ecclesiastes and Song of Songs hold a weak position in the canon. The latter, he believes, depends for its authority on the Church, since Scripture contains no "internal mark" of its canonicity. He held that the gospel was contained in the Old Testament in a hidden way; that it was not on the surface had proved to be a stumbling-block for the Jews and had ultimately become their undoing.[35] He adopted the method (ultimately rooted in Calvin) of establishing a doctrine by working backwards from its clear statement in the New Testament to its hidden formulation in the Old. As an example of his procedure one may take his treatment of Justification.[36] He contends that Scripture in its various portions conspires together as a whole to this doctrine, but he limits himself to showing how several Psalms pray for forgiveness and renewal of life and how a few prophetic passages predict the granting of these things in the Messianic future, and then swiftly passes over to the New Testament teachings.

In the American scene Calvinism prevailed, with some inner dissensions that we need not dwell on. The influence of the Old Testament was large and there was little thought of questioning its authority, though there were Christian men, led by such a vastly influential preacher as Henry Ward Beecher, who put the God of Love and the teachings of Christ at the heart of Christianity and recoiled from the "spiritual barbarism" of Calvinism and of some elements of Old Testament teaching. But they had no clear idea of the consequences for the status of the Old Testament to which such a position was bound to lead. But German higher criticism had entered the American scene in 1843 through Theodore Parker's translation of De Wette's *Einleitung*,[37] and Moses Stuart, though an orthodox scholar,[38] had translated Gesenius' Hebrew Grammar and furthered Hebrew studies, as well as interest in German Old Testament contributions (of the conservative variety). The fires of the higher criticism were thus beginning to smoulder, and as more and more young men were attracted to the German Universities and introduced to the rapidly moving intellectual life that was going on there a dissatisfaction with the tyranny of dogma arose. It needed only the wind of definite occasions to fan the fire into flames. The fact that in the great debate over slavery, prior to the outbreak of the Civil War of the 'sixties, the Old Testament had been much used to defend the supposed divine endorsement of that institution was doubtless a factor making for greater readiness on the part of New Englanders to examine the earlier portion of the canon with a critical mind.

Chapter Seven

THE TRANSITION TO THE MODERN SITUATION

THE enlightenment which went forth from eighteenth-century England to France and reached Germany last returned in metamorphosed form since 1860 from Germany to the tight little isle. The latter had been powerfully influenced by the evangelical movement led by the Wesleys, and now the Oxford Movement led by Pusey and Newman was revitalizing the Church of England. Orthodox biblicism was deeply entrenched once more and it seemed unlikely that biblical criticism of the sort being carried on in Germany could find admission there. But it was overlooked that biblical criticism had arisen on the Continent in emulation of the critical method developed in the study of the Greek and Roman classics. Homeric criticism found a hearing in England and thus paved the way for the application of similar principles to the biblical literature. A series of incidents now occurred which, through the publicity they received, helped to bring about a change.

A situation of pressure demanding some reasonable adjustment of the Scripture doctrine had been created in England by natural science. A nation taught to believe that the world was created in 4004 B.C. was naturally shocked when Smith and Lyell laid the foundations for Geology and made clear that large periods of time were necessary to account for the stratification of rock, and when the historicity of the Flood became very doubtful.[1] Instructed by Moses that man was a product of special creation, it was horrified to have Darwin talk of the *Origin of Species* (1859) and proclaim an evolution of man from lower forms of life.[2] Hardly had the first excitement over Darwin passed when there occurred the *Essays and Reviews* incident of 1860.[3] Seven scholars, six of them Anglican Churchmen, were contributors to this volume, in which were to be found such modern ideas as that the Bible must be interpreted like any other book or that the Mosaic account of the creation of man was not to be taken as accurate history. Under the lead of Bishop Wilberforce of Oxford, who had already played a role in the ecclesiastical excitement over Darwin, the essayists were assailed as "guilty of criminal levity". The Christian public vociferously demanded that they be ousted from the Church. When two of the authors were suspended by their local authorities they appealed to the Queen in Council. Even a man of such lofty character as Pusey favoured their condemnation. But the Court, over the protest of its two Archbishop members, but with the approval of the Bishop of London, Tait, found the suspension unwarranted. After the excitement had subsided some of the things that had been said on the liberal side found response in many quarters and continued to simmer there.

Another incident capturing public attention arose through the publication by Colenso of a work on the Pentateuch.[4] Here for the first time the Anglican fold was actually invaded by the continental type of higher criticism. Pushed off into the African mission field as "bishop of Natal", the scholarly Colenso had through experience in teaching the Africans come to doubt the inspiration of the Old Testament. When making a translation of the Bible into Zulu he sometimes found himself in a tight spot with his flock in certain Old Testament passages. Thus when rendering Exodus 21: 21 (where a master is held blameless, if the slave whom he has chastised dies from the effect, "for it is his money"), a Zulu aide asked Colenso "Did God really say that?" Colenso in that moment realized what it meant to make God responsible for everything that is said in the Old Testament and answered negatively. He now began to study the Hexateuch with a critical mind, and his keen observations in the publications mentioned had their effect on the thought of Continental scholarship, notably on that of Kuenen. But for Colenso himself his venture brought on trouble akin to that experienced by the essayists two years before. He was excommunicated, but appealed to the British courts, which twice rendered a verdict in his favour despite all the influence and power arrayed against him and the public clamour that he be condemned.

But Modernism did not confine itself to invading the Church

of England; it also got a foothold even a little earlier, though less spectacularly, among the Congregationalists, when S. Davidson contributed a chapter on *The Text of the Old Testament* to a revised edition of Horne's *Introduction*. As a result of the protest that arose over it he was forced to resign his chair in Manchester. In 1862, however, he brought out a three-volume *Introduction to the Old Testament* in which that collection was treated like other literature and the presence of myth and legend in it acknowledged. In the same year A. B. Davidson published the initial part of his never completed *Commentary on Job*, generally recognized as the first modern Old Testament Commentary in the English language. But, though affected by modernity, he kept clear of the more controversial matters and filled the role of apologist against Continental critical extremes. His influence on Hebrew studies was considerable, however, and some of his pupils were to attain great eminence as Old Testament critics, *e.g.*, W. R. Smith, G. Adam Smith and J. Skinner.

Meanwhile a new great science was emerging that was bound to have a tremendous impact on Old Testament study— Assyriology. British and French explorers had stirred the imagination by their archæological discoveries of the 'forties. In 1857 occurred the famous incident proving to the numerous sceptics of the time that the decipherment of the Assyro-Babylonian language was indeed accomplished, when five scholars, headed by the master of them all, Sir Henry Rawlinson, separately deciphered a new cuneiform text (a cylinder of the Assyrian ruler Tiglathpileser I of 1100 B.C.) in substantially the same way. And as the vast treasure of the library of King Ashurbanipal of Nineveh was studied a whole literature contemporary with Old Testament times was exhibited to the world, thus creating an opportunity to institute comparisons. In 1876 occurred the startling incident of the publication of Adam Smith's *Chaldean Account of Genesis*, in which that indefatigable decipherer and explorer published for the first time the Babylonian version of the flood story from the cuneiform tablets found by Layard at Nineveh. All the long dispute with science over the Mosaic account of the Deluge now became pointless. To their amazement men learned that the biblical account of the flood was virtually identical with the cuneiform one, with the chances of the borrowing being done by "Moses" being better than even. Apologists of the veracity of the primal history reported in the Old Testament now were confronted with a serious problem. What was illumined here in a momentary flash was to become in cumulative measure a terrible dead weight on the shoulders of any form of supernaturalist belief— viz., the historical conditioning of the Hebrew records, their inextricable entanglement in event, word and thought with the events, words and thoughts of dead civilizations and all the limitations thereby implied.

Under the cumulative effect of all the new learning the resistance to biblical criticism in England was weakened. When W. Robertson Smith published his article on the Bible in the 9th edition of the *Encyclopedia Britannica* in 1875, and in the ensuing years had to undergo heresy trials, the change of atmosphere from that which had marked the trial of a Colenso was curious. Though he was suspended in 1880 from teaching in the Aberdeen Free Church College, the charge of heresy was not sustained and he was merely admonished for having made unguarded statements. His removal from his chair in 1881 in consequence of a further Encyclopedia article on *Hebrew Language and Literature* even aroused a mass meeting on his behalf and led to his being invited to give lectures in Edinburgh and Glasgow.[5]

Meanwhile the vast upward surge of the sciences was taking place and a radically changed spirit was arising. The philosophy of Comte in France had heralded this modern age by proclaiming a total rejection of metaphysics and therewith of the whole philosophical development from Descartes to Hegel, and favouring a "positive" philosophy, based only on the insights obtained by science. The study of Sociology which he inaugurated was destined to have an increasing significance for that of religion. Parallel therewith went the rise of the science of Psychology, the pertinence of which for religion likewise was bound to be great. The importance of Economics was highlighted by Karl Marx's *Das Kapital*, 1867, and a new materialism was permeating life in the wake of the industrial expansion. If Schopenhauer had proclaimed the will supreme and Spencer had raised evolution to a cosmic principle, Nietzsche preached the will to power and drew the consequences of the doctrine of evolution by foreseeing man's rise to a higher and better estate after the hindrance of Christian conditioning was cast off. Finally, nationalism raised its head, as the new possibilities of national self-assertion arose through improved means of communication and increase of military striking power.

A prophetic incident that looms much larger now in retrospect than it did a few decades ago occurred in Germany in 1878, when De Lagarde published his essay on the *Religion of the Future*.[6] Here Christianity is looked at in a critical manner by a man to whom patriotism is paramount. Historically, he regards Christianity not merely as the individual creation of Jesus of Nazareth but as the product of many contributing forces and influences and, with a more or less "political" slant, as essentially a creation of the Roman Empire and the nations united under its sway. It is doomed to perish, he holds, because of the Jewish element which it has carried along through the centuries as part of its heritage. The national consciousness of modern peoples simply cannot tolerate this. A new religion must be constructed by synthesizing genuine Christianity with the natural attributes of the modern nation. Obviously there can be no place for the Old Testament with its Jewish nationalism and racialism in this religion of the future. While De Lagarde seems to think exclusively in terms of his own national scene, he would presumably expect the same judgment to apply for other nations as well, so that the universal religion that Christianity aspires to be would be split up into, or be replaced by, various national religions. (This is indeed what happens temporarily to Christianity in times of war.)

This predominance of a national outlook puts De Lagarde, who regarded himself as a theologian, somewhat outside the theological horizon, and yet it seems necessary to mention him because he brought to light in principle thoughts that cropped out anew in the German scene in terrible realism from 1932–1939, in fusion with absolute political power. The liquidation of that power in the late war by no means puts an end to the significance of De Lagarde's thought, for it is quite conceivable that eventually the same process will repeat itself in other countries and times, wherever or whenever nationalism becomes ascendant. It must be conceded, too, that there is something artificial and incongruous in one's glorifying the past of an ancient Semitic people instead of one's own national past, or the cities and hamlets of Palestine instead of those of one's own land. The hymnology of the Church is particularly vulnerable to this criticism.

Within the process of professional Old Testament study a more immediately influential event occurred in Germany in that same year, 1878—the publication of Julius Wellhausen's great work.[7] It marked the beginning of a completely secular and evolutionistic study of the Old Testament sources. Wellhausen gave convincing demonstration to the thesis, put forward a decade earlier by Graf but not well established by that scholar, that the Old Testament legislation was post-prophetic. By setting up a convincing theory of the structure of the Pentateuch and determining the relative age and succession of its main strata J.E.D.P., he therewith found the key also to the main stages of Israel's religious development. It was now possible to fit all the other materials of the Old Testament into their proper place in that sequence and to obtain the criteria wherewith to differentiate between older elements and accretions in all the other books. The prophets of Israel suddenly assumed a much greater importance. A host of able scholars quickly followed Wellhausen's lead. The outcome of all this tremendous activity, carried on through several decades and with increasing participation of scholars everywhere, was the creation of an entirely different picture of the Old Testament literary and religious history from that held formerly.

The new Old Testament science inaugurated by the movement symbolized by Wellhausen sought to be and was scientifically respectable. It applied methods that had been productive of great results in the study of classical and other literatures to the Old Testament literature. As a result, there came into being an insight into the fact that the Hebrew religion had undergone a historical development.[8] It matters little, as we now see it, that the development is not one of such steady upward evolution as was first thought. It is enough to say that there was flux and change, and that it was affected by historical circumstances, spiritual movements, as well as by the actions and influence of individuals. This history has not yet been adequately written up and probably never can be because of the fragmentary information at our disposal. We must divine more than we can see. The materials we have all fit somewhere into a picture puzzle, but the trouble is that a great number of pieces are missing which, if we had them, would make the picture clear and meaningful. But the mere circumstance that scholarship, from Wellhausen on, established the fact of religious *change* in Hebrew history and discerned important aspects of it, made forever impossible the belief on the part of the intelligent portion of humanity that the Old Testament writings were a supernatural communication of the Holy Spirit.

An awareness of the secular forces operative in modern theological trends was shown by Delitzsch,[9] a man who deserves to be remembered when the roll of Old Testament scholars is called, because of the great usefulness of his Old Testament Commentaries and the inspiring role he played as a teacher. He was a supernaturalist, strongly influenced by the pietist school. But at the same time he preserved a somewhat open mind in critical matters. When he gave in to such results of higher criticism as the existence of a Deutero-Isaiah, the lateness of the Priestly Code, and the Maccabaean origin of Daniel, the fact had a powerful influence in giving criticism an entry into conservative quarters.

In England the higher criticism soon began to make further inroads. W. Robertson Smith, driven out of Scotland, found Cambridge willing to listen. Keble College at Oxford, which had been founded as a haven of orthodoxy after the *Essays and Reviews* incident, produced out of its midst a book of essays entitled *Lux Mundi*, 1889, in which the idea that the Genesis narratives are a historical record was given up and numerous critical views of German and Dutch scholars were espoused. But there was no heresy trial. When a Driver went over to the Wellhausen theory and a Sanday endorsed it in the *Bampton Lectures* (so long regarded as a province of orthodoxy), it began to take on the appearance of respectability, and so English scholarship was set free to participate in the great critical movement.[10]

In the United States, sound philological and historical Old Testament study, but remaining on neutral ground, had been carried forward by Edward Robinson.[11] The higher criticism, however, only invaded America successfully after Wellhausen's demonstration of it. The Baptist C. H. Toy was driven out of his post at Louisville for endorsing it in 1879.[12] But the Briggs heresy trial before the Presbytery of New York did more than anything else to break down the dykes hindering its entry. Briggs was assailed for his 1891 inaugural lecture at the Union Theological Seminary in New York on the *Authority of Scripture.* After proceedings lasting several years he was suspended from the Presbyterian ministry.[13] He was fully supported, however, by his colleague Francis Brown,[14] and Union Seminary severed its bond with the Presbyterian Church rather than drop him. Another able American scholar who suffered a heresy trial was H. P. Smith.[15] In consequence of such events the interest in Wellhausenism was heightened.

While there was still powerful opposition to higher criticism, best represented by W. H. Green,[16] it became increasingly unable to stem the tide. The new University of Chicago, under the aegis of W. R. Harper, cultivated the link with progressive Old Testament study (as with German research in general);[17] in a seat of old congregational orthodoxy such as Yale's Divinity School a Bacon could contribute to Pentateuchal criticism;[18] while in the Andover of Moses Stuart a Moore could arise and wield the higher critical scalpel with the skill of the best.[19] Soon the mighty contenders of orthodoxy were only a memory.

While criticism and historical research were engaged in showing up the Old Testament in its true light against the background of the Hebrew historical process, that process as a whole, with all its intellectual and spiritual content, was being illuminated by Oriental science. The prophetic incident of George Smith's Chaldean Genesis rapidly attained a larger fulfilment than he could foresee. Through the labours of excavators, archæologists, philologists and interpreters of ancient texts and objects, the Oriental cultures were being resurrected, and therewith also knowledge of the literatures and religions of a world contemporary with the Old Testament.[20] It was impossible not to make comparisons between these cultures and that represented by the Old Testament. Yet it came once more as a terrific shock to popular, orthodox supernaturalism when the younger Delitzsch delivered his "Bible and Babel" lectures in 1903 and declared the biblical and Babylonian world views identical and claimed the dependence of the former on the latter.[21] People all over the world felt that Christianity was basically threatened.[22] In reality, the only thing that was threatened—though really not more so than it had been all along—was orthodox theology.

The moderate Delitzsch was soon followed by others who carried their claims to greater extremes. Thus Winckler and Jeremias indulged in the dream of a great Babylonian *Weltanschauung* that was basic for the whole Near Eastern culture including Israel's,[23] and Jensen saw in the Babylonian Epic of Gilgamesh the source of innumerable motifs in the biblical and other ancient literatures.[24] They furnished good targets for the Apologists. But Oriental exploration was vastly stimulated by this publicity, and historical research was in any case making it clear that the Hebrews shared in the ideas, legends and myths of pagan Oriental peoples—something so self-evident that men should have known it anyway.[25]

Chapter Eight

THE OLD TESTAMENT IN SYSTEMATIC THEOLOGY
SINCE RITSCHL

THE Protestant Church of the 'seventies and 'eighties confronted the biblical and notably the Old Testament scholarship of the time with a feeling akin to that which must afflict the hen that has hatched out ducklings and sees them go swimming off whither she cannot follow. The Reformation's setting up of the Bible as sole principle of authority, in the belief that its accurate and impartial interpretation was all that was necessary, had had the unforeseen consequence of proving that it is impossible to use this book as authority in the sense in which this was contemplated. The historical-genetic view of its contents, worked out in co-operation with the higher critical determination of the antiquity and extent of its separate units, was providing a (fragmentary) picture of a great religious history of the past—no exhibition of a single, unified, planned product such as seemed requisite for an authoritative book dictated by the Holy Ghost.

There was abroad an uneasy awareness of the seriousness of the loss for the Protestant Church. The former generations had slept peacefully within the citadel of the Church's ancient biblical doctrine. With an infallible revealed book they had guaranteed information on sin and salvation, heaven and hell, world history and natural science. One had only to quote chapter and verse, rely implicitly on what was written, and the affairs of the universe were comfortably settled. The preacher, learned in Hebrew and Greek, had inherited St. Peter's power of the keys. There was always, of course, a minority of sceptics, agnostics and scoffers, but they stood outside the pale of respectability. The Scriptures were a bulwark from which the fiery arrows of unbelief recoiled harmlessly. In England and America, and in reactionary quarters on the Continent as well, this had still been the situation a few generations earlier. But now this bulwark had fallen.

But providence had ready a man and a new theology for this exigency—at least for all those who could not close their minds to the truth—in the person and work of Albrecht Ritschl. His theology provided the tools for a presentation of Christianity able to weather the troubles caused by philosophy and biblical criticism. If philosophy had on the one hand caused confusion by seeking to dominate theology and on the other hand peril by trying to destroy it, Ritschl, by casting metaphysics out of the theological temple, greatly simplified the theological task. Over against historical criticism he set up the idea of faith, as taught by Martin Luther.[1]

The Reformers' conception of it had, indeed, survived in the consciousness of German Protestantism in theological quarters, but Ritschl saw that for the common man faith meant two things: (1) that one admits that everything in the Bible is the Word of God; (2) that faith at the same time was firm reliance on what is taught and reported in the Bible. This amounted to forcing oneself to accept that of which one was not honestly convinced, and made swallowing of the incredible a merit. The uncomfortable fact remained that this was just the same thing as the Catholic idea of faith. Hand in hand with this went the sham of the pulpit—preachers moving on an artificial plane and delivering biblical sentiments and ideas that were not an expression of their personal convictions. Over against this sort of thing Ritschl stressed faith as something vital and real.

In spite of Ritschl's opposition to philosophy he was governed by one—a dualism. The ultimate terrestrial realities are nature, conceived of as a mechanism, and an aggregate of intelligent personalities whose distinctive quality is ethical autonomy. Ritschl attained a higher unity by use of the teleological idea, in dependence on the philosophy of Lotze. God, imagined as moral will, thus establishes unity by governing the natural order according to the purpose of the moral order. In Christ, Ritschl held, God has revealed that He is governing the world in such a way that a moral goal, in which the individual and community may participate, is attained.[2]

Ritschl's principles were greater than Ritschl's theological system. Once he raised the flag of his principles—and he only did it near the end of his career—he gained a great following. The converts did not follow him in detail but in full freedom. They all concurred in what mattered most: the independence of theology, the true nature of faith and the necessity of relating all Christian teachings integrally with such faith. That meant an enormous simplification of theology and involved relegating many things to the background that had no close connection with living faith. Theology was sent forth courageously into the modern world to win it for Christ (though from the angle of present-day thinking with only a wooden sword). The conservatives and the radicals alike were aroused against Ritschl and his school, and for years there was a tempest over Ritschlianism. But it was the theology of the immediate future, had a standing in the eyes of the intellectuals and even found following in England and America.

Ritschl was deeply imbued with the historical attitude. He had begun as a pupil of the great Baur and wrote at least one historical work of long-time significance. In his systematic thinking he retained something of this historical attitude—a thing not quite consistent with his principle of faith. His views on Scripture and notably on the Old Testament impress one as born out of his historicism.

Ritschl taught that authentic knowledge of the Christian religion and revelation can only be derived from documents close to the founding of this religion.[3] He sees this conceded already in the early Church, for the writings of the succeeding Christian generations are dependent on the thought of the apostolic writings. But instead of asserting that what makes these writings so distinctive and peculiar is their inspiration, Ritschl advances a natural criterion for their worth. The chief difference between the post-apostolic literature and the canonical New Testament writings he holds to be this, that the former authors are incapable of properly utilizing the Old Testament presuppositions of the thought of Christ and the apostles. He believes, furthermore, that the insights of the apostles and New Testament authors into the content, purpose and divine basis of Christianity, as well as Christ's own sphere of thinking, are mediated by an understanding of the Hebrew religion different from that of contemporary Judaism (whether Pharisaic, Sadducaic or Essene). He concedes that in one respect the way was already prepared for the thoughts of Jesus and the New Testament writers in Judaism, viz., by the emergence of the belief in a final judgment, but even here he does not think that the Jewish ideas were merely taken over, but rather that Jesus produced them anew out of His own unique position over against human history. This genuine Old Testament conditioning of the classic writings of the period of Christian origins binds them all together into a group. Discerning their superiority in this respect over other books, he holds, one can refrain from all attempts at justifying their segregation such as that given by the doctrine of Inspiration.

The New Testament writings, then, are the authoritative source of Christian religious ideas for Ritschl. But that does not mean that all the ideas found in them are to be counted valid Christian tenets! He links up with Luther's principle that Scripture is authoritative only in so far as it "treats of Christ", i.e., in the sphere of the direct portrayal of man's redemption. He points out that therein lies a difference between the true Lutheran position and some others. Calvin, for example, took the doctrine of twofold predestination into his system, even though he finds it impractical, just because he thought it was taught by Paul, and he regarded certain ecclesiastical arrangements existing in the early Church and found in the New Testament writings as binding for us. Other Christian leaders have claimed that the communism of the primitive Church of Jerusalem should be regarded as normative for us. Still others, stressing the apocalypticism of the New Testament, have made millennialism important. Ritschl has no use for such biblicism. He holds that the subject of Biblical theology, which must be developed historically and be free from dogmatic interests, is one thing, while Christian Doctrine is another thing. The latter must reach out from the central point of New Testament Christianity and then take in such other elements as hang together with it essentially and integrally. The central point for Ritschl lies in Justification and Reconciliation.

In proceeding to study the New Testament source material that is important for these Christian doctrines, Ritschl everywhere goes back to the Old Testament to set forth the relation between the idea in the two parts of the canon. Since he denies the doctrine of the witness of the Holy Spirit in any form, his touchstone for the authority of the New Testament writings remains this Old Testament background. That makes the task of convincing oneself of the validity of the New Testament teachings a rather complicated one. It seems, too, that he takes the authority of the Old Testament very much for granted. One may well argue that the Hebraic derivation of a concept does not in itself prove its superior value, but may even form an obstacle to our appreciation of it. One must also point out a fact of which Ritschl could not yet be fully aware but which research carried on since his day has made clear, that Hellenism and contemporary Judaism permeate the New Testament writings to a very large degree. Nevertheless, one must see in his approach an interesting effort to find an abiding significance for the Old Testament, and one that has by no means been fully exploited or tried out.

Progress beyond Ritschl was possible in several directions. One was to stress the historical Jesus as bringer to man of the true knowledge of God and as embodiment of an ideal requiring our emulation.[4] Another possibility was to stress the present experience of God in faith, by the Christian individual through contact with the Jesus of history. That was the road taken by Herrmann,[5] whose thought found a considerable echo in both England and America.

Religion for Herrmann is an experience given only to those with a capacity for it, and is authentic only when it has a moral effect. Over against a traditionalist idea which conceives of revelation as a tradition of how the faith of pious men of the past expressed itself, and over against a rationalistic idea which regards reason as the source of religion or as revelation, and over against mysticism which—though it rightly sees that religion must be personally experienced—falsely finds the source of revelation in an excitation of the feelings apart from the realities of our situation, Herrmann sees in revelation an experience that forces itself upon some of us and convinces us of the reality of God. This experience is not only—as Schleiermacher thought—that of becoming conscious of our absolute dependence (though that is included), but also of our becoming conscious of our inner freedom and independence. We have this experience when we know ourselves seized by a spiritual power which works upon us as a manifestation of pure goodness and to which we joyously submit. This experience is given to us, in our living together with other men, when the feelings of awe and trust are awakened in us.

The fundamental thing in Christianity as we see it about us, Herrmann asserts, is the way in which all Christians ultimately derive their spiritual resources from Jesus Christ. We are thus compelled to study the New Testament and to observe how the disciples of Jesus and the early Christians experienced the power unto life that went forth from Him. But we should have an entirely different brand of Christianity from that of the early Christians if we could not ourselves experience Jesus. The New Testament mediates this experience. In defending his position against the alleged results of modern higher criticism, Herrmann argues that, if every fact of the external life of Jesus were uncertain, yet the power that goes forth from His inner or spiritual life, as that shines forth from the record, is so great that we are brought to true faith in God through Him and thus experience redemption.

With such concentration on the Christian experience and on the influence proceeding from Jesus Christ one cannot expect Herrmann to have much use for the Old Testament.[6] While he does not take up this problem of the authority of the Old Testament specifically, he sometimes expresses his reverence for the books of both the Old and New Testaments as the sole tradition in which we can find Christ.[7] He sees in the knowledge of these books a means by which we may come nearer to the historical Jesus, and asserts that for this reason we desire no other kind of preaching than that which interprets the Word of God to us from Holy Scripture.

But for Herrmann, God alone and not a book is the authority to which we subject ourselves. Scripture has authority only where and in so far as a man by virtue of his faith already understands the God who is speaking to him.[8] Hence Herrmann can use the Bible where it suits him and set it aside where it does not. Thus, in his discussion of the doctrine of man, he contrasts the idea of the image of God in man found in the Old Testament with that found in the New Testament, and, after adopting the New Testament idea, adds that the rest of the "anthropological" ideas found in the Bible have no place in Christian doctrine because we cannot see how they can be made to arise in our minds anew through the faith that the inner life of Jesus creates within us.[9] His ethical emphasis, primarily Kantian, does give him a friendly attitude toward the ethical insights of the Old Testament prophets, and, of course, he clearly perceives the Old Testament heritage in the mind and soul of Jesus.

In Herrmann, the historical is first abandoned, and then brought back by a new route. He attempts to make Christianity independent of the results of the most radical historical criticism. Revelation has its reality only in the framework of the practical, ethical existence of man and therefore cannot be theoretically studied but only recognized in ethical decision, in a surrender to it. But the reflection of the spiritual (Herrmann says "inner") life of Christ in the New Testament (which is thus accepted as providentially provided and substantially dependable, in spite of the inaccuracies of the reporting of the external circumstances of His history), is the saving factor in our situation. In reality, therefore, a faint supernaturalism still stands in the background of his thought.

But while the Ritschlian theology enjoyed the greatest amount of esteem, notably because it commanded the allegiance (in principle) of so many scholars who did great work in the area of New Testament and other early Christian literature, other theological trends, too, remained in the field.

Among the conservatives of that period Martin Kaehler looms up as a particularly significant figure.[10] He attempted to grapple with the difficulties created for supernaturalism by the modern world-view on the one hand and by historical criticism on the other. Relating the divine activity to history rather than to nature, he understood it (in analogy to contacts between persons), as a contact of God and man. The decisive category for the history of revelation in this ontology is *Das Uebergeschichtliche* or "the transcendent"—a thought later seized upon by Karl Barth. Here is an attempt to get outside of the natural process—to take the "nature" out of supernaturalism. The "transcendent" in history differs from the historical in the ordinary sense in that it is due to the immediate activity of God, has a universal significance as work of His saving purpose and is always presently influential in God's dealings with men. Historical facts therefore are not as such revelation but only in so far as they have such a transcendent character. The Bible becomes the interpretative witness of the divine activity and performs its living function in the present as it has performed it in the history of the Church in the past.

The biblical problem was particularly alarming in Kaehler's time. He was deeply influenced in his youth by J. T. C. Beck, for whom Systematic theology was still "biblical dogmatics". But though his mind was steeped in the Bible, Kaehler had a very clear conception (gained during prolonged activity as New Testament exegete) of how criticism must deal with the Bible, and what rather radical results inevitably flow from a rigorous application of scientific method. In a series of important lectures he sought to persuade laymen, who were deeply shocked by much-publicized developments in biblical research, that criticism had its place and function, and tried to set up guide-posts for them in their perplexity. He distinguished rather sharply between the empirical, inductive method applied by research (usually culminating in a welter of conflicting opinions and hypotheses) and a theological approach which puts a transcendent Word of God at the centre of everything and proceeds to illuminate Scripture from that angle. He recommended this latter method to those who would really serve the interest of the Church.

In his chief work he reveals a strong predilection for Old Testament ideas. Justification by faith is considered the true ecumenical starting-point for the theology of Protestantism. In the light of this, Christianity must be understood as faith in the Messiah, in so far as He sets up a new covenant in place of the old. For in Jesus the Messiah or "Christ" the final and conclusive "Word" of God's self-revelation was given, and man's deliverance from the state of separation from God as well as the assured founding of a divine kingdom embracing humanity were provided. These biblical ideas, Kaehler asserts, well describe the nature of Christianity in such a way that the first, faith in Christ, gives content to all the others, but so that this content is only properly and completely expressed in the others.

It is obvious that from this basic position Kaehler does not view Christianity as something totally new, but rather sees it in its continuity with the Old Testament order. His is a conservative adherence to the terms "Messiah", "Old" and "New Covenant", in the manner of Von Hofmann and of the "federal" school. From this angle the Messianic expectations and predictions of the previous order are important. The Bible of two Testaments is a witness of the abiding significance of this historical connection between the two orders. The Judaizing and paganizing aberrations that have arisen in the life and teachings of the Church in the course of the centuries show how necessary it is to take the preparation and the fulfilment together to do justice to the whole Messiah.

Kaehler occupied himself with the problem of the Old Testament in a special paper. Since he holds that Jesus Christ came into the world and did His work within the framework of a divinely-willed historical plan, it is not enough to conceive of this in terms of causality and evolution. Christian faith requires the belief that God guided this history to prepare the way for Him through whom He desired fully to reveal Himself. All that is known about that preparation appears in the collection called the Old Testament. The only adequate light on the meaning of Christ was found by the New Testament writers in the Old Testament—not in contemporary Judaism which did not understand or recognize Jesus.[11] Through Jesus and Christianity this Old Testament collection of books became a mighty factor in the history of mankind. The moral insight of man was nurtured by the Decalogue; the Psalms taught men to pray; the figures of Old Testament narrative replaced the old heroes of the national sagas; the prophetic sayings of judgment, reassurance or consolation have, since Jesus, stood like the stars over the beds of the sick and dying. "We are all Semitized, and we would have to dissolve our religious thinking, and our Esthetics, as formed by our greatest artists, as well, if we wanted to pull out these fibres of Semitic thinking."[12] Can we imagine Jesus taking a serious interest in the Agora at Athens or in the Forum at Rome? It was only possible for His message to be appreciated where the ground had been prepared for it by Old Testament history! Through Jesus and Christianity the Old Testament is continuously serving to lay a similar foundation in our present life.

Kaehler stresses the authority of the Old Testament as a *whole*, which according to him implies no compulsion to concede great importance to every book (e.g. Esther) or of claiming equal value or perfect comprehensibility for all its varied contents. The Old Testament element in Christianity—and it continues into the New Testament (cf. the Sermon on the Mount)—is, he declares, the pedagogical element in it, which continuously does its service to those still in need of tutelage (Gal. 3: 24). While the interpretation of the Old Testament in the New Testament is not "historical" in the sense of reproducing the exact meaning of the Old Testament writers, it is nevertheless "historical" in the larger sense. Who to-day would wish to write the history of the Napoleonic wars according to the horizons of the contemporaries?[13] The New Testament writers, too, could not ignore the fact that something very tremendous had occurred since these books had been written, and could not but view the ancient history and writings in a new light. If we were not so curious to know what *really* happened in the centuries before Christ (on the empirical plane Kaehler is a sceptic, who holds we can only know very little of the real facts!) but were concerned about the great creative purposes of God, we would not be so disturbed by the use of the Old Testament made in the New Testament.

Kaehler then declares that the Old Testament collection has the dignity of being part of the Christian canon solely as a *whole* in which the pre-Christian revelation is handed down. Studied in modern historical fashion (*zeitgeschichtlich*) the Old Testament is not canonical, i.e. normative for our own thought and action. Nor is it of any particular importance for us that we should satisfy our historical curiosity by discerning how this or that thought arose and developed in Israel. The Old Testament is important only in its totality, and if we read it as Jesus and His apostles read it—bearing in mind the "but I say unto you" of the Master. No one should be so foolish as to attempt to apply aspects of Old Testament law conditioned by local, national, and historical circumstances to ourselves. Let them read the exemplary discussion of ceremonialism in the Augsburg Confession (Art. 26) and learn with the Reformers how to deal with such matters! Kaehler even goes so far as to assert that the Old Testament collection only has canonical validity for us when interpreted in Christian fashion. In its original meaning it has no relevance for us! It will be seen that these admissions of a great conservative are not really far removed from the claims of the radicals.

Kaehler, however, has a rather unique tenet with which he counterbalances this liberalism. It is a really new and peculiar principle of biblical interpretation, arising out of his category of the transcendent happening, and he emphasizes it over against the purely historical approach. He believes that a deeper insight into the real significance of many a portion of Scripture may be gained from heeding its *effect* in the history of the Church than by vainly trying to recover irrevocably submerged situations of the past. Thus he finds that two great episodes of Christian history illuminate the Epistle to the Galatians better than antiquarian exegesis ever can do: the role it played in Luther's criticism of Catholicism and the place it held in the gigantic Hegelian effort of F. C. Baur and the Tübingen school to interpret the early Christian scene.

In a valuable study on the history of the Bible in its effect on the Church, Kaehler has a section on the "Old Testament and the Church" in which he applies this principle.[14] The significance attained by the Old Testament in Christian life and history is, he claims, ecclesiastically speaking, far more important than what it meant originally to the Jews and how it came into existence. If one considers the lessons of this history of the Old Testament, the following points stand out. While the covenant of God with Israel was superseded by the new covenant established by Jesus, this does not mean that the earlier arrangement has lost all its meaning. Even where "law" and "gospel" are used as characteristic designations for the old and new orders, it must be recognized that there are elements of law in the New Testament and of gospel in the Old Testament. The Protestant Reformers rejected the Antinomian position out of a realization that one cannot appreciate the gospel without being aware of the demands of the law. Out of this insight into the difference as well as the similarity between the two orders there follows the inference that they belong together. They do not merely stand in a historical relationship of past and present; together they form the unified heritage of the Church of Christ. One cannot understand the biblical gospel without the Old Testament, for the content of that gospel is the Son of God, the Messiah of the Jews and the goal of the law. But one also cannot understand law and promise without the fulfilment effected by Him who was put under the law. As He has been set over the House of God, so He has also been set over Scriptures and rules over them. Henceforth the important thing about the Old Testament is not the temporal, but the eternal, not the letter or flesh but the spirit. Still, since the eternal element was clothed in the temporal shell of the letter or flesh for pedagogical purposes, this shell, too, continues to have a pedagogical value. Under the Christian dispensation the Old Testament is in a continuous process of becoming antiquated, but at the same time continuously serves Christianity by preparing the way for it, as well as by illustrating and showing up the basis of various errors into which Christianity may readily fall.

Kaehler finds abundant traces of the Old Testament heritage in Christian history, many of them none too praiseworthy. He points out how Protestantism from the beginning assailed the "Judaism" of the hierarchical Churches. Already the Christian development after Paul illustrates this trend back toward a mere religion of the law. Everywhere the pagan impulse of man—and that is the natural human one—adapts itself more readily to the external order of the Old Testament than to the gospel. The Roman bishop becomes a high priest after the manner of the Jewish high priests; sacerdotalism, the sacrifice of the mass, vows, good works, etc., all represent a renaissance of Judaism within the Church. The Reformation at first was a rebirth of New Testament Christianity, but a similar relapse into Old Testament mentality shortly took place, when Bible and Confessions were treated like codes of law. The Old Testament element in Calvinism and Puritanism also comes to mind in that connection. Kaehler is inclined to view all this rather philosophically, however, and to regard the Old Testament as continuing to do yeoman service in repeating the ancient function of the whole Old Testament order of being a "tutor unto Christ". He finds that there is a radical difference between the early Christian community, composed as that was of people who had become Christians by personal decision, and an institutional Church into which ever new generations are born without having made such personal decision; this institutional Church is in a role much more like that of the Jewish Church, and the Old Testament heritage performs a valuable preparatory function in training this humanity and preparing it for the gospel of Christian freedom.

Kaehler, of course, does not wish to excuse too obviously Judaizing aberrations, but he maintains that they are not the fault of the Bible of the two Testaments. This unified Bible corrects itself where necessary, and when properly handled— with due attention to all the self-criticism found in it—will do no harm at all, but rather provide the most valuable guidance. But he warns that Protestant Christians are all too prone to make the Bible the vicar of Christ on earth. The Bible is not the only form in which the Word of God comes to us, and it is wrong to put demands on it that it cannot possibly fulfil.

Kaehler's position on the Old Testament is inseparably entwined with a theology that leans rather close to the conservative line in Paul. If one is willing to stress the radical line in Paul and is not quite so philosophical as to the rather preliminary character of the Church or the tolerability of sub-Christian viewpoints and horizons on pedagogical grounds, one will immediately come to a different conclusion.[15]

But the Erlangen school, too, retained a following and received a new leader in Ihmels, who sought to modify the position of Frank on Christian certainty in order to meet the criticism of subjectivism levelled against it.[16] In connection therewith his thought on the Scripture problem is of interest.

Christian certainty, Ihmels says, rests on personal experience, which he defines as present communion with God, rather than as that of regeneration (as Frank had taught). He thus veers rather close to Kaehler for whom everything flows from the experience of justification. In granting His fellowship to men, God strives to elicit faith on the part of man. In this act of faith, certainty concerning the reality of the divine revelation, in and through which God seeks us out, is implicit. Revelation and faith are correlatives.

Christian certainty embraces three things: (1) It is a certainty of the historical revelation of God. (2) It is a certainty of the Word of God, which for Ihmels is the living Word of God embracing both "law" and "gospel" and by no means identical with Scripture. (3) It is a certainty about Scripture. The latter testifies to that revelation of God which comes to us in the living Word of God. The Christian attains a growing certainty about Scripture in a threefold manner; firstly he becomes convinced that the present Word of God has its source in an original revelation. Secondly, all insight that comes to him in the living Word of the Church is clarified and even mediated in a unique way through Scripture, so that this progressive growth in certainty includes also a certainty concerning the testimony of the original witness of revelation. Thirdly, while a formal certainty about Scripture is not obtained in this purely religious way it must be remembered that Scripture as a canon is primarily given to the Church. But since it also is to serve the individual to encounter God, a certainty concerning the testimony of Scripture emerges to the extent that this purpose is realized.

The last point in this general theological background is naturally the one from which Ihmels' evaluation of the canon as a whole and of the Old Testament in particular must stem forth. His previous definition of the Word of God as both law and gospel augurs a relatively favourable attitude toward the Old Testament (on which, however, he does not elaborate). But Ihmels cannot attain certainty concerning the canon as a whole for either Testament. In affirming that the Bible is given to the Church he has some protection for the traditional canon, but he concedes that the Church's attitude is nothing that is fixed with absolute finality and hence grants that criticism of the canon on theological grounds is certainly admissible.

A unique figure among the pre-war theologians was Schlatter.[17] He deserves some attention here, in spite of the fact that he neither founded nor continued a school of theology. Of Swiss birth, he exhibited leanings toward the Reformed type of Christianity more than the Lutheran, and also betrayed the strong influence of the Pietism and Biblicism of Beck. He was strongly anti-Kantian and willing to trust reason much more than those deeply impressed by that philosopher's teachings. He virtually re-establishes a sort of Natural theology and deduces much insight concerning God from nature, notably in his theological anthropology, which for him is the basic starting-point. This would seem to put Christ and therewith the revelation in History in a supplementary position. He defends himself against attacks on that score by saying that this arrangement of material is due to the intellectual objective of Dogmatics: to set forth the knowledge of God. In other writings, when not governed by that special interest, he proceeds from the vantage point of New Testament Christianity, stressing the Christian community or congregation.

For Schlatter, the authority of the New Testament is greater than that of the Church because Christ is irreplaceable and Scripture alone brings us into relation with Him. This does not mean that no thought or act is justified which is not found in the New Testament; Christ rules to-day and His grace is alive in our midst. Nevertheless the radius within which the Church may move is governed from one point—the Word of Jesus and the apostles. The authority of Scripture is thus a derived one. The authority really resides in Christ and His apostles. "Authority" is a word that in human relations often spells tyranny; but the authority of Scripture is based on the divine grace—it should not oppress us but rather strengthen us. Wherever Scripture is used as a substitute for our own knowledge of God or where an unreasonable obedience to it is demanded, there we have a relapse into the carnal idea of authority. The orthodox Protestant Scripture-doctrine treated Scripture as though it were timeless. In that way Scripture becomes a burden instead of a help. It no longer influences knowledge or the will. Since the higher criticism was a serious menace to that kind of Scripture authority, orthodoxy developed an opposition to Criticism. But Scripture must be subjected to criticism—not only historical but "dogmatic". For every biblical writer or personage (including Jesus) is a part of the web and woof of his time and we who are part of our time cannot just take over as normative any biblical statement. We are constantly called upon to differentiate between what we can accept and what we must reject in the light of all the other truth that God gives us to-day. Even the richest words of Scripture are historically conditioned.

But Schlatter takes no offence at this close fusion of the eternal and the transitory. To him the human element is ever undergirded by the divine grace, and with all his obscurities the biblical writer remains the servant of God. The false judgments concerning Scripture that have been rampant so long are due to the intellectualistic approach to which the western world is so prone. We are apt to be disturbed by the "poetic element" of Scripture (as Schlatter, rather euphemistically, describes what other scholars call myth and legend) or by the fact that it leaves so many questions unanswered. The infallibility of God does not transmit itself to man or to what men write. There is no use in constructing a revelation apart from men or one that makes the human element disappear. Scripture puts us in relation to God, not primarily in the sphere of thinking but in that of the *will*.

Schlatter holds to an inspiration of the apostolic (and prophetic) personalities. As every personal relation with God is mediated by the Spirit, so the apostolic and prophetic work has the same presupposition. Only in this way does a Word of God to man result. But inspiration is misunderstood if thought to bring about intellectual correctness or to produce timeless truth. It affects the entire life and makes a man able to speak the Word of God. It is not a case of passive receptivity. The individual consciousness is not destroyed but is utilized.

Schlatter stresses Messianism, therein continuing the line of J. T. C. Beck. The Christ, he asserts, was preceded by the long series of Hebrew prophets. He points out that there is objection to that statement from several standpoints. Those who see nothing new in Jesus but regard Him merely as another Jewish prophet or teacher object to giving Him an independent position and putting Him in juxtaposition to the prophets. On the other hand, those who are embarrassed by Jesus' connection with Judaism, and who prefer not to see Christianity burdened with the difficulties arising from the Old Testament and with the objectionable elements of the Jewish character, also dislike the statement. Both objections sacrifice the Messianic idea. As the Christ, Jesus is set apart from all His predecessors as well as from His successors by the uniqueness of His office. At the same time Messianism is inseparable from Israel. Christ was not only prophesied—His work was made possible by what went before.

Schlatter then rejects as false several ways of describing the religious change wrought by Jesus; He did not, as is sometimes asserted, reject the national community and replace that by "religious individualism"; He did not set up a religion of the gospel as opposed to the religion of the law; He did not concentrate on the purely spiritual. The difficulties of the Old

Testament cannot obscure the fact of the indissoluble fellowship of Jesus with Israel. Our historical and ethical insight does indeed transcend that of the Old Testament; but this is a result of the coming of the Christ. With Him, religion ascends to a new level. Jesus' own attitude, he holds, gives us the directives for the right use of the Old Testament—to be bound and at the same time free, the eye fixed upon God.

Schlatter believes in the unity of Scripture, which, he says, does not mean uniformity. This unity results from the fact that the history which created Scripture and to which it testifies has its unity in Christ. He accepts Luther's formula of "whatever treats of Christ" as an excellent yardstick, when taken properly, in the sense of considering how a given section hangs together with central Christian positions. He recognizes that there are parts of lesser and of greater importance in the Old Testament. But on the basis of Paul's argument concerning the different parts of the body and their functions (Rom. 12), he finds a value even in the lesser members of the scriptural organism. The nineteenth psalm may not be as important as the eighth chapter of the Epistle to the Romans, or Ecclesiastes as important as the First Epistle of John, and yet they have their value within the scriptural body. For from every point of Scripture we are led forth into the whole. In individual life this may be a slow process, but the life of the Church vindicates the fact.

Schlatter thus succeeds in maintaining the importance of the Old Testament canon, but his assumption that Scripture is an "organism" is a survival of Beck's idealizing view. He actually devaluates the older order by viewing it as preparatory to the new. He avoids speaking of revelation, since his conception of the latter is very broad. If Schlatter had not been so conservative in his literary criticism of the New Testament, or so deeply imbued with pietism, his thinking might have carried farther in the radical direction.

In sharp contrast to the approach of Schlatter stands that of Schaeder.[18] Indeed, he criticizes all theology since Schleiermacher for being anthropocentric, and seeks to set up a theocentric viewpoint, therein being a forerunner of Barth. An impact on him from the Old Testament side is particularly noticeable in the use he makes of the 139th Psalm at the begin-

ning of one of his books. We shall here, however, confine ourselves to analysing a study of his which chronologically belongs
to the post-war period and shows him reacting to the situation
created by Barth, but which on the whole remains within the
orbit of his own earlier thought.[19] He has a particular interest
in the doctrine of the Holy Spirit, but he links the Spirit entirely
with "the Word of God". The Spirit begets faith in the Word
and thereby creates the Church of the Word, and in so far as He
prevails in the Church He makes it the place in which the divine
sovereignty dwells. That is the starting-point of his cogitations.

The Word of God is not, however, identical with Scripture for
Schaeder. The Word is the oral message that deals with God
as the Lord of the world and of man. Everything communicated
in that Word concerning God, Christ and the Holy Spirit
stands under this unifying principle of the divine sovereignty.
Schaeder's idea of God is primarily that of a majestic, voluntaristic deity who carries out his purpose irresistibly. Even
justification of the sinner through faith is seen as an act of the
majestic grace, rather than of the love of the deity. There is thus
a Calvinistic sternness, ultimately resting on Old Testament
influence, in his approach.

The Scriptures for Schaeder are no external principle of
authority. Faith bound to the Word of God (in the above
described sense of the message of the sovereignty of God) sets
up its own articles of belief, and contemplates Scripture in full
freedom, judging it in accordance with its relation to the Word
of God as defined above. But in the last analysis, he concedes,
his freedom from Scripture is at the same time also a tie with
Scripture, for ultimately the Word of God is mediated to us
through Scripture. The judging of Scripture is a continuous
process, in which the individual, the congregation and the
Church as a whole—not merely of the present but of all generations—take an active part, simultaneously bound and free in
the sense indicated.

For the Christian, Schaeder holds, the normative portion of
Scripture is the New Testament. Faith is for us faith in the God
who is in Christ. We only have an interest in the Old Testament
in so far as the New Testament compels us to have it. Scripture
throughout is a series of documents testifying to God's relations
with the world, as manifested in certain actions. Directly or

indirectly it is the book of divine works, or divinely wrought circumstances which have a more or less immediate significance for the congregation that hears about them. The divine actions necessarily occur in space and time. The knowledge of them is mediated by, or associated with, historical circumstances and personages. So close is the fusion between the eternal and the temporal that it is impossible to disengage the former from the latter. The actions of God, such as those described with relation to Greeks and Jews in Rom. 1–2, 9–11, do not hover, like ideas, above the earth, but are deeply woven into a concrete historical process. Nevertheless, for faith, the eternal side of that which took place in this history is the thing that is paramount. The Spirit of God, though He leads us into His living creation with all its details and in all its concreteness, nevertheless makes us free from all this in view of God and His Christ. In this sense Schaeder favours a "spiritual" type of exegesis—but not in what he believes to be the impossible sense of separating the temporal from the eternal (cf. p. 174).

While the New Testament is gospel, since it preaches the Christ who Himself is the Word incarnate, in whom and through whom the goal of history—God's sovereignty—becomes a reality, the Old Testament does not attain to this rank. It is the first duty of any consideration of the canon to make this difference between the two Testaments clear. But the Old Testament writings, too, are testimonies of faith; they affirm God to be the Creator, the Lawgiver and Judge, and the one who is going to bring to a realization the goal that He has set for history of man—that state of affairs in which His reign will become complete. All these elements of the Old Testament message are not gospel, but they form the inseparable pre-supposition of it. If God were not Creator and Lord of the world, He could not mould history in sovereign grace. If He were not the Lawgiver, He could not free us from the effect of the curse of the law and from its external, formal authority, as he actually does in His justifying grace. If He were not Judge, the abolition of His judgment over us in the atoning death of Christ would be incomprehensible and impossible. If, finally, the God of the Old Testament witness points both in preparatory actions and words to the goal of history—the establishment of His sovereignty over the world—then that sovereignty is on the way. It has not arrived yet, since Christ is not here, but it is coming. Thus, the New Testament gospel draws the afore-mentioned elements of the Old Testament to itself. Even though these elements reappear in the New Testament in a purified form, the Old Testament cannot be dispensed with. For the elements described do not stand alone in the Old Testament but form the basis for the preparatory process leading to the gospel. It is one and the same God who is operative both in the prepara-tion and in the gospel itself.

In short, the Christian theologian who chooses the Word of the New Testament as his standpoint is driven by that very standpoint to take the Old Testament in its main, dominant lines (creation, law, judgment, and promise) into consideration in determining the contents of the Word of God. Attempts to set aside one or more of these elements as below the evangelical level must have their repercussions on the attitude toward the New Testament which likewise contains them.

Realizing the connection between the Old Testament heritage and Christianity, one must concede to the former an inalienable significance for faith in the Word of God. But this significance is not to be set forth on the basis of any external, biblicistic, authoritarian approach. It is reached only by a faith that seizes intuitively upon the main lines of the organic connection exist-ing between the order of the gospel and the order that prepares the way for it in the form of the promise, and of setting up the abiding basis of both orders, viz., knowledge of the reality of God and of His relation to the world that is implicit in the order of creation.

But is that in the Old Testament which we may call the Word of God so pure in content and so unobjectionable that Christian faith is not contaminated by taking this Old Testament element to its bosom? This question subdivides into two separate ones: (1) Does this Old Testament Word of God in any way mis-represent the divine reality or the will of God as focused on us? (2) Does it represent a lower stage in the self-revelation of God which is superseded in certain respects by the revelation in Christ?

In examining the first of these questions Schaeder dwells on the idea of God as the Creator. From the Christian standpoint we can only be satisfied with a purely theistic view. If it should actually be the case that the writer of the Creation story holds matter to be co-eternal with God (exegetically it is by no means absolutely sure that the "created" of Gen. 1 : 1 is a *creatio ex nihilo*) we would have to reject that aspect of its presentation as sub-Christian. When the Old Testament from its first to its last page proclaims the God of the law, who asserts Himself over against both the sinful group and individual, does He always at the same time appear as the God of Love who accepts the repentant sinner? Is the wrath of God in the Old Testament always the expression of an eternally pure will, bent on warding off the evil, or conceived of as analogous to human passion, jealousy and other impure human attitudes? Does the Old Testament idea of righteousness always exclude the thought of merits? Does it reveal an insight into the corruption of the human will? Does it leave room for the sole validity of repentance and faith in the sight of God? And when we turn to the large area of the Old Testament future expectations must one not above all ask whether the destiny of Israel as chosen people is always seen as due to the free grace of God, irrespective of any national virtues of this people?

Schaeder concedes that lapses into lower moral levels occur in the Old Testament all along the line. Faith thus has every reason to use the critical plumb-line in dealing with that book. He realizes that an improperly used Old Testament can have a confusing and baneful effect on Christendom. Faith must eliminate these elements in constant effort. To determine what elements in the Old Testament are authoritative for us is a never-ending task both of the individual believer and the Church.

The second question to be considered is whether the Old Testament does not represent a lower stage of the self-revelation of God than the Christian revelation and how it is to be related to the latter. One must, for instance, recall that Old Testament law makes certain concessions, which are transcended in the New Testament—so in the marriage question, or that as to who is one's neighbour. Furthermore, there is the whole cultic-ritualistic legislation which we regard as having lost its importance with the coming of Christ. So far as Old Testament prophecy is concerned the question arises to what extent it really prepares the way for the Christ of the New

Testament. In particular there is the matter of Messianic Prophecy, or the question of what elements of the Old Testament witness actually have been fulfilled in Christ. This can be stressed in such a way that the preparation sheds light on the fulfilment, or, *vice versa*, that the preparation receives light from the fulfilment. The Christianizing and sublimating of Old Testament passages after the manner of the New Testament writers, however, should be abandoned. Finally, there is the subjective piety, notably in the Psalter, the expressions of which belong to the Word that is valid, wherever they grow out of a "pneumatic" and godly understanding of the Israelitic prerogatives, and dwell on the line of penitential faith in God's elective love.

Thus the relation of faith to the Old Testament canon is one of being bound to the Word of God in that work, but mediated and conditioned by adherence to the New Testament and, therefore, one of selectivity. No one can make a final statement as to how we are bound by the Old Testament "Word". But the living process of faith in the individual and in the Church of Christ will always combine, in ever new decisions, the link with the God of the Old Testament who is the God and Father of Jesus Christ and the rejection of that which is erroneous or exaggerated in the preparatory order.

The culmination of the pre-war Liberal theological development is to be found in Ernst Troeltsch.[20] More than any other Christian thinker he has yielded to the impact of modern scientific method and insight. It will be of interest to see what standpoint he takes on the matter of Scripture doctrine in general and the Old Testament in particular.

Of fundamental concern, of course, is the question of revelation. There are three points at which the Christian claim to revelation, as hitherto formulated, clashes with reason, and Troeltsch thinks that reason here has the better of the argument. In the first place, reason asserts that the whole of reality is subject to its arbitrament; it cannot grant that there is any special area which is unattainable to reason and which can only be apprehended with the help of revelation. In the second place, modern reason with its relativistic view of nature asserts that there are no isolated facts, no islands of unreality in the historical process; it is impossible to see the special presence or activity of God in certain facts of history. In the third place, recent philosophical thought convincingly asserts that there is no unity and no teleology in the historical process and therewith undermines the assumption that a historical entity (Jesus Christ) can be a valid revelation for all mankind.

In seeking for new positions that will not be exposed to a direct clash with modern insight Troeltsch does not cling to compromises like the Ritschlians but goes to the end of the road marked out by the modern world-view, courageously sacrificing various Christian beliefs that most people would regard as essential. He uses the term revelation to describe the apprehending of the unified nature of things (i.e. God) through religious feeling. That which is thus apprehended is beyond rational understanding and can only be believed, and the term "revelation" expresses this aspect. It is rational only in so far as it has the striving toward totality and final values and thus can serve reason in the solution of its ultimate difficulties. It can be experienced by all those who are capable of harbouring religious feeling.

A link not only with Fries and his emphasis on intuition but with Schleiermacher, who stressed feeling so prominently, seems to appear in this line of thought, but Troeltsch broadens the base by not limiting the feeling to dependence, or the object toward which it is directed to a personal God. He also has more use for the historical than Schleiermacher. The productive power of the average religious person, he argues, is very slight and requires stimulation from without. The strongest stimulus is afforded by a religious tradition which unites in itself the religious impression left by certain favoured individuals and the aggregate of the religious forces of whole generations. The prophetic individuals, who are the starting-point and centre of the great world religions and about whom the whole heritage of their religious sphere centres, naturally furnish the very strongest stimulus. The belief in a revelation in the narrower sense is most strongly developed and most clearly exhibited in this area.

From this angle it can be seen that Troeltsch will take a friendly attitude toward the Old Testament, since it increases the range of our knowledge of religious experience. At the same time it is clear that he cannot stop there, but must see a value in religious experience outside of Judaism and Christianity. For contact with rival religions and their equally exclusive faith in their own revelations creates the necessity of comparison. This, he says, soon leads on the one hand to the assertion that revelation was laid down in a particular institution or book and, on the other hand, to a denial of or attack upon the validity of alien revelations. Better knowledge and understanding eventually produce the realization that all religions partake of the character of revelation. Comparative evaluation of their religious and moral ideas results in the conviction that Christianity is superior to all the others, but not to a certainty that it is the absolute religion.

Troeltsch's approach to the Old Testament is highly modern.[21] He points out that in the popular mind undue stress is laid on the untenable narratives of Genesis and on the Messianic predictions, as though these things were the most important elements of the Old Testament. That, he declares, is entirely unhistorical. He takes up the problem from a more organic, sociologically oriented angle. The history of Israel, he declares, has a deep significance for our whole historical sphere —both for Islam and Christianity. He formulates his views as follows:

(1) The recognition of Christianity as the supreme revelation includes also the recognition of the religion of Israel as preparation for and presupposition of this revelation. Without it Christianity is incomprehensible; it must constantly be taken together with its rich Old Testament background. (2) The function of the religion of Israel, historically considered, was to break through the area of nature-religion in every sense of the word and to establish ethical monotheism. In that respect it is absolutely unique. The religion of Israel through the mediation of the prophets marks the release of the Deity from the bondage of nature and the placing of Him above all the world as creative will.

Troeltsch then develops this along three lines: (a) This signifies that the Deity is conceived of in anti-rationalistic and anti-naturalistic manner as "living will"—incomprehensible and not to be measured by man—and thus involves the idea of Creation; (b) This will, furthermore, is directed toward obtaining the recognition and worship of the divine holiness in active moral obedience, in contrast to all cult and ceremonial religion, and over against all worldly, eudaemonistic conceptions of human destiny, or all pantheistic or unworldly and passive mysticism; (c) Since the idea of God is governed by that of a morally conceived purpose set for man, there results a trend in the direction of its illustration by history and its vicissitudes in the personal life of the prophets and in the great national destinies, while the illustration by nature and abstract regularities recedes entirely.

(3) In these three respects prophetic monotheism is an original religious creation, entirely in contrast to the rest of the world, and hence there lie in it the germs of the finally humanized ethical religion of a personal Christianity. The limitations of the religion of Israel lie in its nationalism, never entirely overcome, in the legalistic shell in which the ethical religion of mankind here is encased, and finally in the narrowness of its religious view of history, with its small horizon, its nationalistic and apocalyptic goals, its crude belief in the miraculous and its trend toward eudaemonism in the ethical sphere. But the great thing about this religion is the one-sidedly voluntaristic idea of God. It feels no need of including the unity and connectedness of the life of the world in its idea of God, and therein differs strongly from all Indo-European religions.

(4) This abiding significance of prophetism, which must be recognized despite all limitations, finds expression in the fact that its precipitate (the so-called Old Testament) has become a Christian document and that Christianity designates the prophetic religion as the "Old Covenant", "Old Testament" or "old dispensation" of God which prepared the way for the "New Covenant" or "new dispensation" of grace. This estimate remains permanently valid. It involves at the same time an elimination of the nationalistic elements of the Old Testament and emphasis on the prophetic elements. The latter in their simplicity and strength have the abiding function of holding Christianity firmly down to its basic, ethical moorings, and to keep it from falling into sentimentality, subjective mysticism or intellectual dogmatism.

Troeltsch's essay on the Old Testament prophets shows him deeply influenced by Max Weber's sociological thinking, though carrying it further in theological reflection, but otherwise does not add much to the fundamental aspects of his position. Its importance lies primarily in the field of the historical understanding of the spirit and motives of prophecy and the influences it exerted on Hebrew life. Those who would make the prophets of Israel exponents of democracy or social justice will get little comfort from it. He argues that the message of the prophets has absolutely nothing to do with law deduced from reason, and is no proclamation of social morality.[22] With humanity or liberty or even democracy and socialism in the modern sense, this ethic does not have a single thread in common. The ultimate fact about prophetic religion is that it is the religion of a passionate, transcendent, voluntaristic God and of the human personality that is formed in the fellowship with Him. Because of this the prophetic ethic is full of activism and of an exertion of the will analogous to that of the Creator. But in spite of this activism and voluntarism, it is indifferent toward the world and civilization in the occidental sense,[23] as well as toward all moral values that lie outside the sphere of the personal orientation of the individual toward God and the mutual, divinely oriented fellowship of the group. This trend attains an even sharper and purer expression in Jesus (cf. Matt. 16: 26). The effects of His attitude flow through the whole of Christian history. It is the struggle between the radicalism of faith and the inclination also present in religion to fuse and compromise with cultural trends.

In a manuscript note, posthumously published,[24] Troeltsch set down the thought that the manner in which the prophetic idea of the Old Testament was disengaged from its sociological ties (including nationalism) and became a religious-ethical principle in Christianity is particularly noteworthy. The difficulties which this principle encountered and still encounters, when applied to other and more developed social situations of life, are due to its origin and constantly compel an increasing spiritualization. All these obstacles, however, have not hindered it from becoming the most powerful religious principle in the world, as the religion of theistic reverence, ethical purity, humane love of man, repentance and pious interpretation of nature and destiny. Contact with all concrete relations of social life has been wiped out or become peripheral. The very difficulty of applying it has elevated it to a radical requirement, which confronts the secular life with an alternative and which the world, under the curse of sin (which in Christian re-interpretation no longer signifies Israel's apostasy and worldliness but rather general human selfishness and inertia) does not seem to be able to meet. The necessity of choosing between God and the world has become basic for this whole ethic and its necessary consequence is the doctrine of an involvement of all men in the sins of self-love and love of the world. But at the same time this faith appears as a summons to repentance, as an appeal to the free will to choose between two ways. "Repent" was already the call of the prophets; choice and decision remain the high point of all Jewish ethics; repentance and change of heart are the theme of the initial message of Jesus. It is the religion of those that choose, the religion of decision, of the radical "either—or".

Within these two poles—the ethical-personal idea of God and the fateful, world-encompassing idea of sin—the faith of the prophets, after its general human content had taken on a new form in the preaching of Jesus and of Mohammed (but in a fully humanized form only in that of Jesus), became a spiritual power of the first magnitude in the occident and in the Islamic world, even where men are unaware of it. True, Christianity has within itself a large number of other forces beside "Hebraism" and enjoys its eternal influence just because of its combination of these diverse elements into a new spiritual world, superimposed upon Hebraism but not identical with it. While it must be conceded that European religion, activism and wealth of contrasts did not spring directly from the Hebrew religion, they nevertheless show themselves led, dominated, nurtured and regulated by it.

Since Christianity is no mere refurbishing or further development of Hebraism, it follows that the latter, in spite of its fusion with Christianity, also has played and continues to play a separate role. The Old Testament never merely remained an earlier stage and means of interpreting the New Testament. The hard, strict virility, the reverence and ethical simplicity of its religion of humanity, the poetical nature-piety, the kinship with stoicism (a movement that also has extended its influence through the centuries), finally the fusions with neo-platonic mysticism and pantheistic interpretation of radical monotheism

—all this has given the Old Testament an independent influence as well. It is especially discernible at the very beginning of the modern intellectual life.[25] Troeltsch sees a trend in the world of religious ideas of his day toward eliminating the gnostic, supernatural, mystical-sacramental elements from Christianity and reverting to a Hebraism with Christian modifications. The attempts of theologians to go back to a simple gospel of Jesus,[26] usually resulting in a more or less rationalized Hebraism, are significant of this. He concedes that a simplification of Christianity is not possible in this "historical" form. The need is not for a reversion to an earlier form of Christianity with some modernization, but for a great synthesis in which its basic theistic-personalistic trend is fully expressed, without petty anthropomorphism and anthropocentrism.

Troeltsch obviously has seen the character and significance of Old Testament religion against a larger background than any one since the days of German Idealism. His thoughts on the matter, however, can only appeal to those who have emancipated themselves from biblicism. His emphasis on religious individualism, furthermore, is strongly tied up with the intellectual climate prevailing before the First World War, and fails to satisfy us entirely to-day. He fittingly marks the end of an era.

Chapter Nine

THE APOLOGETIC OF BIBLICAL SCHOLARS

WITH the passing years the differences between conservatives and liberals in the Old Testament field became more and more meaningless. There was scant comfort in the fact that a staunch exponent of supernaturalism like E. Koenig[1] dated the Pentateuchal sources differently (E before J) and earlier than the liberals, and defended the substantial historical reliability of the Old Testament narratives. He had accepted the documentary hypothesis in principle and the consequences of that were inescapable, no matter how obstinately he might refuse to draw them. The dividing line between conservatives and liberals was partly this: that the former were disposed to haggle about how much had to be conceded to criticism, while the latter went blithely from one destructive result to another; partly it was also in an underlying religious attitude. The liberals were content to view the Old Testament in a more or less humanistic light, with some mild emphasis on its literary excellences, moral and religious values, but full and frank admission of all its backwardness and defects. The conservatives, while compelled to agree with most of this, took refuge in the doctrinal position which the theology of a von Hofmann and others had created for them, viz. that the revelation of God was one that had taken place in history, that the Old Testament literature gives us knowledge of that history and of that revelation, and that this literature itself, in its full reality, belongs to the revelatory process.[2] In the course of the latter, backward or primitive elements were gradually overcome. Their survival in the record is instructive. From the citadel of this position they could participate freely in Old Testament criticism, believing that truer historical insight achieved by the best available scientific means was bound to be helpful in giving us a better understanding of the history of the revelation in question.

It may be useful to consider a few instances of what might be called the professional apologetic for the Old Testament on the part of leading scholars, from the period succeeding the triumph of criticism to 1914. We will first glance at a lecture Marti gave to clergymen in Switzerland in 1893.[3]

The lecture had received considerable publicity. Marti finds that in some quarters there was excitement over it; the more benevolent critics were concerned about the salvation of the author's soul and the others lamented about this horrible example of infidel scholarship. At the occasion of its delivery, he finds, there was either baffled silence or outright unwillingness to accept such views. But he holds that the new insights are far too well established to be set aside on emotional grounds or with an appeal to the faith of the Church. He hopes for a better response from a larger public; may it remind timid souls how often the doom of Christian faith has been foreseen by theologians, if this or that position were true. He emphasizes the Reformed position that the Bible itself holds first place, and that its realistic study, therefore, and the truth concerning it are not to be judged by faith. Even if scholarship proves some traditional ideas to be untenable, that does not matter; faith in the grace of God awakened through Jesus Christ is immune to any danger. The Church can rather rejoice at the growth of insight; the ever-increasing knowledge of revelation must serve to put Christ as basis of our faith in a clearer light than ever before. He rejects the idea that such discussions as the present one should be kept secret on account of the weaker brethren; silence has done more harm than the truth could have done, which could before this have helped people to a right understanding of Scripture.

Marti rejoices that Old Testament study has ceased being an innocuous pursuit. Time was when men were encouraged to undertake it in order to render them harmless; thus in 1818 Monod's thesis on the *Divinity of Christ* and another on *Prayer* were rejected by the Geneva faculty, but one on the *Authenticity of the Pentateuch* proved quite acceptable. To-day, Old Testament study touches vital matters.

After describing the view of Old Testament religion now developed by biblical scholarship, Marti sets forth how it affects the study of the History of Religions. The latter subject has all along been hampered by the claims, based on the Old Testament, of a monotheism at the beginning of things, from which a degeneration supposedly took place. This has now been done away with and the evolution of the Hebrew religion itself out of primitive beginnings discerned. Therewith the comparison of the biblical religion with other religions takes on a fresh significance. It will result in establishing the superiority of that religion. Finally, the intensive study of the development of the Old Testament religion that has been carried on recently will sharpen the eyes of men in studying the phenomena of other religions also and thus greatly fructify the subject of History of Religions as such.

For one who has occupied himself with this Old Testament religion in the modern manner it is clear that in describing a religious development one should not merely consider what ideas of God a people had or what teachings it held to be true, but rather discern above all what influence a religion had on morality, whether the two became joined and to what degree such union was demanded. For the right conception of God only becomes valuable as it represents an ethical force. Hence he would not join a Jewish apologist's claim that the monotheism achieved by the Jews was their supreme glory. The Old Testament development exhibits monotheists whose belief had little effect on their morals; Ecclesiastes is a case in point, and so are the ritualists who emphasize the Kosher or certain ceremonies. The Old Testament teaches us not to be impressed by zeal for cult or a refined scholasticism, since they do not prove that a religion is in flower, but are rather symptoms of its decadence. The value of a religious life is demonstrated only in moral conduct.

If the History of Religions has obtained an increased significance through modern Old Testament criticism, Dogmatic theology can be said to have declined in importance as a result of it. In addition to the complete revision of the doctrine of Scripture that such criticism has necessitated, it has brought about a decrease in emphasis on exact formulation of Christian teaching. Like cultic or liturgical forms, the intellectual formulæ mean little in comparison to the proof of faith in living deeds and trust in God as exemplified by Israel's prophets. Next, Old Testament study had shown the futility of Natural theology and of efforts to prove the existence of God, such as were so long a feature of the *Prolegomena* of Dogmatics. The prophets would have regarded that sort of thing as unbelief. They were overpowered by God and then saw His activity in history and finally also in nature. This points the way for Dogmatic theology, too. Furthermore, Old Testament study has relieved Dogmatic theology of all the fruitless discussions about a history of redemption, based on the idea of repairing the damage done by Adam's fall, or all speculations about the origin of sin, or debates on supra- and infra-lapsarianism. Then, too, God is no longer to be considered as governed by the laws of the Priestly Code in His dealing with man. The doctrine of the atonement, in particular, is thereby relieved of all juridical elements.

For real knowledge of God's ways one must turn to the prophets, who teach one to understand Jesus and His message of the love of God. All dogmatic concepts need to be examined in the light of whether they have been unduly affected by extraneous ideas, foreign to or not on a level with prophetic thought. Even in using New Testament concepts like Kingdom of God, Marti thinks, we should not just accept New Testament usage, which in this case has been influenced by contemporary Jewish eschatology, but rather go back to the genuine ideas of the great prophets, who expected a kingdom that would come through moral and spiritual regeneration, such as Jesus then brought about in those who believed in Him. Finally, Marti claims that the prophets give us the best means to understand Jesus. Standing in the counsel of Yahweh and trusting in Him they were free from all traditionalism and fear of men, discerning the falsity of the things on which men relied, and pointing them to Him who alone can save. If we view Jesus in similar manner we will, he thinks, have a higher and better appreciation of Him than by having recourse to lower stages of the earlier religion in which "sons of God" played a role (Gen.6:1f.).

In this manner, Marti thinks, Old Testament criticism vindicates its value for theology. By showing the line that leads from the great prophets to Christ it replaces the purely external juxtaposition of the two Testaments that has hitherto prevailed with the far better one of an organic connection existing between them.

Equally interesting are the thoughts of a more conservatively minded scholar like Dalman.[4] He is fully aware of the inescapable necessity of historical research and of the consequences it must have when applied to the Old Testament sources. Christianity, he reasons, comes to us in the form of a teaching that belongs to the living tradition of the Church; this teaching bases its certainty on a collection of writings received from the past. The Old Testament portion of this collection is the sacred collection of the Jewish Church of the time just preceding the rise of Pharisaic-Sadducaic rivalry. It gives information (1) concerning the origin and nature of this Church and its divine services—from Genesis to Esther; (2) concerning words of God that were given to it—the Prophets and Daniel; (3) concerning the religious feeling prevailing in its midst— Psalms and Lamentations; and the thinking done in it— Proverbs, Job, Ecclesiastes; (4) concerning the way in which it ordered the natural relations of life—Song of Songs, Ruth.

This scholar would thus seem to stress the intellectual aspect of Christianity and see the importance of the Old Testament in the historical information it gives us about the background out of which Christianity came. Dalman is of the opinion that the Christian Church should not have taken over Old Testament books like Esther, Ecclesiastes and Song of Songs that were of doubtful canonical authority at the time of Christ. He is not particularly disturbed by the fact that criticism has shown that we cannot depend absolutely on biblical history as reported. "It has not pleased God to inform us about that ancient era in the form of completely indubitable historical documents. Hence the external particulars cannot be the important thing for us here." He admits that materials that *per se* are nonreligious are to be found in the Old Testament and holds that the prophetic light shed on them by editors and revisers is ofttimes the only religiously significant thing about them. That is the case with the Book of Judges: only the framework, into which the older elements have been put, gives the book the character of revelation, and only because of this framework did it become part of the canon. In some other instances, too, the canonical claim of a book and of its contents hangs close together with the position and significance that redaction gave to the individual entity. Historical and canonical evaluation have divergent laws and go different ways.

Dalman is not troubled by such a matter as the historicity of the patriarchs. He believes that our sources are not of sufficient antiquity to prove anything one way or the other. The real question is merely whether the early Hebrew story is dependable when it asserts: (1) that Israel's special place came about through divine election; (2) that human conduct counted only in so far as Israel endorsed this election in faith. Dalman thinks it is. He finds the Holy Spirit active in a three-fold manner in the bringing forth of Old Testament Scripture collection; first, as decisive force in individual personalities whose word becomes the vehicle of divine revelation; second, as decisive force within the congregation whose spiritual life became capable of expressing in a literary manner the revelation given by word and to judge it in literary productions; third, as decisive force causing the origin of a whole collection that is suited to serve in the further course of the history of the congregation as record of its founding. In this sense, Dalman thinks, we can still hold fast to inspiration to-day. The Old Testament for him is a document of a divine revelation that is still *en route* to its goal. As such it is an important object of theological study, though not without the New Testament. To discern the individual thing in the Old Testament in relation to the whole and the whole in its relation to Christ, and in this way to apprehend the consensus of Holy Scripture progressively and in accordance with the current needs of the Church—that he described as the true task of Old Testamant theology.

It is apparent that Dalman has here combined a conservative loyalty to the Old Testament heritage with all the concessions that criticism demands. Realistically minded, he does not believe in saying what God should have done, but accepts that which actually has taken place in the historical process as divinely willed. But that a modified supernaturalism stands in the background is nevertheless clearly discernible.

Of similar spirit is Kittel's inaugural lecture of 1899.[5] It begins by describing the crystallization of the modern theological situation. The question is whether by drawing the Bible down into the historical process the very basis of faith and the future of the Church are not being menaced. The theological attitude must proceed from the fundamental principle of the Reformation and of the Protestantism that has been built on it. The cardinal principle of Protestantism, he asserts, is the freedom of the Christian man, who is responsible to God and his conscience but is no slave of an institution or tradition. On this principle is based the right of free research in pursuit of the truth. Wherever historical problems arise they must be dealt with in a scientific manner. But at the same time all freedom has its limitation at some point. That point for the Christian is the gospel of Jesus Christ: our standpoint can only be within its radius. He concedes that one who approaches the Old Testament materials with non-Christian presuppositions will deal with the larger aspects of any problem they present in a different way. But then it is merely a case of one dogma standing against another. Divergences in result already appear where one proceeds on an inner-Christian basis, depending on the standpoint taken. But this is inevitable. Convinced of our faith in Christ, it will be possible for us to discern the traces of God's gracious will and activity in history and therewith to see and recognize in the development mirrored in the Old Testament the revelation of our God. Kittel thus concedes as much as possible to criticism, while at the same time holding to a belief in a modified supernaturalism.

Soon after the turn of the century Kautzsch dealt with our subject.[6] His essay was aimed against various kinds of agitation intended to do away entirely with the Old Testament. He demands that the defenders of the Old Testament must first of all refrain from resorting to untenable kinds of argument. Such, for instance, is any doctrine of inspiration which claims infallibility and equal authority for every letter of Scripture. In practice, most people are sensible enough to differentiate between what is of greater or of lesser importance, but dogma has not yet arrived at that point. Over against the unfortunate Christian habit of treating all Scripture as of equal rank, we must remind ourselves that even the Jews who gave us the Old Testament canon did not do this. Such differentiation as is practised by the Synagogue in ascribing different degrees of authority to the three divisions of their collection, shows that it is by no means out of place for Christians to differentiate between more and less authoritative portions of the Old Testament. Another foolish thing is to defend the Old Testament ethic at every point. He points out how Jesus discriminated between things in the Old Testament of which He approved and others which He found morally or religiously insufficient. It is doing the Old Testament a disservice to defend things in it that belong to a lower level of moral insight. A similarly foolish thing is to defend the religious level of the Old Testament at every point. On the basis of the old doctrine of inspiration it was claimed that no imperfect or erroneous ideas could be attributed to the Holy Spirit. The zeal to prove the correctness of the Bible in such matters as the harmony between science and the first chapter of Genesis is something utterly useless. False in the third place is the spiritualization of Old Testament ideas in the interest of their better utilization for religious purposes. Old Testament Messianic prophecy provides much temptation along this line. Not only is it used to demonstrate the exact correspondence between prophecy and fulfilment, but the allusions of the former to Jerusalem and Zion are even transmuted into descriptions of the kingdom of heaven. Kautzsch thinks such procedure unwarranted and finds that the Templars, who urged the emigration of converts to Palestine to help prophecy to become fulfilled at the place to which it refers, or those Jews who travel to Jerusalem to die in order to be close to the scene where the resurrection is to take place, are at least obedient to the literal meaning of Scripture. But these instances show how impossible it is to stick to the letter of the Old Testament. We must not, however, twist and change the meaning of the Old Testament surreptitiously. It behoves us to recognize the limitations and inapplicability of certain passages in order that we may admire all the more those in which such limitations are overcome.

Kautzsch is not opposed to lines of thought stressing the value of the Old Testament from a purely historical or æsthetic point of view. But he rightly realizes that the mere fact that the Old Testament has had a large influence, and contains admirable and stimulating literary material, does not really prove that it has a living relevance for to-day or to-morrow. These are only the outer works of the citadel. Its actual invulnerability can only be demonstrated if it is irreplaceable for morals and religion.

In trying to demonstrate the moral irreplaceability of the Old Testament, Kautzsch insists that in spite of all the defects found in the book, which make it impossible to defend everything contained in it, there still remains a large amount of material that is valuable for the moral education of man. Here he dwells on the Old Testament expression of moral law and on certain of the more impressive Old Testament stories. But the thing he stresses most is the fact that all moral conduct in the Old Testament order is religiously permeated and grounded. This in his opinion is entirely unique and hence gives the Old Testament everlasting significance.

For the religious irreplaceability he points first to the purity of the Old Testament ideas of God. Of course he recognizes that there are outgrown stages, both primitive and mythical, in many an Old Testament passage. But they only serve to make the more remarkable those areas in which the Old Testament idea of God rises to the full stature of monotheism. The great thing about this monotheism is that the world-God does not become a mere abstraction but remains a living God. He contrasts the scholastic discussions about the eternity of God with Psalm 90 and those about the omniscience and omnipresence of God with Psalm 139. He finds it quite understandable that the proof-texts for a great many religious concepts formerly used by theologians in elaborating on the idea of God were chiefly drawn from the Old Testament. The New Testament really did not have much to add to the idea of God as expressed in these basic passages and itself continually reverts to Old Testament quotations. Opponents of the Old Testament argue that such use of classic Old Testament passages should continue, but that there is no necessity for burdening oneself with the whole apparatus of Old Testament viewpoints and phraseology. This Kautzsch rejects—claiming that the outstanding statements in such Psalms as 90, 103, 139 can only be appreciated out of the totality of those psalms. He points out how the same thing applies also in Psalms 37: 25 and 73: 26.

Secondly, Kautzsch emphasizes the abiding significance of Old Testament prayer. All the theories about prayer and its effectiveness are overshadowed by the demonstrations the Old Testament gives of how piety expressed itself in prayer in the lives of the Old Testament saints. But even these prayers cannot be isolated from the source from which they flowed—the whole Old Testament religion. But the third and decisive thing for Kautzsch is that the Old Testament proves for us the existence of a divine plan of salvation which then finds its perfection and consummation in the person and work of Jesus Christ. He rejects the counter-claim that this is purely a matter of faith. He sees the phenomenon of prophecy as proving that we are not dealing merely with an evolution of human ideas in Israel. In prophecy we can study divine revelation better than anywhere else except in Jesus Christ. To give up the heritage of Old Testament prophecy would be to close up a well of inexhaustible religious knowledge and certainty of faith. Hebrew prophecy, it is true, has its links with allied pagan phenomena, but the important thing is that in Israel this institution stands in the service of a divine plan of salvation from which it cannot be disengaged. Could one imagine Greek seers like Teiresias or Cassandra serving a plan of salvation of Zeus or Apollo? The Old Testament prophet is under the compulsion to speak the Word of God even against his own will. This irresistibility of the divine commission is illustrated in the much misunderstood Book of Jonah, in Amos 3: 8 and, above all, in Jeremiah 20: 7 f.

In setting forth the goal of prophecy, and the reasons for God's having employed it, Kautzsch would not stress Messianic prediction. In its personal form the latter occurs only sporadically and is conspicuously absent in long sections of Old Testament prophecy. It always is something conditional that can only be fulfilled after certain presuppositions have been met. The presuppositions themselves form the real burden of Old Testament prophecy: the recognition of sin and guilt, the yearning for redemption. These are the foundations on which the New Testament messages of John the Baptist and Jesus, with their call to repentance, are built. In this way the New Testament message links up with prophecy and bears witness that the God now revealing Himself is the same as the one who revealed Himself in the earlier order.

It is thus a modified supernaturalism that comes to the surface here at the very end of Kautzsch's line of thought. In the main, however, he develops the religious and moral "values" of the Old Testament literature—a secular line of reasoning which can be applied to any literature equally well.

Representative of the emphasis on the saving events of history (*Heilsgeschichte*) is the study of Koeberle.[7] He steers his ship into the channel marked by two guide-posts—the special significance of the Old Testament for the Church as affirmed by Christ and the apostles, on the one hand, and the merely preparatory character of the Old Testament on the other. For him the problem is to find a definition of the Old Testament that will stay within this groove. In attacking the problem of the authority of the Old Testament he says that this is tantamount to investigating the question whether it partakes of the character of divine revelation at all. He recognizes that there is a considerable difficulty in defining revelation and quotes Schleiermacher who, unwilling to concede any theological usefulness to this term because of its haziness, says: "Not only do some consciously play hide and seek with revelation, but even those who use the term in good faith can only with difficulty come to an agreement as to what they mean with it." Without going into the question of principle thus raised, Koeberle proceeds to describe the present crisis. On the one hand, the school of comparative religion, by considering the Old Testament religion as one of many manifestations of human piety, is undermining the belief in revelation as such, and on the other hand, historical criticism has destroyed the orthodox view of the Old Testament. In the face of this situation, is the Church's procedure of continuing to use the Old Testament as Word of God in doctrine, preaching, and religious education at all tenable?

Koeberle thinks that even on the basis of the comparative religious approach it can be shown objectively: (1) that the Old Testament is unique and far superior to any other collection of religious documents, and (2) that it has a unique importance as preparatory to Christianity. It then only remains to show that God was operative in bringing about these situations and the revealed character of the Old Testament is proven. He realizes, however, that this third thing is not objectively demonstrable. Yet it is the decisive thing on which the use of the Old Testament in the Church, as it has continued in practice to this day, depends. We must take the position that this God who speaks in the Old Testament is our God and that the history which He gave this people concerns us religiously more than the history of any other people; the plan of salvation which God has for humanity according to the Old Testament is not merely a lofty religious notion but a reality. The words that he spoke through the prophets were not idle fancy, but were actually divinely inspired. The self-revelation of God of which the Old Testament testifies is real; the salvation which he promised His people is not an illusion; it has partly been realized in Christ and is partly still on the way to fulfilment. These positions, he admits, do not permit scientific proof—they are articles of faith, but they are the certainties for which the Church must fight in connection with the Old Testament. He defends this position, on the one hand, against those who would speak disparagingly of scholarship and foolishly hide behind outworn defences of external "proofs" for Scripture authority, and, on the other hand, against those who think that by scientific means they can disprove such tenets of Christian faith, or that the Church could content itself with a comparative-religious demonstration of the superiority of the Old Testament over other documents of human piety.

The important thing for Christianity is that the Christian Church accept the history to which the Old Testament testifies as preparatory history of salvation. This history concerns us immediately and personally as the presupposition of the salvation that appeared in Christ. Everything that God did for the preparation of this salvation, anything whatsoever that affected this development in any way, belongs to this history. The completed Old Testament partakes of the character of revelation too because it mediates the knowledge of this history that is essential for our salvation. In particular, we recognize the divine working (as a result of which we ascribe to the Old Testament the character of revelation) in the following facts:

(1) God is operative in a peculiar way in the historical experiences of mankind and in those of His people. While we realize that the total historical process cannot be embraced in this framework, the religious side of it can be. The Old Testament story-tellers recognize that there are areas of additional interest which are not their immediate concern when they refer to sources of purely historical information that they did not choose to take over (e.g. II Kings 10: 34). (2) The appearance of religious personalities within the web of the history of the people is the work of God. The prophets and the interpreters of past and present who speak to us in the writings of the Old Testa-

ment were among them. (3) Out of the interaction of historical experience and religious personalities the nation, under divine guidance, attained the status where the situation was ripe for the coming of Christ.

Since the Old Testament gives us knowledge of these things in such a manner that we recognize this history of redemption for what it is, and in such a way as is necessary to grasp it as the divinely wrought preparation for Jesus Christ, it partakes of the character of revelation, and that is why we consider it as belonging to sacred Scripture. Everything, of course, depends on one's attitude toward the salvation of which the New Testament testifies. With that New Testament salvation stands and falls the preparatory history of redemption in the Old Testament. The proof of its revealed character cannot be formal, but must be developed on the basis of content. It applies, first of all, to the Old Testament as a whole; the individual component part partakes of the character of the whole, but the character of the whole does not rest upon the equal value of the individual parts. Everything that does not stand in a close connection with the divine redemptive plan belongs to the contemporary shell (basically Luther's principle). In essence, the Old Testament revelation is to be described as preparatory to Christ; its limitations are its national character, its legalistic form and its application more to a future than present salvation.

But as every age must take its special message from the Word of God, so the Old Testament has a special one for our own time. How mightily it preaches of the significance of the moral forces in the lives of nations! That God governs justly in history and punishes wrong, that deceit and untruth, no matter how successful they may appear, finally perish of themselves, that social injustice, oppression of the weak, violation of law and immorality bring about the ruin of nations, that belief in God's just government makes peoples and individuals strong, and that faith is the most powerful force—all that is expressed in the Old Testament in classic manner for all time. And the same thing applies even more to the purely religious content of the book, from Genesis 1 to Isaiah 53, from the story of Abraham and Joseph to the prophecy of Malachi; everywhere the Christian finds new confirmation of what Jesus said of the Old Testament writings: "They are they which testify of me" (John 5: 39).[8]

We may cite here one more German attempt to deal with the problem. It reflects full realization of the situation created by modern historical study and is from the pen of Gunkel—a man who carried the purely secular study of the Old Testament to new heights by giving heed to the literary techniques and forms employed in the Old Testament story-telling, poetry and prophecy, thus taking up the century-old legacy of Herder.[9]

He grants at the outset that the Old Testament appears to us in a different light than it did to former generations. Modern biblical science has virtually destroyed the belief that it is the inerrant Word of God and a safe guide to true religion and morality. The respect it formerly enjoyed was shaken by the disproof of the traditional authorship of numerous writings, by the casting of doubt on biblical narrative, whether on grounds of natural science, or contradictory statements in the record itself, or criticism of its religion and morals. But merely to discard the Old Testament is not the correct thing either. What is needed is an intelligent use of the Old Testament based on the knowledge provided by modern Old Testament science. The latter has studied this book as one produced by human means and in human ways. By this approach, he believes, it has rediscovered its true significance for the history of the world. Actually, he asserts, we have a very great treasure in the Old Testament!

The line he then follows carries forward the principles of Herder in a modern form. He sees in the Old Testament an almost illimitable wealth of artistic stimulation. He dwells on the charm of the Old Testament stories, on the power of Old Testament prophecy, on the marvellous production of Old Testament lyric poetry, on the titanic character of its one extensive poem (Job), and on the amazing objectivity and simplicity of Old Testament historiography. After thus pointing out the excellencies of the various types of literary material found in the Old Testament, he contemplates what a loss it would be if people no longer were to become acquainted with all this glamour.

Then he comes to the matter of the religious value of the Old Testament. In general, he holds that we cannot dispense with it. The fact that the Old Testament is necessary for the understanding of the New Testament and that Jesus and His apostles

held the Old Testament to be sacred Scripture carries great
weight with him. He also stresses the thought that the decision
of the Church on the Old Testament was rendered at the time of
Marcion and that it is improbable that history will retrace its
steps in this regard. "The Christian Church—a mighty structure—will unfold its nature in the course of its growth, but will
only change it at the cost of serious convulsions; and one of the
foundations of the Church is the Old Testament." When it
comes to particulars, however, he concedes that the Old Testament is inadequate in many respects and insists that this must
not be covered up by artificial interpretation but be honestly
admitted. He grants, furthermore, that some things formerly
held to have a religious value can no longer be so regarded. In
addition to mentioning sections or books that have no discernible religious bearing, he points to the close connection of the
Jewish religion with the Jewish nationality, and the intolerance
of the Hebrew religion toward all other religions, as things that
are indefensible.

Gunkel sees, on the other hand, in the Old Testament things
that can never become obsolete, for they lie at the root of all
modern thinking, whatever attitude men may take toward
Church and religion. They are expressed in characteristic simplicity of thought and are rammed like posts into the soil of our
civilization. The principles of morality taught in the Ten
Commandments, the tenets of monotheism and of the divine
retribution of good and evil are of this sort. But he also stresses
the new conception of the relation of morals and religion that is
emphasized by the prophets, and points out how all modern
social legislation is an outcome of Old Testament prophetic
spirit. He sees the prophetic eschatology, with its hope of a
better day in store for God's people, living on in the forward-
looking attitude of modern man. He furthermore finds certain
aspects of Old Testament belief valuably supplementing the
New Testament. In the latter, God's activity in the realm of
nature has receded very much into the background. The re-
awakened modern feeling for nature, which can become an ante-
chamber to the temple of religion, finds notes struck in the
nature-hymns of the Old Testament which awaken an echo in
our hearts. Even in the national religion of the Old Testament
—*per se* on a lower level than the New Testament religion of in-

dividual salvation—thoughts were born which are still of value for our time. That an interest in politics and patriotism on the one hand, and piety on the other hand, belong together, that there is such a thing as a universal history (an insight given to mankind by the Book of Daniel), and that God's sovereignty is its goal, are thoughts of this character possessing an unforgettable value.

Gunkel then lists other virtues of the Old Testament such as the sheer simplicity of Hebrew thought, which is good for us whose spiritual world has become so complex, and the magnificent utterances of religious emotion. What he has to say on the latter score about the extremes of passion or even fanaticism to which that emotion often grew is not entirely a recommendation from the point of view of religion and morals, though it may be enlightening from the angle of knowledge of human life, or be highly pleasurable or stirring. He takes recourse here to Nietzsche's oft quoted remarks about the great men and things in the Old Testament—a quotation that in our opinion should not be used, for what that philosopher considered great in the Old Testament were things a Christian consciousness regards as shocking and even horrible.

Gunkel describes certain aspects of the idea of God in the Old Testament. He dwells notably on the sterner side of that idea such as the connection of the deity with volcanic phenomena and His being a God of War. He speaks of the dreadful deeds done for this dread God and of the greatness of some of His representatives from Moses and Elijah down, and shows the power of moral passion that dwelt in them. He next speaks of the grandeur of the Hebrew conception of God as illustrated in the sublime narrative of creation in Genesis 1 and in the disdain of the use of images in the Hebrew worship. The profound feeling for the greatness of God accounts for the prominent role hymnody played in practical religion. The fear of the Holy God is another valuable element, Gunkel feels. "The Old Testament in its rugged strength would be as iron in the blood for our time which has become so soft, so irresolute, and so out of joint." But he also sees gentler and more tender notes expressed in the Old Testament religion. One thing he finds common to all these writings and utterances—absolute religious certitude. To these men of Israel God is no mere postulate of reason, but a living and real God. That is why the religious heart of all ages has loved the Psalms, for we find here something we long for and lack. The great achievement of Israel, realized through the influence of prophecy, is that it produced human personality living its own life in the presence of God. What a rich and varied gallery of such personalities the Old Testament contains! Other Oriental nations had nothing comparable, and we of the machine age are coming to the point where great personalities are no longer being produced. After some practical counsel on how knowledge of the Old Testament should be taught in various stages of education, Gunkel concludes by asserting that history has made the Bible (both Old Testament and New Testament) and the Greek civilization the two pillars supporting the civilization of the Christian nations, and that it would be a revolution the effect of which no one living can estimate if either of these pillars were to fall.

We hear nothing in Gunkel of supernaturalism. The Old Testament merely has great aesthetic, moral and religious "values" which mankind for cultural reasons cannot afford to do without. But no divine authority is invoked to buttress these values, which must stand entirely on their own merit or generate their own power. This type of Old Testament study has put aside the sun-glasses of theological reflection and views the Old Testament with the naked eye—in full realism, though with wonder and admiration over the religious capacities of the human mind and soul, and with a mild belief in a divine providence standing in the background.

The logical outcome of the scholarly study of the Scriptures of both Testaments under the German liberal theology was that proclaimed in the title of a lecture by a master of historical-critical exegesis in the New Testament field, von Dobschütz: the abandonment of the canonical idea.[10] These writings bear witness to the religious life of Hebrews and early Christians, and as such are permanently valuable and stimulating, but not normative.

In England George Adam Smith's book fitly leads the parade of twentieth-century reflections on the Old Testament.[11] In the main it is of an informative nature, seeking to present the results of modern critical study and to show how with their help the Old Testament comes alive. His own enthusiasm for the new approach is so great and his personal piety so serene and unshakeable that the problem of our present concern plays no great role in it. But it deserves a permanent place in the library of books about the Old Testament.

The disturbing aspects of the new knowledge come to the surface more vividly in McFadyen's work.[12] He sought to bridge the gulf existing between the modern critical viewpoint and the Church, by putting criticism within its proper bounds and discouraging any irreverence on its part, and by showing the Church the necessity, and even the advantage, of criticism. He believed that criticism leaves the religious message of the various sections of Scripture intact. When it comes to the decisive question: "Standing, as we do, in the full brightness of the revelation of Christ, holding as we do that the truth which He teaches is final, are we in a position to dispense with the Old Testament, or have those Churches been right which have sought to reinforce their faith and hope through psalm and prophecy no less than through epistle and evangel?" he asserts that history has decided in favour of the Old Testament.

In particular, he claims for the Old Testament a twofold value—absolute and relative. It lives both because of what it is in itself and of that for which it prepared the way and which without it would have been impossible. There is no part of the Old Testament in which we cannot see the finger of God, shaping the institutions which were largely to determine the practice of the Christian Church. Were there no New Testament with its perfect revelation of God in Christ, the Old Testament might yet in its own way bring us into the presence of God.

McFadyen stresses what it meant to Jesus. He even finds that in certain directions the Old Testament has been able to help men more than the New. We see in it the history of a people unfolded in a wonderful way, with the divine purpose working through it. There is no history like Israel's for convincing us of the transcendence of God, and no book like the Old Testament for teaching the inner meaning of history. He finds the prophets standing nearer to modern needs and meaning more for our time than the apostles, because they teach us to relate religion to public life. He finds the Psalmists teaching us how to enter into the sanctuary of our hearts and commune with God better than the New Testament does. Speaking of its relative value, he views it as preparing the way for Christ and the New Testament order. The New Testament is practically a dead letter to one who chooses to ignore its historical relations. Over against those who would have the Church become "contemporary", he insists that she must also continue to be historic.

Another significant British production, and perhaps the most massive and thorough attempt to deal with all aspects of the problem raised by the higher criticism, was the book by James Orr,[13] to which reference was made in our Introduction. He lays it down as axiomatic that, whatever they may be for others, these ancient Scriptures can never have less value for the Christian Church than they had for the Church's Master— Christ himself. Believing scholars of all standpoints, he boldly asserts, may be trusted to agree in this. He has a deep realization of the gravity of the situation created for supernaturalism by Old Testament research. The great problem of the Old Testament, as he sees it, is, "How are we to conceive of the religion which the Old Testament embodies and presents to us in its successive stages, as respects its nature and origin? Is it a natural product . . . or a result of special supernatural revelation to Israel?" Orr condemns Old Testament critics from Eichhorn and De Wette on to Wellhausen and Kuenen for operating in a manner discounting the supernatural. He wants to prove that the Old Testament's claim to be the record of revelation is not affected by higher criticism when the latter is reduced to conservative limits. His book is largely concerned with discrediting the more radical theories which seem to him inimical to maintaining that claim for the Old Testament. But Orr also has valuable chapters of a positive nature. His discussion, in his second chapter, of the Old Testament from its own point of view, where he deals with such matters as its organic unity, the fulfilment of the Old Testament in the New, the teleological character of the history it mirrors, the unique ideas of the religion it contains, and the revelation it represents and reflects, are all worthy of attention to-day. Particularly significant, too, is the third part of the final chapter in which he discusses the progressiveness of revelation. He holds: (1) that revelation at whatever point it is to begin must take man up at the stage at which it finds him; (2) that revelation can only be held responsible for the new element which it introduces—not for the basis on which it works, or for everything in the state of mind or limited outlook of the recipient with which it happens to be associated; (3) that it is the function of revelation to lay hold on whatever better elements there may be in that state of mind in order by their means to overcome the imperfections and create something higher. Orr, then, views revelation as an organic process, with adaptation at every point to the stage of development of its recipients. "Its higher stages criticize its lower; shed off temporary elements; disengage principles from the imperfect forms in which they are embodied, and give them more perfect expression, yet unfailingly conserve and take up into the new form every element of permanent value in the old."

Turning to the American scene we find that Old Testament scholars, when they wrote about Old Testament criticism, were chiefly engaged in justifying it, or in imparting some knowledge of its results. Perhaps the best known book of this kind was that of Kent,[14] which in its title echoed that of Kautzsch's contribution already outlined. Kent enjoyed a large audience and so this book passed through several editions. Like Smith of Glasgow he had enthusiasm for the Old Testament and gave little heed to the theological problem connected with it.

We shall content ourselves with mentioning but one further book from the American quarter—that of Fullerton.[15] His concern is not with the Old Testament as a whole, but only with the prophets. But what he has to say on the subject is of general significance. He sees the Protestant Church enmeshed in an untenable dualism—adhering to the dogmatic view of Scripture established in the Reformation, and at the same time appropriating the results of modern research in every other field. Protestantism, he holds, must come to terms with itself, as to its own fundamental principle—the Scripture principle—and must frankly adopt the results of modern scientifically pursued biblical scholarship. Over against millennarianism, which operates with the orthodox Scripture doctrine and dwells particularly on biblical prophecy and apocalyptic, Fullerton seeks to show that the belief that the Bible tells what is happening now or what will happen at some point in the future has been maintained only by means of false principles of exegesis, and that the adoption and recognition of correct principles will automatically eliminate it. Accordingly he discusses the change that has taken place in the interpretation of predictive prophecy from the patristic to the modern periods and ends by showing that a purely historical interpretation is alone legitimate.

But Fullerton does not make clear to himself the full consequences of a complete surrender to the modern scientific method for all forms of Protestantism; the theological problem involved has not entered his field of vision. Hence the value of his book lies chiefly in its historical studies on the history of interpretation.

In retrospect, then, the apologetic of biblical scholars of the period covered in this chapter shows a widespread acceptance of critical results and a desire to make them palatable to a larger public. Whether the credit should be given to such apologetic or to some other factor, it is clear that a vast change took place in the attitude of the average Christian during these decades. The phrase "higher criticism" virtually passed out of existence, while the thing for which it stands was accepted in all but the most orthodox quarters as something self-evident—and quite boring.

While biblical scholarship did little in America to show to men any positive meaningfulness of the Old Testament, a movement arose from the side of practical application of Christian ethical thinking which was of considerable importance in that direction. Fully aware of the social crisis brought about in capitalist America by the rise of modern industrialism, Rauschenbusch,[16] with prophetic zeal and fervour, demanded that Christianity furnish its contribution of moral and religious power in the struggle for social improvement. And here, quite naturally, not only the ethics of Jesus but also those of the prophets of Israel, so much emphasized by the modern critical school, were invoked to furnish directives. This social gospel had a wide appeal and gave fresh impetus to the Churches to come out of the shell of passive orthodoxy into active participation in the great current of life. Its influence abides to this day, and one still finds leaders of liberal religious thought in America stressing the social message of the prophets, when there would not appear to be any warrant for according them any authority under the Scripture doctrine presupposed.

Chapter Ten

HARNACK AND DELITZSCH

IN the situation immediately after the First World War the problem of the Old Testament lifted its head very noticeably in the German scene. While it may seem out of place to couple the names of the two men who aroused so much debate on the subject, because the first addressed himself to theologians and theological students while the second, though a distinguished scholar, sought the limelight of publicity and poured grist into the mill of the anti-Semitic agitators, they do supplement each other. For Delitzsch gives the detailed indictment of the Old Testament that Harnack only hints at, and both in effect desire the same thing and for the same reason.

The problem of Christianity and the Old Testament had occupied Harnack throughout his long career. He reverts to it time and again in his studies and treatises dealing with early Christian literature, quite often in a manner that suggests a vacillation in his own attitude. While the main tenor of his remarks is negative, he occasionally pulls in the opposite direction. Even a friend of the Old Testament can take no issue with such a statement as this:

> The Church is younger and older than Jesus. It existed in a certain sense long before Him. It was founded by the prophets, at first within Israel, but already at that time it pointed beyond itself. All the developments that took place later are refashionings. It was present at the moment when a fellowship tending toward universality was formed within Israel, striving out of darkness into the light, out of national and legalistic religion to a religion of the spirit and saw itself led to a higher level of humanity on which God and His holy moral law exercise sway.[1]

Harnack thus clearly discerns Christianity's connection with Israel. But that evidently did not compel him to believe that

Christians needed the Old Testament. In his work on Marcion he came out with a completely negative declaration on the problem.[2] In appraising the significance of the great heretic he claims that what Marcion had wanted was basically right: the Old Testament should be deposed from canonical rank. He concedes that Marcion went too far in considering the Creator God and the Christian God two entirely different gods, and grants that the Christian will want to preserve the belief in their identity. But that, he argues, cannot save the Old Testament. The intellectual history of the eighteenth and nineteenth centuries has made it evident that the Old Testament simply cannot be a part of the Christian rule of faith and life. The trouble with the Churches is that they are too timorous to admit the truth. Let them consider the harm the Old Testament does their cause. Much of the opposition to Christianity in the modern world is based on the Old Testament which affords so much opportunity to people to attack and ridicule the Bible, and thereby to justify their standoffishness toward the Church. The heroic action demanded of Protestantism to-day is to acknowledge this situation and do something about it. He warns that it is almost too late (and for the German scene, as events soon showed, his warning would seem to have been well-founded). He rejects the excuse of the clever ecclesiastical politicians who say that since the authority of the New Testament in the old sense of the word has also been dissolved, one may as well leave Old Testament and New Testament together. Granting that the idea of the authority of the New Testament has undergone a change, he, nevertheless, considers it to be the true canon of the Church, "because a better collection of documents to set forth what is Christian cannot be made."

He concedes no weight to the argument that because Jesus recognized the Old Testament as Holy Scripture we, too, must do so, and that it is the great document for the history leading up to Christianity. Jesus Himself dismissed the idea of the continued importance of earlier stages of revelation when he said in a most solemn saying that henceforth all knowledge of God is given through Him (Matthew 11: 27). The idea, furthermore, of combining the document for the preparatory history of Christianity with its own original documents on one level is not a religious idea but a secular one. The trouble with Marcion was that he had to portray the Old Testament as a false and ungodly book in order to preserve the gospel. This difficulty no longer plagues us. We are not bound by certain Gnostic limitations at which the Church rightly took offence. The Old Testament, Harnack believes, will receive its full significance and appreciation only when put at the head of the books which are useful to read but not authoritative (i.e., the Apocrypha). These were impressive words, spoken by one of the most widely known scholars of Christendom.

The chief weakness in Harnack's presentation was the fact that it was put forward only incidentally in speaking of a figure of a remote past. He did not—and could not in that connection—restate in full the arguments against the Old Testament that arise in men's minds to-day. Delitzsch, however, had, several years earlier, made himself a spokesman of the present and had carried forward the attack against the Old Testament in a two volume work.[3] We have already referred to the stir previously caused by this author in his "Babel-Bible" lectures in 1902–05. His new venture did not have such far-flung repercussions, but nevertheless received large publicity in Germany, where it coincided with a mounting wave of anti-Semitism. Delitzsch, of conservative Lutheran origin, son of Franz Delitzsch, who had been one of the foremost Old Testament scholars of his day, disclaims anti-Semitic intentions and points to his friendship for numerous high-minded Jews and to the help he had given to Jewish students as indications of his true position. We may well believe that his opinions on the Old Testament could have arisen apart from any anti-Semitic bias, and, in the cases where it would seem to appear, discount that element as a post-war accretion (or a part of Schopenhauer's legacy?) that has no integral connection with his main argument. A detailed review of his position will be given, because he strives to show in some detail and with strong arguments why the Old Testament is unfit to be used as normative Scripture by the Christian Church.

Delitzsch puts himself on the plane of the intelligent layman who is reading the Old Testament connectedly with a critical mind. He assumes that this layman has been taught, as he himself was in his orthodox home, that the Old Testament is the Word of God, and his book reflects all the reactions of complete disillusionment on that score. Delitzsch's critics quickly attacked him as incompetent in Old Testament science. We would hesitate to join in such condemnation, for Delitzsch's contributions to Old Testament study, notably to its philological side, are substantial. That in publishing this new work he did not think it necessary to occupy himself very fully with modern Old Testament criticism is comprehensible enough, because the standpoint chosen by him seemingly made that unnecessary. He wanted to point out what anyone could see without taking recourse to the technical literature of critical interpretation. In the Preface he tells what a shock it was to him as a student when he took a course on Old Testament Introduction and heard his teacher admit that Deuteronomy was not written by Moses, in spite of all its pretensions to that effect. "Then Deuteronomy is a falsification?" he asked the professor. The reply was: "For God's sake! That may be true but one mustn't say such a thing." Since German biblical scholars of those days were by no means safe from being investigated by heresy-hunting ecclesiastical authorities, the professor's caution is quite comprehensible. But it had an unfortunate effect on this particular pupil. He makes the words "For God's sake" the motto of his book, believing that the truth and nothing but the truth should be told "for God's sake". The incident, among other things, reveals Delitzsch's fine feeling for that which is ethical. And herein lies the explanation of his whole attack on the Old Testament. In a nutshell, he considers it a book full of fraud and immorality, that has damaged the moral fibre of Christendom and should be no longer read as sacred literature by Christians.

In the first volume Delitzsch tries to elaborate on this by dwelling in some detail on three sets of Old Testament narratives —the accounts of the conquest of Palestine, of the revelation at Mount Sinai, and more briefly the stories of the early prophets. It is obvious that he has chosen areas of Scripture which present great difficulties to most people and for that reason are not read or studied anywhere with unmixed delight. As to the first theme, he mercilessly shows up the falsity, self-contradictoriness, yea monstrosity of the conquest narratives when read as though they formed a single continuous account (as the untutored reader might naturally do). In some instances Delitzsch places undue historical reliance on some aspect of a particular story, as well as on his own imaginative reconstructions of what happened. Thus he utilizes the incident of the scarlet thread of Joshua 2 : 18 to insinuate that Jericho fell through betrayal by a *bribed* harlot who admitted the Israelites to the city. He treats that fanciful reconstruction of what happened as a proven fact and considers it a terrible indictment of the morals of the Israelites that the spies went to a harlot's house! More convincing is the way in which he sets forth the absurdity of the narrative of the march around the walls of Jericho. He reasons that since the walls of the ancient city have an actual circumference of only 750 metres, as measured by modern excavators, it would have taken 15 hours and 10 minutes for the 531,150 men allegedly composing the invasion host to march around them if they went 5 deep; how then, he asks, could they march around Jericho seven times in one day? As a matter of fact, 1300 men would completely ring Jericho at a bowshot's distance from the walls! But a person of any insight knows that this absurdity of the present narrative has merely resulted from combining the fantastic figure of the number of Hebrews that went out of Egypt, as given in the P source, with the older narratives that presupposed no such numbers. Would it not be better to provide the layman with the key to the understanding of the narrative than to ridicule the effect of the compilation? These matters have long been recognized and are among the things that show the need for biblical criticism. If Delitzsch is merely arguing to convince naïve literalists of the impossibility of numerous statements made in the Old Testament narratives as they now stand, this is really gratuitous.

Weightier than this is his revulsion of feeling at the murderous mentality reflected in the Book of Joshua. The God of the Hebrews commands the extermination of the Canaanites—the horrible, callous murdering of captive men, women and children. Why did He not send a merciful plague to destroy them instead of ordaining this ghastly carnage? (Here Delitzsch might well have compared the more mercifully-minded Babylonian deity that rebukes Enlil at the conclusion of the Babylonian flood story.) Delitzsch then dwells on the inconsistency between the divinely given prediction that Israel was to possess a realm extending to the Euphrates and the historical fact that it did not obtain even the present limits of Palestine. The Old Testament scholar who does not consider the prophecy as actually focused on the conquest, but rather on a future to which the authors writing much later were still looking forward, does not feel as shocked over that as Delitzsch. He then points out that the extermination command is given its basis in the supposed immorality of the Canaanites. But Melchizedek (Gen. 14) and Ephron the Hittite (Gen. 23) show on the contrary that the Canaanites were good people, while the record of the Book of Judges reveals the moral depravity of whole Hebrew tribes (Benjamin, chapters 19–21; Dan, chapters 17–18). The divine command to exterminate the Canaanites could not even be carried out, as Judges 1 and the taking over of Baal worship by the Israelites clearly show. The God Jehovah who has been unable to make good His promises thus supposedly stands convicted of impotence—He is an *ellil* (a "nothingness") just like all the other Oriental gods!

Turning to the Sinaitic revelation, Delitzsch first dwells on the picture given in Exodus 25–27, 35–40, of the Tabernacle. He shows that it is a purely imaginary projection of the Jerusalem temple into the Mosaic era. The whole Priestly Code is a forgery attributed to Moses but written 900 years later. Deuteronomy is another forgery written 680 years after Moses, and the Book of the Covenant (Ex. 20: 23–23: 19) a still earlier similar forgery. This is a very harsh judgment and overlooks the ancient fondness for literary masquerade, of which even Christians still made use without much sign of scruple. Coming to the Decalogue, Delitzsch points out how monstrous it is that its text as given the second time in Exodus 34 does not agree with that given the first time in Exodus 20 on the tables broken by Moses. He dwells on the crudity of the theophany situation —the elders of Israel "saw God, ate and drank!" And after all the experience of the theophany and while Moses was on the mountain with God, the people could make a golden calf and worship it! How totally absurd everything is. Why, there is not even a mountain in the Sinaitic peninsula around the foot of which a million people (once more a naïve acceptance of the Priestly source's imaginary figures) could have congregated!

After so many "deceptions", Delitzsch comes to the supreme

one—originally a self-deception of the narrators—that this divinity Jehovah (he refuses to accept the pointing "Yahweh" that is customary in literature on the Old Testament and uses the form Yaho which appears in so many Hebrew names, e.g., Jehoiada, instead) is identical with our God. He grants that it was consistent enough for Israel to elevate its own god to the rank of God of gods, just as other people, like the Babylonians and Assyrians, did with some of their gods. But the fact remains that Jehovah is always and exclusively the God of Israel. The finest passages of the Old Testament speak of this God's care and love for His people and have no relevance for the Christian reader. All non-Israelites are excluded from the benefits of this religion, or are only dragged along if they attach themselves to Jewish coat-tails (cf. Zech. 8: 23). How incredible that the God in whom we Christians believe, who knows no partiality and is Father over all that are called children in heaven and on earth, should have elected one people as His own, and condemned all others to perdition (cf. Spinoza)! Delitzsch is shocked by such a statement as Amos 3:2: "You only have I known of all the families of the earth", the naked meaning of which is that God has only concerned Himself about the Hebrews and no others. This election is grotesque already on Old Testament grounds, since that book in hundreds of passages shows that the Hebrew people did not even want to have Jehovah for a God or be loyal to Him. Who can believe that God could have chosen one people and conferred idolatry— a thing punished in Israel with death (Deut. 17: 3 f.)—on all the rest of mankind, as Deuteronomy 4: 19 claims? He then points out that the God Jehovah moves on a low moral plane—giving unethical or inhuman commands in the matter of robbing the Egyptians (Ex. 3: 22) and of chastising a slave with impunity to the point of causing his death (cf. above, p. 90). Particularly objectionable and ethically inferior to the Babylonian law which Delitzsch knows so well are the supposedly divinely given Hebrew marriage laws, which left a wife without rights and made divorce at the whim of the husband possible.

To the religious and moral grounds that rule out the identification of Jehovah with our Christian God must be added the cultic manner of His worship, fixed most strictly by the Priestly Code, and involving bloody sacrifices, exactly like those brought to the idols of Western Asia, and, above all, the narrowest of all narrow ideas—the Deuteronomistic centralization of worship at Jerusalem! Delitzsch finds the Canaanite cults on every hill and under every green tree, that the prophets condemn, "poetic" by contrast—an absurd, romantic idealization that he might better have omitted.

This deception, that Jehovah has anything to do with our Christian God, is an unheard-of fraud perpetrated on all humanity, says Delitzsch.[4] The way for it was already prepared in pre-Christian Judaism and was greatly furthered by the use of the word *Kyrios* (lord) in place of the name Jehovah in the Greek translation of the Bible. Jewish Christians like Paul espoused the idea. Identifying the Church with a "spiritual" Israel—a purely allegorical, unjustified interpretation!—they arbitrarily appropriated the Old Testament for Christianity. In Ephesians 2: 11 f. the apostle reveals himself enmeshed in the horrible Jewish philosophy that God left the Gentiles "strangers from the covenants of promise, having no hope and without God in the world". How unworthy this is of the Almighty who looketh only on the heart of man (here Delitzsch forgets that he is quoting the Old Testament I Sam. 16: 7), and who loves all peoples equally.

Delitzsch then turns to the narratives of the early prophets. These men are exponents of a fanatical Hebrew racialism, and have infused their excessive nationalism into supposedly divine oracles and predictions. At the same time they were skilful politicians who understood how to dominate the people and the kings—sometimes, in fact, demagogues of the worst sort. Their interference helped to undermine the authority of the kingship, which alone could have preserved the state. He points to the role of an Ahijah of Shiloh (I Kings 11: 29 f.) in provoking a revolution that destroyed the unity of the kingdom and produced bloody civil war (I Kings 14: 30, 15: 7), and to that of an Elisha, who in the name of Jehovah incites a revolution and lets the terrible murderer Jehu loose on his own people; the latter exterminates the whole house of his master Ahab, and is then even praised and rewarded by Jehovah for his foul deed (II Kings 10: 30)! To add to one's confusion the same Jehovah inspires the prophet Hosea to threaten Jehu's house with punishment for the crimes of "Jezreel" (Hos. 1: 4). Is not

the presence of such contradictions in the records an indication
of the abuse that the prophets carried on with the assertion of
their inspiration? After a few kind words for the prophets as
preachers of social justice, Delitzsch gives instances of crude
and absurd miracle stories about the prophets from Kings and
Chronicles, and points out that these stories have had a warping
effect on people's ideas of the divine ways, giving encourage-
ment to fantastic hopes of miraculous divine interpositions, and
have stultified the intelligence of a humanity that is supposed to
accept this preposterous stuff as gospel truth.

This sketch of Hebrew prophecy is supplemented in his
second volume, where Delitzsch shows that the prophets are all
bound by one and the same dogma: there is no higher God than
Jehovah and Israel is Jehovah's people.[5] He rejects the idea
that Isa. 56:7—"Mine house shall be called a house of prayer for
all peoples" (which, he had been told, is engraved above
the door of many a synagogue) is in any way an expression of
liberal sentiments; these Gentiles, he points out, all have to
accept circumcision, i.e., become Jews, and he reminds of the
comment of Duhm that in spite of the promise of verse six the
foreign born were not admitted to the great day of prayer
after the first correctly celebrated Feast of the Tabernacles
(Neh. 9:2). Actually, the idea that Gentiles should join in their
national worship is an abomination to the prophets. O that
Christian leaders would be able to discern this clearly and
acknowledge the truth! If Isa. 2:2–4 speaks of the peoples
streaming to Jerusalem for instruction, the parallel, Mic.
4:1–5, puts a damper on it by adding "For all people will
walk everyone in the name of his god, but we will walk in the
name of Jehovah our God for ever and ever"! He finds a
callous indifference to the fate of other peoples vividly reflected
in these words. The prophets, he claims, were not "inspired"—
they were speakers of the Hebrew national genius as embodied
in the supposed god Jehovah! Their sayings are composed of
purely human combinations, inferences, hopes and fears. He
cites Jeremiah's idea that the proof of the inspiration of a
prophecy is its coming true (28:9). What a lot of prophecy
falls to the ground when judged by that principle! He gives
three examples of unfulfilled prophecy.

(1) The predictions of the fall of Babylon. In Jeremiah 50–51

and in Isaiah 13–14: 23, 46: 1 f., 47: 9, 11 the catastrophe be-
falling Babylon is described in lurid colours. Nothing of this
kind ever came to pass. These prophets were completely mistaken as to the divine plan, for Babylon opened its gate to
Cyrus and was absolutely untouched to the time of the Seleu-
cids; it just died a natural death. Its ruins remained till to-day
a veritable mine for building stones for the inhabitants of the
neighbourhood, putting to shame Jehovah's alleged saying in
Jeremiah 51: 26. (2) The prediction of the fall of Tyre. Ezekiel
was so firmly convinced of the fall of Tyre at the hands of
Nebuchadnezzar and foresaw in it such a display of Jehovah's
power that he revelled in the idea (26–28: 19). Obviously his
god had not taken him into his confidence, for that which he
expected did not happen. Nebuchadnezzar's siege was un-
successful. (3) The return of Israel to Zion. How vividly the
prophecies, notably those of Deutero-Isaiah, speak of the
glorious return of Jehovah's people, and what promises of
future prosperity they make! They remained unfulfilled. When
the opportunity came to return, Israelites and Jews, in cool
calculation, stayed where they were better off materially.

Delitzsch then takes up what he considers to be the lack of
any real value in the prophetic books of the Old Testament.
He asserts that the speeches of a Jeremiah or an Ezekiel are
entirely ephemeral and have not the least religious interest for
those living to-day. All of their hymns of hate against neigh-
bouring nations, with their predictions of doom, have already
been proven valueless by history, since these nations outlived
the Kingdoms of Israel and Judah. He has sharp and not
entirely unjustified words for the prophetic misrepresentation
of idolatry, notably in Deutero-Isaiah. The Babylonians, he
asserts, did not pray to the idols of wood and stone; they
prayed to celestial divinities of which the idols were mere
artistic portrayals.

The Psalms, too, come in for a discussion.[6] From the first
to the last, Delitzsch holds, they are full of the particularistic
Jewish view of God. The Gentiles are only called to praise
Jehovah because He has blessed Israel, and must become Jews
to share in any way in Israel's blessedness. Historically he has
great respect for the Jewish element that returned from the
exile and rebuilt its destroyed national home, passing through

a fire of trials. But that has nothing to do with the question whether the Psalter is a book fit to serve Christian religious needs. That imputation must be entirely rejected.

In the first place, the Psalter rests on the Torah. The Torah, as Jewish law, is a thing of the past so far as we are concerned. If the Psalter divides people into two classes, the godly and the ungodly, depending on whether they observe this Torah or not, that is a totally remote situation for us who enjoy the glorious freedom of the children of God through the new message of Jesus Christ. Still less are the references in the Psalms to past events, such as that of the exodus from Egypt, of any use to us. The Psalms even justify the low cunning practised by the patriarchs and later by the departing Israelites (cf. Ps. 105: 13–15, 37). In other respects, too, he finds the Psalms defective— he stresses their materialism and their melancholy view of life after death. Only two or three references to the immortality idea are found in them, and in these it is confined entirely to the pious, leaving the rest of mankind to a dismal Hades. Not a single Psalm is devoted to the theme of the love of one's neighbour (limited at best in the Old Testament to one's fellow national). Everywhere there are thoughts of hatred for the personal enemies of the psalmists. How few are the Psalms that have any value at all! He concedes that Ps. 73: 25–26 is indeed, a fine utterance but asserts that the Old Testament scholars who praise it to high heaven are thereby tacitly condemning the whole previous history in which they can find no such expressions of religious sentiment. It is an isolated saying, expressed at the very end of the Old Testament development, and occurs only in a Psalm influenced by the imported (Delitzsch erroneously says: Sumerian) immortality idea.

In passing, Delitzsch ridicules the Catholic priests who are obliged to pray the whole Psalter once a week in Latin, and gives examples of Vulgate renderings which are so obscure that they can convey no intelligible idea to the reader's mind. He speaks of the inappropriate use made in thousands of Christian homes of Psalm 90 when read as a Lesson for New Year's Eve; its cheerless melancholy sentiments should not be those of the Christian at that season! He mentions the impudence with which in the last decade before Christ so many obviously late Psalms were ascribed to David (cf. Ps. 138 f.) and even linked to certain definite situations in his life. The tendency to put a halo around the head of that king may be understandable, but a man whose ruthless acts, crimes and immorality are a matter of record does not deserve a place of honour in the Christian Church and is not worthy of being considered the ancestor of Jesus.

The summary of his indictment that Delitzsch gives, after reviewing the favourable reactions his first volume had elicited from various quarters, may be quoted here:

> That the Old Testament is full of deceptions of all kinds: a veritable hodge-podgè of erroneous, incredible, undependable figures, including those of biblical chronology; a veritable labyrinth of false portrayals, misleading reworkings, revisions and transpositions, therefore also of anachronisms, a constant inter-mixture of contradictory particulars and whole stories, un-historical inventions, legends and folktales—in short, a book full of intentional and unintentional deceptions, in part self-decep-tions, a very dangerous book, in the use of which the greatest care is necessary. I repeat: the Old Testament in all its books is full of linguistic beauties, of archæological information, and retains its value as a historical document in spite of its defects, but it is in all directions a relatively late and very cloudy source, a propa-gandistic document from the first chapter of Genesis to the last of Chronicles.[7]

There is little in this recapitulation with which the Old Testa-ment scholar needs to take issue except with his over-emphasis on "deception". As though conscious of a weakness in his argu-ment, he adds the words "and unintentional" to "intentional". Self-deception is, indeed, a great element in narratives far removed from the times of which they speak. Historical memory fades very quickly. In the crystallization of stories about things past that bubble up anew out of the wellspring of the popular thought and life the facts are often distorted beyond recognition. It seems to us that wilful deception, though perhaps present in some instances, is not as prominent a factor as wishful thinking. Delitzsch gives Old Testament scholars a sorely needed lesson on at least one biblical narrative in which few had hitherto realized how much it distorted the actual events—that of Sennacherib and Hezekiah (II Kings 18–19).[8] To what extent this is an instance of an intent to deceive remains debatable. The natural tendency to forget what is painful and unpleasant, the upsurging of a nationalistic-prophetic attitude which accepted the dogma that Jehovah protects Zion, could have produced gradually a form of narrative concerning that episode tending to be more satisfactory to Hebrew religious and patriotic feeling than the transmission of naked and shameful truth. There is an unconscious "drift" in the development of popular narrative of which the scholar should be aware. For this Delitzsch seemingly has no understanding at any point—he thinks it was malice aforethought that produced the result.

In his presentation of Jesus and Christianity as differing radically from Judaism, Delitzsch has some interesting things to say. He argues that Jesus was no Jew, but a Galilean, in whose veins may have rolled blood of the "Cuthaeans" who had come from the Sumerian plain. The real Jews had all been removed from Galilee. His ancestors can only have been people of Ituraea (cf. Luke 3: 1), whose inhabitants were compelled to accept circumcision and Jewish law by Aristobulus I, one hundred years before Christ.[9] As a member of this Galilean group of mixed derivation, Jesus could, on occasion, be defamed as "Samaritan" (John 8: 48)! If that be rather unconvincing Delitzsch finds further proof for Jesus' supposed non-Jewish origin in His unique mental attitude. His broad universalism and humanitarian outlook are in the sharpest possible contrast to the exclusive particularism of the Jews (which Delitzsch apparently regards as a congenital trait of the Hebrew people). Hence in His use of the Old Testament Jesus saw things that had not entered the consciousness of the original story-tellers at all; thus when He makes a peculiar observation on the widow of Zarephath and Naaman (Luke 4: 25 f.), His statements were so un-Jewish that the men of the synagogue at Nazareth cast Him out of the city. His setting up of a Samaritan as an example of mercy (Luke 10: 33 f.), and of gratitude (17: 15 f.), His association with publicans and sinners in utter disregard of Psalm 1, are all un-Jewish. There is no bridge at all, he thinks, from the Old Testament to the mentality of Jesus. *Christianity*, he says, *is an absolutely independent, new religion—no mere higher stage in the development of Judaism.*   Here one feels reminded of the position of Schleiermacher.

What Delitzsch says about a possible Aryan origin of Jesus is not without interest. But we know too little about the Jewish element in Galilee to say that Jesus was not of Jewish extraction. His broader attitude toward the Gentiles might, for instance, be like that of the Jews of Beth Shean in Maccabean times, whom their non-Jewish fellow citizens protected in an era of persecution—doubtless because they had conducted themselves blamelessly.[10] Certainly some late books of the Old Testament like Jonah and Ruth show the existence among the Jews (albeit in pre-Maccabean days) of kindly humanitarian attitudes. Could not Jesus have been an outflow of a stream of this type within Judaism? We cannot set up an *a priori* picture of what the Jew must have been like and then, when we find one who was not like that, deny that he was a Jew! As nearly as we can judge, Jesus does not act as He does because of a non-Jewish background, but because of what He (rightly or wrongly) felt was in accord with the noblest strain of the religion of the Old Testament. That the intellectual and moral sides of His environment contained numerous stimuli of non-Jewish origin need not be denied.

Delitzsch casts ridicule on the "medieval paper dogma" found in so many books on Old Testament theology, according to which God supposedly elected Abraham's descendants that they should observe justice and righteousness, and that later on all nations should share in this blessing. What a clumsy pedagogue this Jehovah must be! he exclaims. The pages of the Old Testament show that this people, instead of serving such an end, were the breeding ground of the worship of the golden calf and of a lawlessness and immorality that its own prophets had to condemn. How monstrous from the standpoint of Christianity that the all-wise God should have chosen as His favourite people one that was to crucify the Son of God and entertain for Him and for Christianity as such a deadly hate through all the centuries. Thanks to this hate with which the Jews of Arabia defamed Jesus as "Esau" and Christianity as "Edom" (by way of wishing Old Testament curses on them), Mohammed got to know Him as "Isa", with the result that 250,000,000 Moslems are unwittingly continuing this Jewish defamation of Christ.[11] If some liberals claim that there has been an upward progression in Israel from an original particularism to a universalism leading to the idea of Christ, this would, if true, prove that the greater part of the Old Testament ought to be eliminated anyhow; but he sees no such universalism—prophets and psalms prove the very opposite. Everywhere there is nothing but Jewish nationalism.

Delitzsch concedes that certain passages of the Old Testament can, indeed, be utilized by Christians. He doubts, however, whether they are numerous enough to compose a whole devotional book such as a popular author had suggested. He thinks such a collection would have to be supplemented by the many beautiful sayings of Gentile poets and thinkers. However, he lays the foundation for such a collection by listing a number of outstanding Old Testament passages.

Delitzsch thinks that study of the Old Testament as a theological subject should be abolished. It should be handed over entirely to the secular sphere of Oriental studies and History of Religions.[12] He believes it an absolute waste of time for the average Christian theological student to learn Hebrew.[13] The expenditure of effort necessary for that purpose, he thinks, might better be utilized in acquiring some knowledge of the social sciences, along with some History of Religions. A brief general course in Hebrew history, literature and religion should give the theological student all the Old Testament background he needs.[14] He recommends studying the use of the Old Testament in the New Testament with the help of books by capable scholars; the student will then discern how the unfortunate effort of Jewish evangelists and apostles to find the teachings and the history of Jesus indicated or foretold in the Old Testament, by means of false translation and interpretations, drew the New Testament into a dependence on the Old Testament that is no longer bearable. In short, the New Testament must be freed from its artificial embrace by the Old Testament; the teachings of Jesus must be worked out in their purity for the blessing of every Christian and especially every future servant of Christ, and therewith of the whole Christian Church. Above all, the theological student should begin as soon as possible to become a practical follower of Jesus by being the embodiment of loving, kindly service to his fellow men. That Delitzsch, like

Harnack, has the welfare of Christianity at heart and is fully sincere in his belief that the Old Testament influence does irreparable harm is quite obvious.

If we take Delitzsch's books at their face value (disregarding the unfortunate way in which anti-Semitism capitalized upon them and for which his emphasis on "deception" is partly responsible), we do not find them as worthless as is commonly claimed. He has made his readers conscious of the limitations of the Old Testament. Christians have been too prone to read the terrible and shocking things contained in that book in a sort of pious daze. This has doubtless been seriously detrimental to the moral sense of Christendom. The constant uncritical acceptance of the most monstrous contradictions in the record, furthermore, has helped to lull people's critical faculties. If the Church was shaken by having this said, it well deserved to be. Delitzsch has shown how necessary it is for theology to find a better basis for its retention of the Old Testament than antiquated constructions of philosophy of history, or a mere reliance on the Jewish traditionalism on the part of certain New Testament writings.

But while Delitzsch's attack illustrates the impossibility of certain orthodox views of the Old Testament which no enlightened admirer of that book has any desire to defend, it leaves out of consideration the benefits which the Old Testament properly understood may be able to confer, and hence is too one-sided. The question can only be whether it is possible to get into the popular mind an idea of the place of the Bible as a whole, and the Old Testament in particular, in our religion which will be more tenable than that which Delitzsch takes to be the self-evident and accepted one and which alone makes such attacks as his possible. The flood of literature by Old Testament scholars in reply to Delitzsch did not come to grips sufficiently with this theological issue, but was primarily focused on giving the scholarly slant on the Old Testament to the public. But in this scholarly slant the doctrine fixed in the popular Protestant mind was sacrificed by implication. These men were not fighting on the same front with the churchmen. Thus Delitzsch's results seemed at least partly vindicated in the eyes of the impartial observer.

Harnack had expressed the wish that Marcionites should

again be found in the Christian chorus of to-day. Delitzsch fulfilled that hope before the utterance of it saw print. Marcion's church did not survive any more than did the opposite extreme of Judaistic Christianity. Harnack himself, in a vacillating moment, infers from this that possibly neither alternative can be carried through.

Chapter Eleven

SYSTEMATIC THEOLOGY AND THE
OLD TESTAMENT AFTER 1918

IN the disintegration and despair of continental post-war
Europe the entire range of human values and beliefs was
shaken. New philosophies arose seeking to probe life and
reality in a new manner. Behind them stood a great scepticism
as to all previously accepted truth. We are like the blind man
who has to grope his way and try to comprehend the mysterious
character of things in gradual and circumstantial approach; and
beyond those immediate things lies the great world of the unknown. The phenomenology of Husserl was particularly important here; his method was to get at the "meaning" of a
given entity by determining its place and approaching it intuitively from various angles. Soon there arose the existential
philosophy of a Heidegger and Jaspers. Under impulses deriving
from the gloomy Dane, Kierkegaard,[1] a view putting personal
existence before all compulsion of ideas or abstract concepts
was promulgated. Existential thinking, therefore, is concrete
thinking. Every thought-form is dependent on the form of
existence represented by the thinker; the axis of philosophizing
is the illumination of the existence of the inquirer. From this
angle belief in the objectivity of most social sciences and of
philosophy as well became dubious.

Out of the same Kierkegaardian roots emerged also the
theological movement of Karl Barth, who prefers that it be
called the "Dialectic theology".[2] Dialectic is the art of dialogue,
be it with another person or with the self. The designation
"Dialectic theology" is derived from the conviction, shared by
Barth and the circle about him, that theological statements can
be made only in the form of human speech and response, in full
consciousness of the impossibility of drawing near to the divine
reality. In the Hegelian dialectic, thesis is followed by antithesis, and then by synthesis, in which the contrast is dissolved.

In the new theology the thesis is God, the original given entity. The antithesis is: God is unapproachable. The synthesis is the paradox that the unapproachable one has made himself approachable. Since a metaphysical entity, God, is involved here the dialectic is merely "analytic": i.e., the "thesis" is not changed, but only limited in the antithesis, and defined as to content in the synthesis.

Behind this theology stands an experience of the sovereignty and unapproachability of God, and of our human limitations; it holds that we cannot draw near to Him, either theoretically or practically, unless He Himself draws near to us first. All speaking of God, therefore, must be positive, in the full consciousness of our being under God—God cannot be dealt with as an object of debatable reality. Another significant fact about this theological attitude is its dependence on the basic doctrine of the Reformation—*justification* with the emphasis on God's declaring sinful human beings just. This puts the concept of God's "speaking", or his "Word", or "revelation", in the very centre of things.[3] On the surface at least this linked up with the basic Reformed position.

For the Dialectic theology, revelation is not a mere divine communication of teachings as for orthodoxy, or a limited portion of a historical process in which God revealed Himself in events and in inspired interpretations of these events, as for the modified supernaturalism of the nineteenth century. The teaching of Herrmann that revelation is a *present* reality, encountered when the individual meets God in personal, ethical experience of the saving power of Jesus Christ, was adapted by Barth to suit his new starting-point. The question that concerns Barth is the crisis of human existence (for which reason his theology is sometimes called the "Theology of Crisis"). What is this crisis? Man, thirsting for life, is delivered over to mortality; yearning for goodness he is unable not to sin, etc.

This crisis is increased and becomes an acute one where man is conscious of standing before God. God speaks to man in this situation; such speaking is revelation. It is the answer to man's question as to how he can bring his existence to its desired realization. God is veritably in His Word (not at all identical with Scripture), and His Word is to be heard by the human heart. The Word thus cannot be adjudged by man as Word of

God on the basis of various characteristics or of its content but confronts man with absolute and unquestionable authority. Barth recaptures something of that complete certainty concerning the divine Word that one finds in Luther. Since God answers our existential question in His Word, this speaking is not ended so long as our existence endures; we can never talk about His Word as though it were a completed product. It is a reality not given to us like the objects of the world about us. If we speak of it in positive statements as orthodoxy does, we make it a part of the world, "forgetting that as a solution of our existential need it stands absolutely beyond our existence with its physical and metaphysical realities."[4] If we speak of it in negative statements, we still remain in the area of that which is in our own control and do not establish a bridge to the unattainable positivity of God. The only thing remaining is to point to the impossibility of exercising any control over God's Word either in substance or by concept. Positive and negative thus stand dialectically side by side; we speak positively of the positivity of the Word of God, but put alongside of it the negative statement that this positivity does not belong to the series of positivities under the control of man. But this dialectic is only the form in which we must speak of God. Revelation itself completely transcends reason and is entirely under God's control.

The Word of God which is so completely transcendent to reason and of which one can only speak dialectically is for short "Jesus Christ". But the Dialectic theology here faces a dilemma: If taken as the answer to the existential question, revelation or the Word of God cannot be a historical fact in the ordinary sense, for man can control, or attempt to control, historical facts but not the Word of God. And yet, at the same time, this theology does not wish to give up the Christian claim that revelation occurred at a point in time and thus must be reported by a tradition subject to critical control. It asserts paradoxically both that it is historical and not historical. History is a predicate of revelation but revelation is not for that reason a predicate of history. God acts in history, but history is not itself the revealing action of God. Revelation, therefore, is no category of the general concept of history. Indeed, history as such is never revelatory. "In history *per se*, as far as the eye reaches, there is nothing that could provide a basis for faith." "In history *per se* everything could always be regarded in a different light."[5] Revelation is an historical event, but only in so far as the event transcends the historical is it revelation.

The Dialectic theology denies that one can speak of the "being" of God in revelation on the basis of general philosophical presuppositions. No ontological concept can be found in advance to provide a niche for revelation. It is something completely apart and above the process attainable to natural reason. What revelation is can only be determined through revelation itself. The necessity for a theological ontology which then will spread light also on the reality around us, thus looms up on the horizon. Over against historical relativism, the Dialectic theology asserts that the Christian claim of the revelation through Christ as central for humanity is not to be defended with a unified teleological philosophy of history that is subject to the attacks of reason, but with a "theology of history" that understands history in other terms than that of a progressing dotted line. The nature of history and the place of Christ, as well as the relation of revelation and Scripture to each other, are to be interpreted from the vantage point of faith in revelation.

If Herrmann had emphasized the present nature of revelation, Kaehler had provided the idea of the transcendent or suprahistorical (*das Übergeschichtliche*), which likewise proved stimulating here. The fact that God speaks with *us*, who are bound by space and time, makes His speaking historical; but the fact that it is *God* who thus speaks, makes the speaking more than historical; something eternal enters the here and now and this bit of history takes a transcendent aspect. Barth unhappily coins a term for the higher unity of the historical and transcendent—"primal history" (*Urgeschichte*), a word ordinarily used for the prehistoric era of human life on earth.

Barth considers the Incarnation the real "primal-historical event". The deepest meaning of history is revealed here: the victory of God in man's clash with God (which Christian insight sees as going on through the ages). No other point in the historical process takes on the same character of "primal history", except one in the future—the final redemption.

It is at this point that the attitude of Barth toward Scripture in general (and the Old Testament in particular) becomes understandable. Scripture has a revelatory authority only because it is witness of the "primal revelation". It is set apart by the fact that its authors had an immediate relation to the divine revelation—a relation very different from that of other men, even the greatest teachers of the Church. "The circumstance that revelation begat the witness of Scripture and speaks for itself in Scripture, makes Scripture the Word of God, without its ceasing for that reason to be simply and historically the word of the prophets and apostles, sharing in the relativity, the ambiguity and the remoteness, which pertain to all that is historical."[6]

Barth holds that the Word of God in Scripture is by no means confined to that which impresses *us* as the Word of God. God Himself and not our ever-limited insight determines what is His Word. According to the testimony of the Church, the Bible as a whole is the Word of God. This statement does not require us to believe all Scripture to be the Word of God, but says to everyone, no matter how much or little of this may actually be recognizable to him, that over against this literature *as a whole* we are confronted with the task of the discernment of that reality.

Barth regards the whole of Scripture, both Old Testament and New Testament, as witness of this "primal history" in Christ. Unlike the historical process, "primal history" is not bound to historical succession. The Old Testament testifies to the coming "primal history"—not to the when, where and how of its temporal appearances (for the prophets were no clairvoyants and self-evidently thought and spoke in their own historical sphere), but to its reality. Messianic prophecies are not the main thing in the Old Testament, but are only the exponents of the basic and decisive thing that they proclaim: the God who speaks in Christ; the Word that becomes flesh; the *deus absconditus*, who as such is the *deus revelatus*. For just this God, the inscrutable, strong, powerful God of Moses, Jeremiah, Job, the 39th and 139th Psalms is also the God of Capernaum and Nazareth, of Gethsemane and Golgotha. The New Testament takes its place alongside the Old Testament as witness to the "primal history"—not as a second and higher stage but as a witness of the succeeding one alongside of the preceding.

Barth thus proclaims the singleness and continuity of revelation in such a way as to put the Old Testament on a level with the New Testament. He views the New Testament Christianity as looking forward to a consummation, like that foreseen by the Old Testament saints.[7] With Christ present in the Old Testament (he stresses Christ's pre-existence) and the men of the Old Testament still with us as a cloud of witnesses (Heb. 12: 1), the two Testaments are merely testimonies of before and after the Incarnation. He asserts that only a secular thinking, which confuses the Incarnation with the so-called origin of Christianity, can attribute a lower dignity to the Old Testament.

Barth wants to maintain the designation of the Bible as the Word of God.[8] It makes clear that which is the object dealt with in this literature: the Word, heard—not spoken or written—by its authors. Since the Church knows the Word only through this medium it can call the medium itself the Word of God. But he rejects the Roman position that it is the authority of the Church which established the authority of Scripture; the canon was merely *declared* by the Church after these writings had *proved* themselves to be the Word of God. Barth recedes, however, from the older Reformed position that the canon is definitely fixed for all time. He theoretically concedes the possibility of widening or narrowing it, but holds that only the Church can act in this matter.[9] In individual experience, he admits, other things may be more important than the Bible, but for the Church the priority belongs to the latter. He dismisses the doctrine of verbal inspiration as unknown to the great leaders of the Reformation, and contents himself with the position of merely affirming that "God speaks to us in the Bible". This conviction is not one to be demonstrated, but is axiomatic (though of course not immediately acceptable to reason like an axiom in mathematics). It is implied in the Christian faith from the outset, for Barth holds with Calvin that a believer is one who subjects himself to Scripture.[10] God Himself speaks to us in and through the Word and thereby gives evidence of Himself (the so-called internal testimony of the Holy Spirit).

Serious dangers, Barth warns, beset all efforts to be more precise. If one stresses the objective reality of God's speaking in the words of the prophets and apostles, one gets the conception of a mysterious book, out of which one vainly tries to hear the Word of God. Or if one stresses the fact that the Spirit testifies in us to the reality of the revelation given to the prophets and apostles, then there is a tendency to exalt mystical experiences on the part of the individual. Barth affirms that both things are true: God speaks in the Word and God (the Spirit) speaks within us. But the light that goes forth from the Bible and the eye that sees this light cannot be separated. Both factors together constitute the single voice of God.[11]

Dialectic theology thus tacitly accepts the validity of the objections reason had advanced against supernaturalism and tries to find an unassailable position for revelation.[12] It concedes that the assertion of an absolute revelation in Jesus Christ is impossible according to reason, but paradoxically asserts that it is a reality none the less; it grants that a historical event can have no universal significance, but asserts the universal significance of this one. Over against the claim of reason that there is no special exempt area in which revelation imparts truth rather than reason, it radicalizes revelation, as something apart from knowledge and as a mystery and paradox even to the believer.

Here Kierkegaard's thought on the paradoxical was influential. The paradox, according to the Danish thinker, is present whenever one thinks that things are other than they appear to reason. In philosophy one speaks of antinomies—truths that seem mutually exclusive and yet are valid; behind them stands a paradox. There is an irritating border-line for reason in every paradox—reality asks reason to take a step which reason according to its own laws is unable to take. To live in the face of this border-line becomes a practical attitude, in which theoretical considerations are no longer decisive.

In this new manner, then, revelation is upheld over against reason. And at the same time theology shows up the inadequacy of the modern world-view; it points out that it disregards the very heart of all reality—human existence—and necessarily so, because, since one stands within it, one cannot see it from the outside, objectively. One can only speak of existence in terms of one's own concrete existence and only in a confessional manner. Revelation, it is claimed, addresses itself to and operates in this centre of reality. The Dialectic theology thus could claim that it had given revelation a deeper and more genuinely theological form. Over against the "heteronomy" of Supernaturalism and the "autonomy" of a liberalism that was in league with philosophical Idealism it had created a "theonomy", a god-centred approach. The impact of this thinking on all fields of theological study, including that of the Old Testament, was bound to be great.

In the early twenties the Dialectic theology, while important, was not yet dominant; there were other lines which also had their dignity and following. Perhaps the leading systematic theologians of that period were Heim and Otto. We need not enter particularly into Heim's theology, for in spite of his links with Pietism and love of the Bible he is primarily concerned with problems arising in Christianity from the angle of the natural sciences.[13] When he steers toward a positive presentation of the Christian message he goes directly to the experience of the forgiveness of sins through Jesus Christ. Old Testament categories thus do not basically affect his position, and there is no occasion for the problem of the Old Testament to come into view. In such an essay as that on the Biblical World-View,[14] however, his affection for the Old Testament is revealed, and he looks for insights of abiding value in much that others consider purely mythological.

Of greater interest for our theme is the work of Otto, whose viewpoint may be described as a combination of historicism and mysticism. Here are world-wide horizons with attempts to understand and interpret appreciatively the non-Christian religions, and a feeling of ecumenical Christian unity together with practical concern with the modernization and enrichment of the worship of the Church. Here is interest for the tie-ups with philosophy (notably the Kantian as modified by Fries) and a psychological approach to the study of religious experience in the whole great sphere of the History of Religions.

Limited by the task in hand it cannot be our function here to dwell on all aspects of Otto's theology. It is obvious that one so deeply and reverently concerned with religious phenomena everywhere will have a very great partiality for the Old Testament. In his *Idea of the Holy*,[15] which had a vogue comparable to Schleiermacher's *Reden*, the strain of Old Testament influence is very marked. Indeed, one may doubt whether Otto would have been led to describe the experience of the Holy as the basic thing in religion without that collection of Sacred Writings. We must differentiate sharply, however, between a religious philosophical observation, viz., that in empirical religion the idea of Holiness is basic, and a theological-normative statement that it *ought to be* basic. Where the latter standpoint is taken the Old Testament strain in Christianity will be very large and will veer toward Calvinism. Otto's ideas seem to have run along that line—as his efforts to enrich the liturgical element in the Church service reveal—but he did not give any systematic presentation of that viewpoint. That the atmosphere he created with his emphasis on the non-rational and the awesome in the experience of God helped pave the way for an increased success by the Dialectic theology, which similarly stressed these aspects of the idea of God, seems patent.

But modern individual psychology, which under the leadership of William James had interested itself in the religious experience of the present-day individual, also found favour with certain theologians. Thus Wobbermin produced a Systematic Theology written from this angle.[16] He holds analysis of the psychical as well as the logical structure of the religious consciousness to be the fundamental preliminary task that needs to be performed before any theological statements can be developed. The basic religious conviction is viewed as taking root in the individual experience of faith. Through consideration of the latter the attempt is made to fathom the meaningfulness of the content (*Sinngehalt*) of religious faith on the basis of its own motives and to the exclusion of all motives, ideas, and concepts of an extraneous origin. This transcendental-psychological manner of inquiry stands close to that of the phenomenological school in Philosophy (cf. below on Tillich). The effort is to do justice both to the object and subject side of the faith-relation. The object, God, not being directly controllable, it is necessary to consider the historical objectivation of religious conviction and relate that to subjective conviction going back to personal experience. This historical objectivation is found primarily in Holy Scripture as the historical document of the divine revelation culminating in Jesus Christ—His life and teaching, death and resurrection. The primacy of Holy Scripture is recognized because there is no Christian experience that does not depend on it directly or indirectly. Indeed, Scripture is viewed as the sole source of evangelical teaching. It is apparent that in such an approach room can be found for the pre-Christian revelation, though there is no need for especial emphasis on it.

Individual-psychological interest also governed the theology of Karl Girgensohn. He undergirds his outline of Christian doctrine with Psychology and Philosophy of Religion.[17] Stressing the non-rationality of Christianity, he rejects Troeltsch's demotion of it to one religion among many and tries to develop the distinctive character of Christianity by means of partly contrasting and partly harmonizing thought. He distances himself from the Erlangen theologians by making subjective experience only one of the sources of doctrine—the other two being Scripture and the Confessions (in broadminded manner he welcomes use of the Reformed Confessions as supplementary to his own Lutheran). His views concerning Scripture are those of a moderate. He stresses revelation and inspiration of the men behind Scripture, but limits the infallibility of Scripture to the sphere of that which concerns the preaching of the saving purpose of God and the manner of its realization. That smacks somewhat of the same artificiality as the Catholic doctrine that the Pope is only infallible when he speaks *ex cathedra*.

Girgensohn's views on the Old Testament may be inferred from the way in which he discusses the Jewish religion of the law. He restates Christian criticism of the latter, in the light of Paul's contribution, and hence must regard the Old Testament as a partially outgrown stage of the biblical religion.

To Girgensohn the theology of that decade owed a renewal of the plea for an improvement in the method of Scripture interpretation.[18] Since that was bound to affect the Old Testament problem, we may dwell on it here. The post-world-war generation of theological students, which had seen life at its grimmest on the battlefield, had little equipment for or patience with the scholarly type of biblical exegesis, which sought to set forth the meaning of the biblical writings in their true ancient colour with the aid of the tools of philology, and of antiquarian research. Those who went into the ministry complained that the biblical exegesis which they had been taught, or which was available in critical commentaries, did not enable them to preach on the Bible, or even hindered their preaching. Girgensohn was particularly impressed by the fact that professional exegesis of Scripture failed to raise the question of the abiding worth and significance of a Scriptural thought. It was becoming increasingly useless for Systematic theology, for though the theologian cannot be indifferent as to the original historical sense of Scripture, he is really always seeking for the normative element in it. Paul's remark, "the natural man receiveth not the things of the Spirit of God . . . but he that is spiritual judgeth all things" (I Cor. 2: 14–15), suggested to him that there are two ways of interpreting Scripture: the historical-critical type of interpretation which belongs to the horizon of the natural man, and a spiritual or "pneumatic" exegesis, which he holds is the thing that is needed to-day. The term was not new—it had been used, e.g., by J. T. Beck, half a century before. But churchmen hailed the revival of the idea by a responsible scholar with great joy.

Girgensohn's untimely death prevented his publishing a demonstration of the method he had in mind. His idea, however, was that the exegete should extract the timeless element in Scripture from its historical shell and transpose it to a higher plane; and he conceived of this as a service to be done by and for Systematic theology. His much discussed programme was soon crowded off the scene, however, by the rival idea of "theological exegesis", which Karl Barth had introduced and demonstrated so effectively in his *Commentary on Romans*. But Girgensohn's ideas did stimulate biblical scholars to enrich their exegesis somewhat with religious reflection in order to meet the needs of theological students and pastors, without sacrificing critical insight. A comparison of Gunkel's and Weiser's expositions of selected Psalms will vividly reveal the shift made in this direction.[19]

Another important theologian of this period was Tillich. He links up with the phenomenological method of Husserl. As already indicated, the aim of this method is to describe the "meaning" of a given entity in intuitive approach, before deciding to accept or reject it. An interesting example of his treatment of Christian teachings is his lecture on revelation.[20] To him revelation is an idea. An idea cannot be demonstrated— only the place where it appears can be pointed out; whether one sees it depends on one's inner inclination. The idea of revelation is as old as religion; but the concept of revelation was created by late Greek philosophy at the time when there was a complete collapse of existence. In that age of scepticism men turned to the eastern religions, which had revelations in abundance. The concept of revelation is the correlate of late scepticism and the supernaturalism of revelation the correlate of the collapse of the belief in reason. Christianity took over the concept of revelation and focused it on Christ; in Him supernatural revelation was held perfect. Insights obtainable by reason were held to be natural revelation. Both ideas have come down through the ages. Where natural revelation is stressed the supernatural revelation is dissolved into an immanent process— a history of religion. Where the supernatural revelation is stressed, the connectedness of the process is interrupted. In the former case culture becomes hollowed out, in the latter case religion is put in a compartment. Tillich sees a need for a fresh start in examining revelation as well as all other "symbols" of religious knowledge.

Only that can be revealed which is by nature concealed, and revelation pertains to the absolutely concealed. If that be revealed it must be revealed in its quality as absolute and it must furthermore be fully revealed. This absolutely concealed is the utterly strange to which no way can be found out of our reality, but it is also our very own, present whenever a way begins. If that which is revealed is my own it absolutely concerns me. There is no revelation that does not put an absolute requirement on him to whom it is given. Hence it is not possible to receive it neutrally. Only what concerns me is revelation; hence we cannot think of other religions as revelation. How can the absolute enter the connectedness of the conditioned? It must appear in the conditioned, then the connectedness is not broken. The possibility exists *in* the conditioned to experience revelation. An object or being that has become an area in which revelation takes place is holy. Not through itself or its own excellence does a being take on holiness, but only through its character of bearer of revelation. Therewith Tillich believes he has overcome the contrast of natural and supernatural revelation. The idea of "natural revelation", he asserts, is at best an echo of original revelation, but is inadequate. "Supernatural revelation", on the other hand, is either revelation itself or a poor concept, identifying revelation and the bearer and doing violence to the connectedness of the conditioned.

Revelation for Tillich is not confined to the sphere we call religion. It points both civilization and religion back to their ultimate origin in which both are one.[21] Revelation is perfect only in so far as it can again be troubled. When a finite such as Bible, Church, Christianity is put in the place of the concealed absolute then Tillich sees a "demonic" seizure of revelation taking place.[22] A Church, secure in dogma and cult, is "demonizing" the revelation on which it rests.

Tillich aroused special attention with his "Kairos" teaching (Kairos being "the right, the favourable moment") which he made central in his religious philosophy, thereby designating the moment in which man experiences the irruption of the eternal into the present.[23] He regards numerous Christian doctrines as symbols which are produced by the basic forms of being. Thus the "Eschaton", as he calls the sphere of the "eschatological", is a symbol based on being, in so far as it is historical, for the Eschaton is the transcendent meaning of happenings. In this manner Tillich seeks to find the ultimate ground of the various assertions of religious experience or conviction by regarding their traditional form or description as merely symbolical. Some doctrines are undergirded by this procedure while others are devalued.[24] Since Tillich preserves an Old Testament element, stressing sin and the consciousness of guilt as well as the thought of the divine holiness (though at the same time incorporating elements of mysticism derived from Schelling), his attitude toward the Old Testament heritage is by no means hostile. He can afford religious selectivity, and it enables him to stress the elements of it that suit his purpose, without being handicapped by the elements of the Old Testament religion for which he can have no use.

It is of interest to note that the aged Ferdinand Kattenbusch in his valuable survey of contemporary theological trends (1934) saw good reason to stick to the Ritschlian appreciation for the Old Testament.[25] He counselled Old Testament theology not to continue to view the Old Testament in too detached a fashion—without regard for the New Testament. The same thing, however, applies to New Testament theology—it must not continue to view the New Testament without taking account of the prophetic literature of the Old Testament and the mentality that lies behind it. The "pneumatic" Old Testament substratum in the consciousness of the men of the New Testament, notably of Jesus, has not, he thinks, been sufficiently heeded. That the early Church lost its appreciation for this under the dominance of Paul's teaching about the law is a fact. But, he asserts, we here touch on the inability of the ancient Church to create durable formations of dogma. Jesus as the "Christ", Paul and John as those who proclaim Him in this unique exaltedness of person, are only to be rightly understood and theologically evaluated in their true canonicity if one makes clear to oneself that they lived in the old prophetic "pneumatic" atmosphere of an Isaiah or Jeremiah, which was later choked by Hellenism. This programme which, however, is not developed in detail would seem to place on theologians a heavy burden of historicism, especially in the requirement of stressing the Old Testament background of the men of the New Testament. The danger is that by that procedure we shall make them more remote than they already are.

This sampling of significant theological thought between the two world wars must suffice to indicate the range of new stimuli thrusting themselves upon the common mind and thus bound to affect Old Testament study in diverse ways.

Chapter Twelve

APOLOGETIC OF THE 'TWENTIES AND 'THIRTIES

GERMAN Apologetic on the Old Testament theme was of a varied nature in the two decades between the two great wars. It was at first strongly concerned with the situation created by Harnack and Delitzsch. Then the Dialectic theology and its interpretation of the Old Testament, notably by Vischer (see p. 219 f.), entered the picture. Next followed the rise of National Socialism, with an attendant anti-Semitism, bent on eliminating the Old Testament influence from national life. Finally, there was the doctrine of Hirsch representing a compromise between retention and rejection of the Old Testament (see p. 239 f.). Some of the writers dealing with our subject may be found fighting on several fronts at the same time. In England and America the Old Testament theme found increasing attention, but was detached from any special situation. It was merely a case of its being in the air as a result, probably, of the dust it was raising in Germany.

In the German debate over Harnack and Delitzsch two of the leading contributions were those of Eissfeldt[1] and Sellin.[2] The latter in part re-echoes the former, but since Eissfeldt's general position will be reviewed later, we will confine ourselves here to some account of Sellin. He held that Old Testament scholarship was at fault for not having properly disseminated its new knowledge and having left the Christian public bound in the untenable beliefs of the older orthodoxy. Hence the shock given Christian people by the publicity over his two colleagues. He found it necessary to demonstrate to his readers that the Old Testament is no infallible revealed book; it is human literature pure and simple, which, however, testifies to a divine revelation that took place in the history of a people. Revelation he defines as self-communication of the living God for the purpose of granting personal, living fellowship with Himself. Such revelation cannot take place in a manner dissociated from human presuppositions, but takes place in the historical process—in and through the medium of events, personalities and human utterances. It is only recognized in faith—only he who already has a relationship with God will discern His activity and presence in all these circumstances; the others will see only an immanent development. That would seem to leave the decision as to whether there is divine revelation in the Old Testament an entirely subjective one. But Sellin does not wish to grant that— instead he adduces arguments supporting the belief that there was actual revelation in Old Testament history.

The first is based on Comparative Religion; in the light of that subject, he thinks, it can be demonstrated that the Hebrew religion is so vastly superior to other religions in its spiritual insight, purpose and attainments that one cannot explain it on a purely historical basis, but must sense the Spirit of a living, personal God as operative in it. In this way we can lead anyone who is willing to use his eyes to the point where he can at least divine the existence of revelation in Israel. Here he evidently is following in the wake of Troeltsch. The second argument is that since Jesus and the apostles recognized the divine revelation in the Old Testament all those who see a divine revelation in Jesus cannot be indifferent to that book.

After setting forth that the Old Testament exhibits a struggle that went on in Israel and Judah between higher and lower forms of religion, and that Christians, following Jesus and the apostles, can only regard the former strain in it as normative, Sellin turns to Delitzsch's and Harnack's books. He accuses the latter, whom he takes more seriously, of employing a double standard in his treatment of the two Testaments. When referring to the Old Testament, Harnack implies that it must be "holy and therefore infallible Scripture" in order to be retained in the canon, while in speaking of the New Testament he contents himself with the more moderate estimate that it is "a collection of documents for determining that which is Christian". Harnack's criticism of the Old Testament, he believes, would fall to the ground if he gave the earlier collection the same leeway. He rejects, too, the idea that the Old Testament is primarily "law" and therewith the law-gospel contrast.

Sellin then raises the question whether the Church would not suffer serious loss in dropping the Old Testament. Not the

New Testament alone but the Bible of the two Testaments won over the nations for Christianity. While he does not feel capable of setting forth in detail just how the substance of Christianity would be affected by depriving it of a part of its equipment wherewith it has hitherto fulfilled its mission in the world, he makes the following observations:

(1) The Person of Jesus would lose something if no longer regarded as the culmination of a historical development leading up to Him. Even Schleiermacher, with good reason, conceded some importance to Messianic prophecy. (2) Christian piety easily becomes one-sided if it exclusively relies on the New Testament. The latter everywhere presupposes the earlier revelation and the idea of God as Creator and Provider, which finds little emphasis in the New Testament. (3) The Old Testament establishes a bridge between Christianity and the world. Without it an ascetic tendency is apt to prevail, for New Testament Christianity stands under the impression of the imminent return of Christ. (4) In the Old Testament the faith in a righteous but merciful God proved itself in a long history. There are admonitions, impulses, and consolations in this which are of positive value for the nations to-day. Christianity cannot do without this heritage. The New Testament alone is of little help for the historical process, because it is not oriented in the direction of a continuation of history, but looked on the end of the world as at hand. (5) In foreign mission work, especially, the Old Testament serves a useful purpose of drawing people gradually upward to Christ. (6) The Old Testament contains "law". Law and gospel belong together and the grace of God is only appreciated where the divine imperative has first been heard.

In a concluding section of his treatise Sellin makes a powerful appeal to all those who with the best of intentions urge a revision in the relationship of the Church to the Old Testament. He urges them to make clear to themselves what a loss it would be to do without this book. He reminds of the impulses that have gone forth from it on art and civilization, and of the way in which people in the midst of the trials of life have found strength in its utterances. He sees the Church partly responsible for the present crisis. He points to its unfortunate handling of the Old Testament—its inability to teach people to differentiate between what is bygone and eternal in that collection, its failure to make clear the difference in the religious levels of the Old Testament and New Testament and its leaving people under the false impression that it is infallible and verbally inspired Holy Writ—thus giving monstrous offence to reason. The slogan for the Church must be "forward to the right understanding and evaluation of the Old Testament".[3]

Turning to the British scene in the mid-'twenties, we may take from the shelf an important volume of essays by Members of the Society for Old Testament Study which contains two contributions relevant to our theme. The first, that of R. H. Kennett, seeks to appraise the contribution of the Old Testament.[4]

The more we subject that book to critical investigation, he says, the more we find it to contain passages at variance with what Christians believe to be true and right, not merely in regard to history and science, but also in connection with morality and theology. Hence he finds it inevitable that the question should be asked "What has the Old Testament to do with Christian faith?" He would approach the Old Testament critically—scrutinizing every part of its teaching in the light of what our Lord has taught. The result will be that we shall find ourselves compelled to classify these teachings under various categories. Some of its elements are mere pagan survivals, not suited to the needs of higher religion; others, though of pagan origin, are capable of being made subservient to genuine spirituality through allegorization, or may be shown to possess some practical utility. Finally, we must recognize the presence of teaching of an infinitely higher order, which has to a great extent transformed those heathenish elements of which it was unable wholly to get rid.

Kennett finds in the Old Testament survivals of the same primitive, folkloristic thinking that existed outside of Israel, and is not so sure of the superiority of Hebrew religious and moral ideas over those of their pagan neighbours in every respect. It may well be asked, therefore, why the race that produced the Old Testament should have been chosen to prepare the way for Christ. He finds the answer in the resolute monotheism of Israel, and in the combination in its idea of God of qualities such as justice and mercy, which in men might seem incompatible one with another. From these ideas great influences flowed forth. No relationship or activity of life remained unaffected.

But the Old Testament is more than a compendium of moral rules, it is a record of God's revelation (apparently understood as higher religious insight) to Israel. That revelation possesses a unity and completeness not found elsewhere. We cannot imagine any other nation in which our Lord Jesus Christ could have proclaimed His gospel with equal immediate effect. This revelation was a continuous one. It is impossible, however, to understand the Old Testament without studying the history of the people among whom it took shape; for the members of Israel were interpreters of the national history in the light of their belief in Jehovah. If, as they believed, God's mind could be known from what was then happening, it was evident that it must also have been revealed in the events of the past. That gave the history of the past a very great interest.

Kennett then describes various ways in which the teachers and prophets of Israel reflected on the events of the past. He points out, too, that universalism and individualism are attained in the high-water marks of their thinking; and individualism has produced a faith which can move mountains and suffer martyrdom. Though the immortality idea was not fully attained in the Old Testament, Jesus drew the natural inference from the highest teaching of that book when He deduced from Ex. 3: 2 "He is not the God of the dead but of the living". (Mark 12: 27). Finally, the Christian Church owes a great debt to Israel for providing a pattern of worship for us in the hymns and prayers of the Old Testament.

In the last paper of the same collection of essays, G. H. Box deals with the indebtedness of the New Testament to the Old Testament.[5] He finds it necessary to protest against a misguided policy, urged by some, of eliminating the Old Testament from popular religious teaching. He admits that there is much that is fresh and novel in the New Testament, but insists that much that is old is inextricably interwoven with the new elements. The influence, he grants, came via the Septuagint. In speaking of Paul he holds that his thought "was fundamentally Jewish—not Hellenic or Hellenized in any deep sense—and his great ideas go back to the Old Testament. He does, it is true, use Stoic terms and, to some extent, the terminology of the mystery religions; but in all such cases the language is charged with new meaning and content. The determinative element is Jewish." In fine, he sees the New Testament standing in a single line of development with the Old. And here he stresses the fact that it continues Old Testament prophecy, instead of linking up with contemporary Rabbinic Judaism. The criticism of the Old Testament, he acknowledges, by rediscovering that great literature for us, has enabled us to see more clearly than was possible formerly how the New Testament really expresses and emphasizes at their true value the most vital elements of the religion of Israel.

In another British symposium arranged by Jewish scholars, the emphasis is not so much on the Old Testament as on the Jewish nationality. Nevertheless the Old Testament stands in the background all the time. The essay of G. Adam Smith on "The Hebrew Genius as exhibited in the Old Testament" cannot do more than point out the literary and religious heights attained in that literature.[6] Burkitt's contribution on the debt of Christianity to Judaism strives to approach its theme by first clarifying what parts of Christianity are derived from other than Jewish sources.[7] He finds that English Christianity evolved in a Judaizing direction after separation from Catholicism. In the latter, the hierarchy, the creeds, the sacraments are linked with the imperial Roman and the Greek heritages. But there is still much left that was of Jewish descent—notably Jesus and the Bible. This was, and is, an ineradicable and inseparable element. Burkitt finds Reformed Protestantism to have been most deeply influenced by the Old Testament by virtue of a conscious antiquarianism. But there is one point in which all forms of Christianity have been influenced—the view dominating Judaism of a divine purpose manifested in time. Reality, in this view, is a grand drama. Right or wrong, wise or foolish, it is part of the debt of Christianity to Judaism (really to the Old Testament). The noble epilogue of the Jewish scholar, Montefiore,[8] points out that for these Christian contributors "Israel" might as well be dead—their detachment is complete. Asserting, then, that Israel is still alive, he asks whether its contribution to humanity is totally a thing of the past or whether it is still capable of giving. He finds the Jewish conception of God and His relation to man, and the Jewish conception of the relation of religion to morality, akin to but not quite identical with the Christian, and able to complement the latter to the benefit of mankind. Indirectly this becomes a plea for the value of the Old Testament heritage for Christianity and to that extent deserves mention here.

Prominent among those in England who thought much about the biblical question was A. S. Peake.[9] He discussed its "permanent value" in lectures of exemplary clarity. He sees it is a real problem why the Old Testament, the book of an earlier order, should stand side by side with the religious book of Christianity. The expedients used by former generations to meet the difficulty are no longer possible for us. We cannot use the Old Testament and the New Testament to make a composite amalgam of doctrine. We must take the Old Testament for what it is and must see whether we can vindicate for it its position alongside the New. He concedes that it is no easy task, but thinks that if we will only put ourselves at the proper point of view we will accord the Old Testament an inalienable right to be considered part of our Christian Scripture.

With a surprising paradox Peake then argues that the fact that the Old Testament is imperfect is the very reason why we want to keep it in the Bible. Before pursuing that point, however, he speaks of other things that make the Old Testament seem valuable. The social reformer, for instance, finds it precious —the more because the New Testament dwells very little on problems of that kind. "Principles are expressed in the New Testament more universal and deeper and more inward than the principles which were expressed in the Old; but the application to the social and economic conditions, to question of politics, are not made in the New Testament in the same way in which they are made in the Old." Then he dwells on the literary excellencies of the Old Testament. To that class of readers who think the Old Testament primarily gives us the revelation of truths which we could not otherwise have discovered he points out that there are other values besides the intellectual. There is the emotional value which gives the Bible much of its power over the hearts of men. Illustrating with a church hymn how we are stirred by words that *per se* are mythological, he states that the Old Testament moves us in the same way when we find language in it that we may not be able to work into our scheme of theology and which does not lend itself to the scientific statement of doctrine, but that touches us at the elemental bases of our being. Just as Jesus Christ was greater than anything He said, so the religious experience of the Old Testament is greater than any verbal expression of it could be.

Peake then speaks disapprovingly of the older attitude towards the Bible and the Old Testament in particular as being "too atomistic". We must radically break with this way of looking at Scripture. When we are talking about the Old Testament as revelation it is the Old Testament as a whole that is meant. It is true that this view has its difficulties. While there are many passages that have a self-evidencing divine quality to anyone with spiritual insight, there are also long passages which do not speak to our soul at all. The tendency then is to say that these things should not be there. And the matter is even worsened when we find sections that are a contradiction and a negation of what is dearest to us in the gospel, and indeed of much which we find in the Old Testament itself. Nevertheless, Peake wants to form a theory that will accept the whole Old Testament as it stands, for what it is and what it really means to be.

He holds that we must look at the Old Testament as the record of an exceptional movement of the Divine Spirit upon a chosen and a guided people, taking them at a low level and gradually leading them to a higher level until it becomes possible for them to receive the supreme revelation in God's only begotten Son. When we see this, we no longer come to the Old Testament with illegitimate demands on it. If revelation is a process which comes through history we can understand revelation only as we know the history, and in this we find the meaning for very much in the Old Testament that in our first impatience we might have been tempted to cast aside as irrelevant. Even the imperfect or definitely false things found there are not useless. For it was necessary for us that we should see not only the light side but also the dark. Unless we have them all and can paint them all into the single picture of the history of revelation we have not rightly understood the Old Testament. In this way Peake vindicates the paradox statement referred to above. The objection of those who say that, when all is said and done, the Old Testament represents a stage of religion that is superseded, is answered by the arguments that it gives us the only key to the understanding of the New Testament and that Jesus appealed to its authority.

The arrival of the 'thirties brought a fresh outpouring of literature on our subject in Germany. Among those who spoke up was Meinhold.[10] After portraying the situation of the time in which rising anti-Semitism went hand in hand with demands for abolition of the Old Testament from Christian use the author addresses himself to the question: can the Old Testament be taken away from Christianity without its suffering harm from the loss, or is the harm greater if it adheres to the Old Testament? If we would keep the Old Testament must not the use be selective and must not even that which is selected frequently be reinterpreted along Christian lines?

Meinhold then paves the way for further discussion by showing how Old Testament scholarship has liberated us from the nightmare of verbal inspiration, which a false theory of the origin of the canon first laid upon the Synagogue and then upon the Christian Church. Describing the origin of the Old Testament sacred collection, he concludes that the historical process is entirely a matter for scholarly study. The viewpoints which led the synagogue to accept or reject this or that document, in so far as we can determine them, are not binding for us. One may well hold with Luther that some rejected writings might with more justice have been taken into the canon than some which were accepted and are now included—that is if one still cares at all about a term such as "canonical", which originated in dogmatic thinking, and will not simply use it as a designation for the collection made by the Synagogue and Church.

Meinhold then discusses the limitations of the Old Testament. Rejecting all *a priori* dogmatic assertions about inspiration, he urges that the Protestant Christian must follow his conscience and first discern the real nature of the Hebrew religion. He describes it as a national religion and gives an account of various phases of it in the light of modern Old Testament scholarship.

In the final part of the book, however, Meinhold tackles the question of whether one can still speak of a significance of the Old Testament for theology and the Church in the light of such a historical study of the materials. He gives an affirmative answer and then proceeds to justify it with the progressive revelation philosophy (revelation understood as addressed to the intellect). If there is a God for us it can only be one who revealed Himself. It is difficult to see how else He could have revealed Himself except in a national religion. Israel claims that God revealed Himself to it and that it received Him into its heart and soul. The Old Testament is the record of this revelation of God. History seems to prove that this was no illusion, for we still are experiencing the after-effects of this consciousness of Israel through the medium of Christianity; and history knows of hardly any illusions that are operative for millennia.

He then traces the current of ethical religion, as represented in the prophetic and wisdom movements, through the Old Testament and up to Jesus of Nazareth. In Him he finds the conclusion and therewith the end of the religion of Israel. He combined the roles of prophet and sage perfectly and finally in His person. If the Primitive Church sought to prove Jesus the Messiah, this need not greatly concern us—it is merely a token of its inability to get away from Jewish presuppositions. For us Jesus is rather the "saviour" and "redeemer", as the Gentiles, taking terms offered by their own tradition, preferred to view Him. The religious mission of Israel ended with the rise of Christianity, so that it no longer makes sense to regard the Jews to-day as the chosen people. But the Old Testament as well as the New Testament remain documents reflecting the history of the divine self-revelation. They are not the Word of God as such, but they contain it and we have it through them.

In his concluding pages Meinhold discusses the problem whether the plain and unlearned Christian can still use the Old Testament as Holy Scripture. He who has been educated in the study of the Hebrew Scriptures in their original tongue and in accordance with modern scholarship can be expected to use the Old Testament with discretion. It is different with those who have not had this advantage. That the unlearned have in the past derived great stimulation from the Old Testament is revealed by the story of Pietism. But at the same time this use of it by the unenlightened causes all manner of confusion. It is

quite true that we must bear with the weaker brethren, as Paul
says (Rom. 14: 1), but at the same time we cannot suffer them
to rule us with their pretensions. Of such a nature is insistence
by the untutored on the whole of Scripture as gospel truth.
Here Paul's admonition to his converts not to become entangled
again in the yoke of bondage which the Judaizers would foist
upon them (Gal. 5: 1), is apropos. Meinhold's thought is that
the selective attitude toward the Old Testament taken by Jesus
—about which he had already written in 1896 in a manner to
provoke ecclesiastical protest—should be a model for us. He
finds the Primitive Church sometimes failing to live up to that
example; thus, if a series of sayings of Jesus was put together
redactionally into a "Sermon on the Mount" (Matt. 5–7), with
the implication that He was a new law-giver like Moses, this
was contrary to the spirit of Christ, who was not the bringer of a
new yoke and who even replaced the Decalogue with the twin
commandments of Deut. 6: 5 and Lev. 19: 18 (which really are
no commandments at all, since love cannot be commanded),
thereby giving us a yardstick for the right use of the Old
Testament. Jesus was not so much concerned with the correction of external actions, as with improving the inward attitude,
from which right actions then will flow forth. The God He found
in the Old Testament was the one whose voice He heard in his
own heart. And so we, too, can find the God and Father of our
Lord Jesus Christ in the Old Testament, if we read it with
Christian eyes and use it in a Christian sense. Jesus and the
Old Testament on its higher levels are in concord in many
things. The Old Testament, he notes, affords a protection
against a false asceticism, such as crept into Christianity at a
very early date, and has an appreciation of nature and of
natural things that is most excellent. Recalling the way in
which Paul emancipated Christianity from the Jewish nationality Meinhold emphasizes the universality of Christianity as a
way of redemption for all men, and rejects slogans arising from
the lunatic anti-Semitic fringe that was becoming so vociferous
during the years in which he was writing.

But alongside the apologetic directed against the detractors
of the Old Testament in the German scene there was also the
problem of the theological position of the Old Testament as
raised by the Dialectic theology. While among Old Testament

scholars there was as yet no one to participate directly in this approach, a need for some positive attitude on the subject was felt even by those who had been wont to think of this literature chiefly in historical terms.

Thus we find Hempel touching on the problem in the conclusion of a fine study on the Old Testament and History.[11] After describing the distinctive nature of Old Testament piety he raises the question: can a religion of such characteristic stamp, bound with a thousand threads to earlier and contemporary Near Eastern religions, claim to be the religion of revelation? How can a temporal entity be something of eternal value, the beginning of a kingdom of God?

After dwelling on the nature of history, which never repeats itself, and viewing it theistically as governed by God, he sees divine revelation as the working of God in a particular, concrete situation with human beings of peculiar sociological and cultural structure and with all the limitations of mind and outlook that that implies. It is thus not to be expected that Old Testament prophecy should be infallibly true as to coming events, or that Old Testament ideas of the past history should be absolutely reliable. The legalistic character of the Old Testament in its contrast to the New Testament order of grace is not as insurmountable an obstacle as is sometimes thought, for every revelation of the divine will, being an attempt to win man, in the last analysis partakes of the character of grace. So the law, too, has an aspect of grace. The real difficulty lies in the assertion that the Old Testament testifies to a portion of a history of redemption as such. If the actual facts of the divine revelation are often submerged beyond recovery, then the document purporting to tell of such divine action has a value only in so far as it can claim to be a paradigm of how God acts again and again. But since the action of God is not primarily symbolical but rather directed toward a particular situation, this necessary imperfection of the record cannot refute the fact of the divine action itself. He finds that the latter, whatever its true nature may have been, remains tangible in its effects.

But here the doubts from a comparative religious angle claim Hempel's attention. We find similar ideas and conceptions outside of Israel: have we divine influence in the one case and not in the other? Hempel sides with a liberal view here, basing it on the ancient ecclesiastical doctrine of the *logos spermatikos*. But that does not annul the claim of the Old Testament to be the record of a special revelatory activity and history of redemption. He finds that claim seriously threatened, however, where the Old Testament ideas of faith cannot be ours and do not have the internal testimony of the Holy Spirit in their favour. He hesitates to make limited individual experience the measuring-rod, but he concedes that portions of Scripture have lost their ability to convince us of their being actually a Word of God. We have no yardstick for judging whether a thing was *once* the Word of God, if it is not Word of God for us *now*. A certain amount of help is afforded by the thought of a divine pedagogy, but only as an intellectual possibility—not as a certainty of special revelation. One of the great theological tasks of the future, he holds, in conclusion, is to establish a theological basis for the scriptural canon. In connection therewith the question of the relation of the Old Testament to the New Testament will have to play a special role. One will have seriously to apply the idea of the actuality of the divine activity, and avoid all softening up of exact, historical exegesis by Christianizing procedures. But we have no other criterion validating a Word of the past than the testimony of the Holy Spirit. Since we can experience it as Jesus did, we have a right to hold to the unity of the history of redemption and to the belief that God's dealing with Israel forms a part of that history and to sense in it the secret stirring of the spirit of Jesus Christ.

In 1933 Hempel discussed the religious value of the Old Testament.[12] According to him our task to-day in connection with the Old Testament is fixed by the fact that we have such a vast increase of comparative religious material on the one hand and new tools of psychological analysis on the other hand. Our first duty is to find the place of the Old Testament in the development of the religious life of mankind. The second, to understand the special character of Old Testament piety in its finest emotions. He confines himself in this connection to the second of these objectives. The peculiarity of Old Testament piety, he asserts, consists in the realism of its faith. It knows a real God who is active in a real world with its differences and troubles. He then elaborates on the Old Testament idea of God and on the faith which the people of the Old Testament placed in Him. The last word in this Old Testament realism of faith, embracing as it does a realistic view of God, of the world and of sin, is the word "forgiveness". God rules over His own anger, while man is inclined to vengeance (Ps. 103: 9). The Old Testament shows God to be one to whom we can pray: "Forgive us our trespasses."

But we may interrupt here the parade of biblical scholars to let a leading representative of the Dialectic theology, Brunner, tell us how he regards the Old Testament problem.[13] He asserts boldly that the understanding of the Word of God of the Old Testament is decisive for the understanding of the Word of God of the New Testament. In elaborating on that thesis—which reminds one of the teaching of Ritschl—he first shows that the New Testament alone provides a dangerous temptation in the direction of Hellenizing religion. We can see the peril of a conflation of the gospel with Greek abstract thinking illustrated in the case of the great idealistic philosophy, for instance when Fichte makes the Son of God an eternal idea on the basis of the *logos* of John's Gospel.

The normal road for the right understanding of the New Testament, according to Brunner, leads through the Old Testament. He then lists a number of ideas that occur in that manner only in the Old Testament but without which the New Testament is not comprehensible.

(1) There is the idea of Creation and the Creator. The New Testament hardly refers to this at all; it takes it for granted. But we must note how the Old Testament speaks of the Creator. The Creator is He who revealed Himself as Lord of His people Israel. Theology is revealed theology, not Natural theology. Outside of this revelation God is unknown to His people. The world is not like Him and He is not like the world. Hence "thou shalt make thee no image or likeness". God and the world are to be absolutely differentiated. One must come from Isaiah in order to understand the harshness of the statement that God became man.[14] One only knows this God through revelation, not from the world. And one only has this God through election and grace, not by nature. Israel had Him only because God chose to reveal Himself. He is, furthermore, a God who can reject His chosen instrument. He has revealed

Himself in a particular area of history and through persons who proclaim His Word. Therein He is recognized as personal God. For revelation is always given to definite persons at a definite moment.

(2) There is the role of the divine law. God is a voluntaristic God. He wants to take my will captive and bind my existence to Himself. His call can only be answered by life and action. Brunner at this point engages in a polemic against those who find the Old Testament prophets emphasizing an abstract moral law. He points out that they know nothing of a moral law based on reason. They know only of the divine commands, which on occasion may go contrary to what the moral law that proceeds from reason seems to require. He thinks that Luther fell into a grievous error when he identified Old Testament law and general moral law—Calvin adhered more closely to the Old Testament spirit here. Nevertheless, he credits Luther with having made an important contribution in differentiating between legalism and faith. God is not first of all a God who makes demands on man. He gives before He asks. His requirement is that one permit Him to give what He chooses. The very meaning of the law is expressed in the command: "Ye shall be My people"—words that imply a privilege given by God to man. Thus God's holiness can not be separated from His love and mercy. In the Old Testament alone this fusion is found.

(3) The covenant of God with Israel is focused on a goal. It is no stabilization of a *status quo*. The Old Testament is eschatological. God is going to come to His people in a different manner. The message of judgment is an essential presupposition for the understanding of the New Testament religion. One must first know the fear of being lost before one is receptive for redemption. The Old Testament performs an indispensable service here; without it the idea of the love of God is in danger of becoming mere sentimentality. Hebrew eschatology stands in a sharp contrast to Greek thinking for which redemption is apt to become a denial of the world and to lead to asceticism. In eschatology God chooses to bring the world closer to Himself again. The Old Testament is full of the idea of the coming kingdom. The present receives a vast importance in the light of the End. And this Old Testament eschatology is one that takes a positive attitude toward the world. It is so realistic

that at times it seems as though it were an inner, worldly goal that is envisioned. But one must approach the New Testament hope from that Old Testament background, he says, and understand that for Christianity, too, the world is not to be dissolved but rendered perfect.

(4) With this eschatological realism is associated the social viewpoint. God is concerned with the group and with the individuals in so far as they are members of this people. His will is directed toward a fellowship. Old Testament ethic is social ethics. One sins not against oneself but against one's neighbour. The highest good is not ascetic purity but correct conduct toward one's brother. Hence, the Old Testament has an unparalleled drive in its idea of the religious community: that the righteousness of God is to be realized in such a community is paramount. God and one's neighbour belong together. The Old Testament knows of no private relationship with God; there are no individual lone spirits that stand forth in solitary greatness. The prophets are not to be classed as such; their concern is not for their own salvation. That which the God of the Old Testament wishes to bring about is a public thing. It is from this Old Testament angle that we must see the New Testament eschatology.

In all these particulars, Brunner concludes, the Old Testament is the beginning of the New. It is not replaced but fulfilled; through Jesus Christ prophecy begins to become fulfilment.[14]

The spirit of von Hofmann and his *Heilsgeschichte* comes up again in the thought of Procksch. Of his impressive book on Old Testament theology we shall make some mention later. In an essay of 1931 he dealt with the significance of the Old Testament for the Church.[15] He correlates the two entities—both are born out of the Spirit of God and are thus "pneumatic organisms"; the one is the Word of God congealed into Scripture, the other the people of God born in history. But the Word of God is the cause, the people of God or the Church the effect. Procksch first sets forth the dependence of the Church on the Old Testament in the very roots of its existence. Jesus, he says, by being bound to Old Testament thinking forces the Old Testament upon the Church. He does not stand apart from the

Church, but is its Prophet, Priest and King. Procksch sees
Jerusalem as the symbolic centre of the history of the Church.
The latter must always keep its eyes turned in that direction if
it would not lose sight of its goal. This implies a connection
with Israel. The Church must never forget that in worshipping
the Father of Jesus Christ it is at the same time invoking the
God of Abraham and Moses. In its prayers it will never be able
to emancipate itself from the language of the Psalms. The
history of Israel and the history of the Church are undergirded
by the same forces of revelation that manifested themselves in
the great heroes of the faith of the Old and New Covenants.

Procksch then discusses the dependence of the Church on the
Old Testament in its social relations. The Church has a relation
to the nation, but the theme of king and prophet in the Old
Testament shows what stresses and strains may occur in this
relationship. The question of the relation of the Church to the
Jewish people and religion, too, comes up; he thinks that it is
only soluble for the Church on an Old Testament basis.

In the third part of his article Procksch describes the Church's
dependence on the Old Testament in theology. Every theological concept, he declares, (in apparent agreement with
Ritschl), must have a Hebrew basis or it is none. Dame
Theology is a Hebrew, not only in vocabulary but in spirit.
He then proceeds to illustrate this by examining a number of
such concepts. In fine, to pull Christianity away from the Old
Testament is to drag it from its historical moorings and can
lead only to gnosticism or rationalism. The Old Testament is
the regulator of the historical nature of Christian thought and
the thing upon which the latter's health and fruitfulness depend.

Procksch was much taken with Girgensohn's idea of the
desirability of having a more spiritual type of exegesis developed
to supplement the historical critical.[16] He saw, however, that
it would be virtually impossible to carry this through for large
sections of the Old Testament and so suggested particular emphasis on those areas in which the spiritual element actually
comes to the surface.

Another scholar who was prone to think theologically about
the Old Testament was Hänel.[17]

He starts with the assertion that the faith of the Church holds
that we have the Word of God in the Old Testament as in the

New Testament. But he sees a real need for re-examining this belief in view of the fact that modern interpretation is forced to apply a method to Scripture study which has nothing to do with its normative use and even relegates the latter to the background. The handmaiden, historical criticism, nowadays has usurped the place of the mistress, theology. The Church must regard that situation as unsatisfactory. Furthermore, certain valid results have been attained by this scientific method which are extremely disquieting. For one thing the belief in verbal inspiration, on which our forefathers primarily based their doctrine of Scripture authority, has been made impossible. For another thing, the identity of the two Testaments, which seemed so vital a prop for maintaining the authority of the Old Testament, is not easy to defend. The latter work cannot be viewed as on one religious and moral plane, but exhibits different strata, higher and lower. The widespread realization of this special situation is reflected in the fact that nobody to-day undertakes to present the theology of the Old Testament in a systematized form, but that the usual thing is to describe the religion of the Old Testament in its historical development.

Hänel then inquires whether the fall of the doctrine of inspiration actually makes it impossible to believe in the divine character of Scripture. He points out that when this doctrine was at its height it came to be overshadowed by another that really made it superfluous and that remained as a firm support when the other fell: that of the internal testimony of the Holy Spirit. Notably Lutheranism, which combined the material principle (justification by faith) with the formal principle (Scripture authority), was able to employ this doctrine of the internal testimony of the Holy Spirit in such a way as to uphold the authority of the central element of scriptural content. But Hänel holds that revelation has a larger scope than the belief in Justification. The thing common to all revelation, he argues, is the manifestation of the holiness of God and of the absolute contrast between the divine and the human, which reaches its high-water mark at the point where God does the seemingly impossible and regards the sinner as righteous for the sake of Christ. With respect to God's holiness, Hänel feels that he is utilizing the Reformed emphasis on the majesty of God which amounts to the same thing. It is for the sake of the testimony of the Spirit, given in the revelation of the holiness of God, that Scripture which mediates this revelation proves itself to be the Word of God. The Church, he thinks, has rightly held fast to this truth brought forward by orthodoxy.

But Hänel finds it desirable, owing to the fact that many other religions besides Christianity have entered our field of vision, to attempt to reach this same certainty by another route. While reason has been sorely discredited, owing to the speculative excesses of a former era, he regards it as not out of place to reflect rationally on this matter after the manner suggested by the dictum of Anselm, *credo ut intelligam*, "I believe that I may know." His starting-point is the definition of the nature of the Old Testament. While this work is a complex product of various groups of materials, these all have this in common that they are governed by the idea of the divine holiness, though in various shades of import. The most primitive stratum looks on this holiness primarily as unapproachability (I Sam. 6: 20). Another, perhaps representative of the patriarchal era, looks upon it as exaltedness (cf. Gen. 28: 17). A third, perhaps beginning in the Mosaic era, regards it as zealousness (Josh. 24: 19). The climax is attained in prophecy, where Yahweh's holiness is glory (Is. 6: 3) or perfection. Jesus links up with this stage, directly substituting the perfection concept for the holiness concept (Lev. 19: 2; Matt. 5: 48). Post-exilic Judaism viewed the divine holiness primarily as transcendence, as remoteness from this profane sphere (cf. Ps. 11: 4).

Hänel then points out that the concept of holiness is not confined to the Old and New Testaments but occurs in all religions, yea, (in dependence on Otto's famous book), is the very essence of religion; it is the *logos spermatikos* that is embedded in every religion. At the same time, however, this idea is very much corrupted in religions outside of the Old and New Testament sphere. The emphasis on the unholy or unclean is almost as important in the extra-biblical religions as that of the holy, and the latter is applied more to men and things than to deities. Mysticism, too, in its original form, disregards the contrast between human and divine; it therein reflects a lack of appreciation for the holiness of God and reveals its pagan origin. The moral decadence so commonly associated with heathen cults is a proof of a low status of the experience of holiness. From this angle of its higher conception of holiness, Hänel argues for the uniqueness of the Old Testament religion over against all others, and takes that for a proof, sufficiently satisfying to the mind of the believer, that in this religion alone of all pre-Christian ones God truly revealed Himself. In pursuing this line of reasoning Hänel is following the course recommended by Troeltsch, of setting forth the superiority of Christianity over all other religions by comparative analysis.

From the point thus reached Hänel proceeds to inquire how we can imagine the divine influence to have brought it about that the books of the Old Testament became Word of God. He makes light of the importance of any theory on that subject— the character of the Old Testament as belonging to revelation is fixed for us without any such theory. We can either stress the idea of the inspiration of persons, with the Holy Spirit awakening important religious thoughts in them, or we can imagine the Spirit as so organizing the individual religious constitution that it will guide the religious author aright in whatever he has to do for God's purposes. Such a theory must also take due consideration of the fact that the books of the Old Testament have a complicated history, and must regard their evolution to final shape as also having taken place under the workings of the Spirit of God.

Going back to the revelation that precedes the literary process, as experienced by the personalities of prophets and others, Hänel asserts that this, too, is a matter of secondary importance —that the Old Testament is Word of God is fixed for us without any results of such investigation. He concedes that not all of the numerous ideas of revelation found in the Old Testament can be utilized. Who would wish to employ the theophany idea found in the primeval and patriarchal histories, or the notion of obtaining divine oracles through use of the Urim and Thummim? More importance may be attached to prophetic visions and auditions, and the thought of actual inspiration may have to be given more weight in that connection. But we stand on even firmer ground, he thinks, where faith and history meet. We can see how the whole Old Testament religion is dominated by the revelation experienced at the Exodus, and how other historical events are understood as having been brought about by God's government. Revelation comes into being here in that God offers His manifestation of Himself in the extraordinary events of history, on the one hand, and on the other hand in creating the prophetic interpreter who understands and gives the authoritative interpretation of these events (Rothe's manifestation and inspiration). In this interpenetration of divinely wrought history, in which God speaks, and of mightiest faith, which He Himself awakens, the foundations of the temple of the Old Testament, in which God's Word is proclaimed to us, were reared.

Hänel next discusses the topic of the unity of the Word of God in the two Testaments, for he asserts it is a desideratum that such unity exist, if the Old Testament is to be considered Word of God. As an Old Testament scholar of rank, he cannot endorse attempts to Christianize the Old Testament by artificial devices. Even though the God of the Old Testament is our God, it does not follow that He already gave the salvation that was to come through Christ to the Hebrew people. His pedagogy could envision other temporary goals. Nevertheless, Hänel would equally reject the over-emphasis on the differences between the two orders. In spite of all that is bygone in the older one there is an identity of the Testaments which cannot be explained away. It is not true that the Old Testament is only law and the New Testament only gospel. Nor is the Old Testament only prophecy and the New Testament only fulfilment. It is not enough to think of the Old Testament in terms of the clues it gives for the understanding of the New Testament concepts.

Before setting forth the relationship of the two Testaments more precisely one must duly appreciate the majesty of the New Testament revelation. It may be measured first of all by the contrast with the inadequate and primitive ideas found in the Old Testament; but it can also be seen over against those very elements of the Old Testament which represent the latter's high-water mark and for the sake of which one must speak of the unity of the Testaments. We may, for instance, consider the basic shift in emphasis on certain ideas in the two areas. In the New Testament the idea of divine love, as the most exalted expression of the divine holiness, moves into the centre. The Old Testament, too, has penetrated to a knowledge of the divine love, but it is only one insight alongside of others there, and does not hold the centre of the stage. The difference between the two Testaments culminates in the person and work of Christ; for in the Old Testament Messianism is confined to prophetic insights and thoughts, whereas in the New Testament there is the living experience of Jesus the Christ. But in spite of all changes in emphases Hänel would hold fast to the idea of a unity of the Testaments.

There is one sphere in the Old Testament that is a worthy counterpart of the New Testament—that of prophetic religion—or, if one chose to abide by differentiation on the basis of ideas, the area in which the divine holiness is understood as perfection. Here the ideas of prevenient grace and of the failure of the law as way of salvation, as well as the belief in free grace and in vicarious sacrifice, are to be found. Notably Deutero-Isaiah, Jeremiah, Ezekiel, and the Psalms provide material for this insight. If one proceeds from a New Testament basis to consider sin and grace, righteousness and faith in the Old Testament, one can likewise illustrate the approximation of many Old Testament passages to the New Testament level. Indeed, Hänel declares that there is no insight of a basic nature in the New Testament for which an Old Testament counterpart cannot be found. The connection between the two Testaments is not merely genetic. With all due concessions to the distinctive position to be accorded the New Testament we must assert that within the Old Testament there is a world that is substantially identical with that of the New Testament.

In his final section Hänel discusses the unity of the Word of God in the Old Testament. The Old Testament as a whole claims to be authoritative. How can this claim be reconciled with the fact that it contains in itself higher and lower levels of religion? The author rejects the idea of smoothing this over by allegorization. Historical-critical exegesis alone can tell us what a passage means. But he believes that one must proceed from the historico-critical basis to further reflections in the light of a belief in the fundamental unity. One way would be to seek at every point the relationship of a passage to what Hänel believes to be the basic motif of Old Testament religion—the idea of holiness of God. Another way would be always to bear in mind the goal toward which revelation tended and to illuminate every step of the path it took in the light of that goal. He thinks the interpretative method used by Jesus in the Sermon on the Mount stands close to such a procedure, and even sees a value in the New Testament typological interpretation which is to be differentiated from allegorization. To view the Old Testament from a New Testament angle is the culminating function of Old Testament exegesis. We can only do justice to the task, however, if we see it from the angle of the whole Christ—not merely in the light of His person and work, but also of His words and ideas within which they are centred.

The fateful year 1933 saw the ascendancy of National Socialism in Germany.

The crisis that arose for the Church under the pressure of the new political régime from without and the elements from within disposed to co-operate in the idea of creating a truly national type of Christianity that was purged of the Semitic ideas, is well reflected in the contribution of Herntrich, who took his stand with the conservative churchmen.[18]

He insists that religions are born, not made. To manufacture a national religion by setting up some collection of Nordic religious texts to replace the Old Testament, as had been suggested, is not feasible; the old Teutonic religion is little known, remote and dismal. Analysing the motives behind the opposition to the Old Testament he finds that at their root lies an idolatry, a setting up of the nation as an idol. A belief in the idea that man can redeem himself by his own efforts is likewise operative. These things constitute rebellion against the sovereignty of God. The message of the Old Testament God, who demands our submission to His will in consciousness of our guilt, is the one we need to hear. There is nothing Jewish about that message, because the Old Testament shows that the Hebrew people were in constant opposition to this God whom the prophets proclaimed. To attempt to set up a new national religion to-day would involve doing away with final moral standards and leaving the peoples of the earth to follow their lower impulses unchecked. Of what help could national gods be, whose power ends at the boundary lines? All ethical experience of God depends on the idea that He is present and active everywhere and that all men are responsible to Him. Differentiating

between faith and piety, Herntrich asserted that while there can
be various national types of the latter there can only be one
Christian faith, because there is only one Christ. Influenced by
the Dialectic theology at this point he stresses the Incarnation;
this belief implies that God revealed Himself in a definite
nationality at a definite moment; there is no getting away from
it—Jesus was a Jew according to the flesh. But at the same
time he was conceived by the Holy Ghost, and that signifies that
He is not just a Jewish man, but transcends that nationality,
and brings salvation to all men. With Barthian eyes he sees the
Incarnation idea basically operative in the Old Testament
order; there, too, the Word (in the sense of revelation) became
flesh. It was incarnate in the history and life of the Hebrew
people, amid all the limitations their condition and circumstances imply.

After rejecting the doctrine of verbal inspiration which the
opponents subtly fasten on the Church and then make the basis
for ridiculing this or that biblical statement, Herntrich asks
why the link between the Church and the Old Testament must
be held inseparable? He concedes that if Jesus Christ is the full
and perfect revelation of God that would seem to obviate the
necessity of our clinging to that older order. But he finds a basis
for it in the thought that there was a history of redemption and
that Christ is not separable from the divine plan of which He
was the culmination. However, we must carefully differentiate
between the various stages of development in this history.
Even the earlier stages are not without their lessons. Once we
realize that God acted in history and revealed Himself in a
particular time and place we can read the Old Testament with
eyes opened to its importance. He stresses what the modern
nationalists could learn from an Isaiah or a Jeremiah. The
awareness of human depravity that these prophets had shows
that they were realists, while those who ridicule this attitude are
blind to reality. Nations to-day do not want to hear the truth
any more than the Jews of old did, but God rudely breaks into
our history with His Word—His promise as well as His threat.

In closing, Herntrich stresses the need of properly relating the
idea of the nation as a divinely willed entity to a Christian
universalism that knows no race or colour. The misunder-
standings that arise between the nations are to be viewed as due

to sin and in their consequences partake of the nature of divine punishments. The old story of the Tower of Babel already reflects this insight, but the sequel to that also shows how God prepared a way of salvation leading out of that situation through a particular line of His choice. The Christian Church is the continuation of that line into the present and future.

Soon afterward we find three Old Testament scholars of high rank, Alt, Begrich and von Rad, publishing lectures given by them, in which they sought to show how the Old Testament tended to lead men to Christianity—a service it had always performed and could continue to perform.[19]

Alt's introductory general discussion first defends the Old Testament against the virulent anti-Semitic book of Th. Fritsch, which at that time was receiving renewed attention, and then goes over to a positive presentation of the uniqueness of the Hebrew religion, culminating with the philosophy of history in which the Yahwistic writer of Genesis views Israel's destiny as bringing blessing to all peoples and thus as not an end in itself but bound up with the greater purposes of God.

Begrich discusses the prophets. After developing matters of an essentially historical nature opening the proper perspective on these figures, he asks whether the words of the prophets that grip us do not really confront us with the living God. He then stresses Jesus' approval of the prophets and their being an inalienable part of His message. The prophetic line of the Old Testament thought, he says, only reaches its fulfilment and fruition in the New Testament. But it remains the presupposition without which the message of the God of love and reconciliation is not comprehensible. We must avail ourselves of the Old Testament anew as living Word of the God and Father of the Lord Jesus Christ.

Von Rad, in conclusion, then sketches the Hebrew religious development in such a way as to show how there was an advance in insight, in the course of time, involving correction of earlier Hebrew dogmas, and how the whole heritage, preserved in the canon, was available for Jews and Christians in the first century A.D. Each group now claimed that this heritage belonged to itself alone. The rival claims still endure to the present, as the example of Martin Buber on the Jewish side, who denies that Christians have any right to the Old Testament, shows. Von

Rad finds this question decided by the answer given to the other: whether Jesus was the Christ. If the Church were mistaken in this its assertion, then all Christian claim on the Old Testament would fall to the ground. In the measure that we take offence at Jesus the Christ we also take offence at the Old Testament. While we cannot see God in the Old Testament or anywhere else, as the instance of Moses in Ex. 33: 18 f. reveals, we can hear in it the Word of God's grace, and in studying its pages we can see "His back parts" in that unique road on which he led His people Israel through history. This is all professional apologetic on a high level with slants and sidelights that will refresh the Old Testament student.

In 1934 there also appeared a book which in many respects crowned the whole German literary critical movement that began with Wellhausen—Eissfeldt's *Einleitung*.[20] Since the author in a concluding section speaks of the effect the Old Testament has had on mankind we may here develop his standpoint, not only in the light of what he says in that chapter but of other utterances.

Already in 1921, in a study in honour of Harnack, he had registered his opinion that the Old Testament is too deeply ingrown in Christendom to be uprooted and had pointed to certain values that the Old Testament has contributed to our religion. In the book mentioned he speaks of it as having been an object of the most intensive study on the part of both Jewish and Christian scholarship, due to the fact that it is a source of religious life to both communities and—however that may be justified or qualified—a norm for faith and conduct. Scholarship, however, not only receives its interest in it from this circumstance, it in turn helps these Faiths to understand the Old Testament in a more realistic manner. Christian and Jewish scholars can co-operate, learning from each other, up to the point where the ultimate spiritual content of this book comes up for consideration. Here there is a parting of the ways. We thus continue the struggle that began when early Christianity appropriated the Old Testament, and asserted that its promises were for the Church and no longer for the Hebrew people. The influence of the Old Testament will continue in the future in spite of all opposition of the present. Through the fact that Christianity appropriated it the Old Testament was elevated to the rank of a purely spiritual entity, no longer concerned with a particular people and its members, but with nations and men in their relation to God. The way in which those elements in the Old Testament that militate against such spiritualization and generalization were neutralized or brought into line did not remain the same at all times. The New Testament and early ecclesiastical writers used allegory or typology to that end. For us, the historical way of looking at this literature serves the same purpose. In all epochs of its history Christianity has experienced formative influences from the Old Testament, and this is bound to be the case also in the future. The Old Testament played a great role when Christianity came to realize that the end of the world was not as near as the first generations thought and that it was necessary to understand and evaluate properly, from the angle of religion, institutions such as the family and the state which play an essential part in the world of men. For the Old Testament was closely linked with the business of man's living in the world and could show the Christian how he could integrate his higher spiritual existence with life in a human society. Notably the close connection of Old Testament religion with nationality and the state opens the way for Christian appreciation of these entities; at the same time Hebrew prophecy prevents exaggeration of their importance by the polemic of its prophets against that sort of thing. Christian Ethics, furthermore, though it receives its ultimate impulses from the gospel, has up till to-day enjoyed much guidance from the Old Testament and will not be able to dispense with it in the future, least of all in an age when we must rethink the Christian's relation to the world in which he lives. Eissfeldt believes that the influence of the Old Testament is not at an end but rather that a new phase of such influence is beginning.

During the war years Eissfeldt gave utterance to his opinion on the question sometimes asked: whether the God of the Old Testament and the God of the New are the same.[21] While the New Testament writers regard that as a fact, they could have been mistaken. We must discount some of their convictions, e.g., their ideas of cosmology and historical chronology. We cannot, therefore, just accept their belief in this matter either, but must test it in direct approach. He then resolves the question into a twofold one, viz., whether the same idea of God is found in the Old Testament as in the New, and whether the two revelations coincide. The former question can be answered objectively, but the latter involves an inner participation. For revelation and faith are correlates and no generally valid proof can be substituted for faith.

Eissfeldt then compares the ideas of God in the two Testaments. The Old Testament idea represents a long history and may be divided into four stages: the pre-Mosaic, the pre-prophetic (to Elijah), the prophetic and the post-prophetic. He finds that the New Testament idea of God has little kinship with the pre-prophetic (to say nothing of the pre-Mosaic religion about which so little is known), though there is still some survival even in the New Testament of the "numinous" element, as Otto had pointed out. But the prophetic and post-prophetic ideas of God have much more relationship with the New Testament idea. One must take the high-water mark line of Old Testament thinking and compare that with the New Testament thought to perceive their relationship.

Eissfeldt then turns to the second question, as to the two revelations. He sees various answers possible according to the standpoint. He notes that many things that earlier generations found very meaningful in the Old Testament have no appeal for us. He cites as example that of a beloved clergyman whose assistant he once was, who placed a very great valuation on the theme of the Holiness Code of Leviticus: "Ye shall be holy: for I the Lord your God am holy,"—a thing impossible for him. In the days of the First World War, he hints, certain Old Testament passages were greatly appreciated by German people, but now stir them no longer. But then he asks: are there still things in the Old Testament which we can find valuable to-day? This he affirms, and specifies three things: (1) The attitude of individual Old Testament personages towards thoughts about God. (2) Monotheism. (3) Religious poetry and prayers. There is certainly, he believes, a continuity between the Old and New Testament revelations, but there is also tension between them. This leaves him untroubled. He makes an interesting point in the matter of the hurdle we have to take in proceeding from the Old Testament revelation to that of the New, by recalling Alt's thesis that in the Hebrew religion itself there was one such sharp shift, when the God Yahweh was adopted by those who had hitherto revered a God of the fathers. In the new stage of religion it was asserted that the two were the same, and in the narrative accordingly Yahweh says "I am the God of thy father, the God of Abraham", etc. (Ex. 3: 6). This is a bridge thrown across a gulf separating two stages of religion. In the same way the New Testament identification of the Christian God with the God of Israel is such a bridge. He sees an organic growth going on in religion, and in each stage something useless is cast off and something that is useful conserved. The inference is that we must be selective in our use of the Old Testament and employ that which is of value for us to-day. Eissfeldt, therefore, is no biblicist, and the monastic aisles of the history of revelation-philosophy have no charm for him. When he uses the word revelation it is obviously not weighted on the supernatural side.

The theological problem comes into particularly sharp focus in an article by a clergyman, Press.[22] He argues that æsthetic and utilitarian considerations are of no avail for the problem of whether we are to keep the Old Testament. The decisive thing is its religious significance, and even here one cannot be content with general religious "values"; the question must be whether the Old Testament is Word of God, in other words whether there is a special revelation in the Old Testament. If the Old Testament only contained valuable religious documents it could not differ in principle from any other collection of religious texts. The position of the Old Testament must be established theologically or the Old Testament must be given up. It is insufficient to say that it is of decisive weight for us that Jesus saw the Word of God in the Old Testament. This could be taken over from the ideas of His contemporaries and be part of a heritage that must be discounted. One must prove directly from the Old Testament that it contains the Word of God.

Press then shows that it is impossible to understand the whole Old Testament as Word of God. There are large sections which are of no religious value, e.g., the legal codes. It is of no use to defend the law in general with the alleged necessity for a preaching of law alongside of the gospel. The New Testament contains more effective preaching of law. The cultic law of the Old Testament cannot even be understood as expression of the will of God addressed to a certain people at a certain time;

for how then could the prophets have indulged in polemic against it? The thought of a divine pedagogy, too, is not without its weaknesses. The requirements of God must be the same from age to age. We can only do justice to the law if we look at it as a manifestation of the fact that Israel heard God's claim on itself but had not yet attained a clear realization of what constitutes the true service of the Lord. There are two currents in the Old Testament which struggle with each other; one leads to the New Testament and the other to the Talmud.

A sharp line of demarcation, Press says, also goes through the Old Testament between that for which the prophets stand and a false popular conduct and piety that they oppose. And it is here that the Old Testament takes on a real significance for us. The prophets, like Jesus, demand a new life of repentance and faith. The sins that the prophets assail are found among us as well. It is the mind of the old Adam. Over against it stands the ideal of the new man. Is that message not Word of God for us and in full conformity with the New Testament?

Press then sets forth a series of Old Testament thoughts that stand in contrast to the thought of later Judaism, but in principle are on one plane with the New Testament. The purpose of God is to draw men to Himself. All the contrast between the sinner and the holy God in the Old Testament cannot obscure that. Even the prophetic predictions of doom have this for their background, and in eschatology the belief in the realization of this fellowship of man and God is maintained. But the divine purpose rests on God's free grace, not on human initiative. The gracious will of God is recognized in such passages as Hos. 11: 9, Mic. 7: 18, Ps. 103: 3, 8 f. The covenant of God results in the setting up of covenant-statutes. The belief in divine election is the basis of a new morality (Am. 3: 2). The Old Testament does not preach good works, but the life that flows from faith alone. This thought in the Old Testament belongs to the "special revelation" contained in it.

One truth is proclaimed in the Old Testament as in the New Testament, and yet the Old Testament is only realized in Christ. It is not accidental that Jesus grew up in Jewry, where a long spiritual struggle was tending toward its conclusion. Since Jesus and the prophets stand together in a common front, over against sinful man, the Old Testament in its prophetic strata is not antiquated. Though the preaching of the prophets is not in the power of Christ there is an inner unity in both. However, it is only for faith that the Old Testament contains a Word of God. Even though we have the whole Word of God in the New Testament, we cannot give up the Old Testament. It stands in God's choice through which portion of the Bible He first works upon our hearts. Ofttimes the Old Testament serves His purpose before the New. We would lose something of the wealth of form in which the Word of God took shape, if we gave up the Old Testament.

Another scholar who touched on our subject in those years was Volz.[23] He has his eyes focused notably on the preacher's use of the Old Testament and is concerned not only with foes of the Old Testament but with Vischer (see p. 219 f.). Over against the former he sets up the demand that more use of the Old Testament heritage is needed in private study, devotions, preaching and above all regular lectionary use in the service. The Old Testament era was an era of gigantic battle in the religious sphere and the prophets were the great protagonists of God against humanism, against reliance on good works and against rule by priesthoods. They emphasized the moral independence of the individual, and put the Word of God rather than ritual in the centre of things. Prophecy is the Protestantism of antiquity and with its help one can illuminate what Protestanism is and should be to-day.

Volz then discusses the difficulties involved in accepting the Old Testament as normative. Undoubtedly there are things in it which are sub-Christian; we should not be honest if we did not, e.g., see a difference in the level of Ps. 103 and of Gen. 19: 30–38. But study enables us to discern how God's Spirit unveils the divine truth gradually, and how even some of His greatest servants gradually attained a deeper understanding of it than they had at first. Thus if we had I Kings 19: 1–13 among our stated lessons (customary in German Protestant Churches) we could show how God brings Elijah to realize that fanatic zeal and violence in the cause of religion are not in accordance with His will. The instances where prophets used violence in God's cause are to be read in the light of the correction given at that occasion; the danger of a vindictive spirit associating itself with religion is ever present (cf. Luke 9: 54 f.). Other difficulties in connection with the Old Testament arise from the national character of the Hebrew Religion. And yet Jer. 29: 7 shows how these were transcended. Thus the Old Testament contains within its pages the necessary correctives against its own lower elements.

Volz then takes up the idea of the election of Israel, which was particularly offensive to those being influenced by National Socialist doctrines. He finds that this difficulty is easily obviated, if we recall (1) that not the world-rule of Israel but rather of God is the thing the Old Testament emphasizes, (2) that such election is stressed primarily in times of despondency and not without reference to the spiritual calling of the nation, (3) Israel is not just considered a favourite of the deity, but as having an increased responsibility because of its election (Am. 3: 2).

Another difficulty arises for us from primitive ideas of God surviving in the Old Testament. Volz finds these instructive rather than disturbing. We must realize that monotheism had to struggle upward against all manner of opposition, and passages of a backward religious character show how arduous that struggle was. On the whole, he finds, the historical books of the Old Testament provide the chief hurdles. This to him highlights the fact that religious and moral progress came about chiefly through prophecy. The best way to fight for the Old Testament is to set forth prophecy's greatness and divine power.

Volz then turns to the question of the unity of the two Testaments. The idea that the essence of the Old Testament is law is only an echo of the late Jewish view of it. As soon as we emancipate ourselves from that standpoint and look at the Old Testament with our own eyes we find it full of gospel. Its words of consolation simply cannot be spared. In its very nature the Old Testament is gospel and even its law is embedded in the grace and redemption of God. The mission of the prophets reflects the saving will of God. The goal of history is the divine kingdom, the salvation of Israel and the nations. Even the national catastrophes are viewed in the light of a constructive divine purpose that is to be realized through them. As it speaks of redemption and of the love of God, so the Old Testament speaks of the perfect forgiveness of God (Is. 1: 18, Ps. 103, etc.) and is aware of His pedagogical activity (Gen. 22, Jer. 15: 19, Is. 49: 4–6). It teaches the prevenient grace of God, holding

that man can only be converted after God redeems him (Deut.
6: 4–5). If we had Ps. 130 as a stated lesson we could set forth
the unity of the Bible by means of it; it is an exultant celebration of the forgiveness and redemption of God.

Volz then dwells on aspects of the Old Testament that are by
no means superseded. In part their influence continues in the
New Testament, but they are more clearly discernible in the Old
Testament and must be recaptured by the Church. (1) There is
the feeling of God's presence and activity in the larger historical
process; thus Jerusalem receives its fate from the hand of God
(Is. 40: 2); kings are only the agents of God (Is. 10: 5, Jer. 27: 6,
Is. 45: 1) and prophets are his heralds. (2) There is the idea of
responsibility to God in public affairs. The divine message
permeates all areas of public life—law, commerce, culture,
politics; no secular department of life is acknowledged. The
people as a whole must receive the divine imperatives. Whether
God's requirements are practicable does not trouble the prophet
any more than it troubles Jesus in the Sermon on the Mount.
The messengers of God set forth the goal and point out the
sources of strength that make it attainable. (3) There is the idea
of God's universal presence and his interest in men's small,
everyday affairs. How vividly I Sam. 1 and Gen. 24 exhibit this!
Everyone of us has his own problems, and the Old Testament
illuminates a considerable range of these in the light of religion.
(4) There is the idea of the judgment of God. Our own pride
rebels against the pricks of our conscience. The Old Testament
supports conscience by laying low the pride of man, and emphasizing the totality of God's requirement of us. Much of the
wrath men are venting against the Old Testament is because it
tells us the truth about this. (5) There is the idea of the inscrutability of God. While the New Testament in its message of the
Cross shows that God moves in a mysterious way, to accomplish
His ends in the larger sphere, the Old Testament makes this
vivid in more ordinary human concerns. Gen. 22, which speaks
so powerfully of this, combining the divine inscrutability with
His nearness and mercy, should be a stated lesson in Christian
services. (6) There is the Old Testament consciousness of corporate personality; the individual is a member of the group
representing the cause of God. The "thou" of the decalogue is
the congregation and yet at the same time the individual. We

to-day particularly need this feeling of solidarity with our fellow Christians and of a united responsibility. All this wealth of special material in the Old Testament, Volz thinks, needs to be utilized more in the Church than is the case to-day.

The final topic of which he speaks is that of the Christological interpretation of the Old Testament. Here Volz (who once wrote a quite negative critical work on Messianism) is willing to concede that we can, indeed, say of a few Old Testament prophecies that they were fulfilled in Christ (so Is. 42: 1–4, or Is. 53). But we are not in the situation of the Primitive Church and cannot just utilize its mode of Scripture-proof. There is a danger of exaggeration in the Christological interpretation of the Old Testament on the part of Vischer and others. The *richesse* of the Old Testament is lost sight of when everything is studied from the narrow angle of Christological prediction. It is more important to see how the Old Testament *as a whole* prepares the way for Christ, and how the word of the prophets and psalmists lives on in Him. For testimony concerning Christ the New Testament witness is fully sufficient! This new Christocentrism is a veritable dethronement of God, and contrary to the New Testament, which stresses theocentrism most at the very points where it dwells on Christ's exaltedness (I Cor. 15: 22 f.; Phil. 2: 5 f.; Heb. 1; 1 f.). In closing he quotes John 14: 6: God is the goal, Christ the way and the truth, and holds that we only understand the Old Testament aright when we are under Christ.

Turning now to the American scene, we may first consider an address by G. R. Berry.[24] This scholar first speaks of the harm that has resulted to Christian life and thought from the Old Testament, owing to its use as authoritative Word of God. The idea of God has been grievously corrupted by the immorality, injustice, arbitrariness and vindictiveness of the God of the Old Testament narratives. The dogmas of election, and especially of hell and damnation, embody some of the worst features of Old Testament belief. The idea of man, too, has been affected. The dogma of total depravity is based on Gen. 3 and what New Testament writers read out of that passage. Where religion affects society, the Old Testament influence has likewise been harmful. Militarism, slavery, persecution of witches, polygamy, capital punishment, and religious persecution are all justified and demonstrated in its pages. These results, he grants, need to be estimated in connection with other results of a beneficial nature which it has also without doubt produced. But he does not elaborate that part of the picture. All in all, he considers it a real question whether in the past the Old Testament has not been more a liability than an asset to Christianity.

But Berry thinks that whatever harm the Old Testament may have done is due more to the wrong use of it than to its essential nature. It is inconsistent to treat it dogmatically as the infallible Word of God and then evade the consequences by allegorizing interpretation or other expedients. The right view of the Old Testament is that of modern criticism which is inductive, in contrast to the conservative view which is deductive. It asks not what the Old Testament must be, but what it really is. He rejects a mediating position which is often taken, viz., that the Old Testament does not intend to teach history, politics or science, but only religion. In this way many wish to shake off the liabilities of the Old Testament and keep its advantages; so far as this is reading the mind of God it is a matter difficult to prove, and so far as it is reading the intention of the human authors of the Old Testament it may be challenged by the contrary assertion that they were really trying to write history, science, etc. The interest of the Old Testament writers is by no means confined to religion. Whole books like Esther, Song of Songs, and Ecclesiastes are devoid of it.

The historical approach to the Old Testament teaches us that there is an evolution in Old Testament thought and enables us to differentiate between higher and lower stages. Accurately discerning the meaning of given portions of the Old Testament, we can see its lack of unity and appreciate what sections have no helpful message for general use at the present time. Berry then points out in what ways the Old Testament thus studied may and should be an asset for present day use. (1) All the documents, of course, have importance from a historical standpoint, but that use "belongs to the study much more than to the pulpit". (2) The Old Testament is an asset in so far as it expresses religious truth which is universal and permanent. Here he stresses ethical monotheism and the teaching concerning the redemptive power of vicarious suffering (Is. 53). (3) The literary quality of the Old Testament. (4) Those portions which express feeling—notably the Psalms. While they are largely a restatement of familiar ideas, coming particularly from the prophets, and often ordinary or even platitudinous in thought, their feeling gives them an appeal to the human heart at all times. (5) The biographical element in the Old Testament. (6) The element of personal experience. This expression of personal experience and conviction reaches the heart. The heroes of the faith lived in a very real sense in a fellowship with God.

Another American Old Testament scholar who was stirred to speak about this problem was J. A. Bewer.[25] After conceding all the difficulties the Old Testament has caused Christianity, he argues that it is nevertheless too valuable for the Christian to discard. We need it for the true understanding of Jesus and the early Christian writers, especially Paul, who were all rooted in the Old Testament. Furthermore, next to the New Testament, it is our greatest source for the enlarging and deepening of our spiritual life and thought. It is great literature; parts of it belong to the greatest literature of the world, e.g., some of its stories and Psalms, some of its prophets and the Book of Job.

> In it we find the record of the experience of the great men of the spirit, the original geniuses of religion, the pioneers in the moral and spiritual realm. It is a book of power. Here we may nourish our spiritual life by fellowship with the prophets, deepen our sense of the reality of the spiritual world, refine our moral and spiritual perception. Here we may learn from Amos penetrating insight into social conditions, from Isaiah tenderness, forgiveness, and moral redemption, from Ezekiel pastoral fidelity. Here are the sources of the social side of religion, the social ideal of the prophets, the kingdom of God, reformed and deepened by Jesus. Here are the great teachers of prayer, the psalmists who give us the words of worship which we use when we are inarticulate and dumb. Can we afford to forgo all this? Need I mention the wealth of material the Old Testament presents not only for sermons and for religious education, but also for theology, especially for ethical monotheism? One has but to think a little of all that is involved in neglecting or discarding the Old Testament to see how impossible it is for the Christian minister.

The evil consequences of the Old Testament can all be avoided, Bewer thinks, by the truer understanding and use of the Old Testament we owe modern criticism. As significant points in the new view, he lists: (1) We use the methods of literary study to find out what the authors actually mean or say. (2) There is a development from lower to higher religious and moral ideas and ideals, "a progressive revelation" as it has been called. (3) The norm by which every step in the marvellous development is tested: the spirit of Christ. (4) The necessity of distinguishing between the truth and the manner in which it is presented—taking poetry as poetry, etc. (5) Going on to the spiritual appreciation of the truth in the Old Testament.

In a later paper,[26] Bewer sets forth how impossible the former idea of the Old Testament is for the Christian but how the new view has made it fascinating and inspiring. But he discerns a reluctance of the Christian Church to acknowledge this. The danger of which it is afraid is that, in this eager study of the human side of the Old Testament, the reality of the truth and revelation of God in these pages will be forgotten, and the authority of the Old Testament entirely lost. Bewer warns that nothing can restore the authority of the Old Testament in the former sense of the word, once a modern man has read it in the new way. He asks: Is there anything in the Old Testament of such authoritative character that we may say "While indeed the Old Testament as a whole is not the Word of God, it never-theless contains the Word of God"? But where, he continues, is the distinguishing principle that will enable us to separate the imperishable divine from the ephemeral human? The only norm and standard is the Spirit of God as revealed in Jesus. Those things contrary to it or without spiritual meaning to us are for us without authority and not canonical. If, however, this is to have real meaning the external authority must become internal authority: the Word of God in the Old Testament must become Word of God to me in my own heart and conscience.

He sees the Word of God in the Old Testament finding us, striking home, touching our hearts, justifying itself to our minds, commanding our consciences along three lines: (1) That of its moral teachings and precepts. (2) In the spiritual experi-ences of the prophets. (3) Its illustration of the search of the human heart for God in Old Testament prayer. All this is authoritative only to him who believes himself directly confronted and addressed by God. Many read the Old Testament professionally, with unconcerned hearts, and so do not hear its message, and others read it with hearts and consciences only and without discriminating intellect, with equally unfortunate results. Jesus read it with a warm and eager heart, and yet also with discrimination, and His example should be followed.

In a valuable symposium of Old Testament articles that appeared in England in 1938, Lofthouse gave a discussion of our theme.[27] He finds that it is with the New Testament, rather than with Christian theology, that the Hebrew Scriptures can be usefully compared. He begins by pointing out that from the point of view of *form*, the religion of the Old Testament is the religion of promise. For the best of the Hebrews the object of their vision is what is out of sight. They dauntlessly look forward to the coming intervention of God that will bring salvation. The religion of the New Testament, on the other hand, looks from the future to the past. The promise is fulfilled, the deliverance has appeared; though there is still more to come, faith conceives of it as almost realized.

Taking up the comparison from the point of view of *contents* of the two Testaments, Lofthouse first dwells on the two great pioneers of the Christian faith, Paul and John. While they have different slants they both turn away from the old dispensation, even while they breathe its air. They both look to one who is felt completely to transcend what the older writings would suggest—to Jesus.

Turning to Jesus he finds that if the vocabulary of His sayings is that of the Old Testament, the spirit is fresh. He veers especially toward the line of the anti-sacrificial utterances of Prophets and Psalmists. But He did not remove the law to establish the gospel. Properly speaking there is no opposition between the two, for the law was more than a catalogue of burdensome duties—it was God's instruction to men, revealing to them how they could enjoy His favour, and even more it was a promise, though a conditional one. The gospel is a second and this time unconditional promise. It is a triumphant present, though it passes into the future—therein linking up with the Old Testament mood once more. Discussing the New Testament eschatology he says its heart is the approach to God by faith in Christ (itself God's gift), and the welding of all who believe into one great redeemed community; he finds this no mere legacy from Jewish apocalyptic but outgrowth of the work of Jesus.

Lofthouse then discusses another aspect of the Hebrew religion that he considers essential in thinking about the Old Testament promise, as well as about the relation of the Testaments—the Covenant idea. While the word occurs but seldom in the Old Testament, the idea is present constantly. Nowhere is it clearer than in Is. 53, which chapter forms a kind of bridge between the Testaments, and though rarely quoted in the New Testament is, as it were, the *leitmotiv* of the Gospel story. Turning to Christian doctrine and concepts, Lofthouse finds the Old Testament a kind of acid test for the consonance of a doctrine with the spirit of the New Testament. Properly used it could have protected Christendom from the misconceptions of a thousand years of Christian speculation, and he then illustrates this in the matter of the doctrines of God, Sin, Atonement, and the Church.

In closing, he speaks of record and revelation. The Old Testament is a double record, how God dealt with men and how men have felt about Him, and knows a double revelation—a revelation through the world of nature and history, and a revelation given through inspired men. The New Testament is also a record and revelation, but in it the final veil which had remained in the Old Testament is also a revelation of priceless worth, for it brings men to the place where they stand before the last veil that awaits removal.

In the same volume the editor, H. Wheeler Robinson, has a contribution on Old Testament theology.[28] He prefaces his delineation of the characteristic doctrines (God, Man, Sin and Grace, the Judgment of History) with a section on the Philosophy of Revelation. He finds the Hebrews realists, who continually adjusted their ideas of God to the events of life. The strong sense of corporate personality among them, combining ancestors and descendants with the present generation into a single unity, helped to make history the supreme revelation of God. The philosophy of history for the Hebrews thus becomes the philosophy of revelation. The record as given in the Old Testament is dominated by particular theories evolved in the course of the development of the religion, e.g., the doctrine of retribution, or the idea that Moses gave the law in all completeness. The task of critical scholarship is *to get behind these theories to the original history of both the events and the ideas*. This actual history, so far as we can reach it, must be the basis for a modern philosophy of revelation. Only when we have decided on a probable series of events and a parallel series of human reactions to these events can we usefully begin to ask how far and in what way they both in their blended unity really serve to reveal God.

But Robinson does not follow this out. Instead he deals with the "record", speaking of that as "revelation". While Old Testament criticism has removed many former difficulties with which that book confronted us, new intellectual difficulties have arisen for those who believe it to be divine revelation. The very phrase "historical revelation" is a paradox (when revelation is understood as static and permanent truth), for history implies dynamic movement of some kind, whether or not it can be called progress. And how can absolute truth be relative to each of a series of generations? The answer of the Hebrew to the difficulty is a *solvitur vivendo*: he says, "God knows me and I know God in the experience of living."

Robinson finds that this leaves us with the theological problem of the canon. While its precise boundaries have no more than a historic interest this does not diminish the authority of the Old Testament. Both Judaism and Christianity really only made *selective* use of this literature, the one emphasizing the Law, the other the Prophets and Psalms. The authority of the Old Testament thus rested from the beginning on what we call value judgments. No Tridentine decree can eliminate that historic fact and its theological significance. But Robinson insists that this does not entangle us in the slough of subjectivity. Revelation has always been and still remains the unity of the subjective and objective. As the word of the prophet only became revelation when it found obedient and intelligent response from his hearers, so the objective fact of the Old Testament as literary record still awaits the response of the reader through the internal testimony of the Holy Spirit. Such authority is in no way inferior to the authority of truth, goodness and beauty wherever they are found. Secondary authority may rightly belong to the living tradition of the Church, or to the written record of the life that went before it, but only as guides to a goal—that goal being the direct and individual knowledge of God. The authority of the Old Testament depends on the penetrating character of the intuition of the prophets, the rich variety of religious experience, the vocabulary of worship, the picturesque character of the language and thoughts and the dynamic quality of the idea of God behind the record.

In the same year there appeared a book by the present writer[29] which, though it did not deal with the authority of the Old Testament, attempted to interpret a single Old Testament book, that of Job, in a new way. After first approaching it in historical-critical manner, in which form-criticism played an important role, he "stood off" to view the meaning of the whole. For he held that a literary product may in reality have a meaning and message of greater range than its creator realizes at the time of writing, and that this is even more the case with a book like Job, which was taken to be a social product. The meaning Job now conveys was held to be that of the greatest of all theodicies, in which all the important viewpoints that can be adduced are brought in and powerfully presented in poetic form. Whether this approach could be used as readily in the case of other Old Testament writings the author does not know, but he believes it deserves further trial. For there are times when we prefer to read ancient books with an eye to appreciating and enjoying them, instead of getting wrought up over "decisions", "time and eternity" and other deadly serious matters. Such a search for "meaning" of an entity suggests a link with phenomenology and evidently would conform best to theologies of the kind advocated by Tillich or by Otto.

Chapter Thirteen

THE REVIVAL OF THE NEW TESTAMENT APPROACH

UNDER the influence of Barth a trend toward a Christianizing interpretation of the Old Testament arose in the outer fringes of German and Swiss Old Testament study. It was chiefly promulgated by theologically interested clergymen[1] and found great favour with all those who were deeply dissatisfied with what the professionals had to offer. For the scholar's approach demanded toil, critical analysis, and in the end there was no religious profit in it. The Church, bereft of its ancient support by a paternalistic, aristocratic state, was now the prey of the nihilistic forces that were let loose when the thrones sank into the dust. In this situation a liberal was a man with a wooden sword. The crying need was for a more effective weapon. In the Reformation era Protestantism had found the Bible of the two Testaments a sword of the Spirit. The idea arose: we must recapture that standpoint. Barth had provided a great stimulus in this direction and indicated the possibilities. Among the clergymen who came forward with such sentiments Vischer took a leading role.

In an article of 1931[2] he gave an outline of the views he was promulgating and in a work that began to appear in 1934[3] he has been applying them exegetically to the three parts of the Hebrew Canon (taken in their Hebrew arrangement rather than the one accepted in the Protestant Bible translations). We shall deal here with his thought on the basis of his early article, since that gives his standpoint in principle, without encumbrance by exegetical details. By one's surprise at his exegesis one may too easily lose sight of his central positions, and be too hasty in one's condemnation of his approach.

Vischer first raises the question: Is the Christian message of today bound to the Old Testament? He begins with the assertion that there is no getting away from it that Christianity is bound to a fact of the past: namely that God became incarnate in Christ

1–30 A.D. All the lines of a relationship between God and any man at any time intersect this particular point in history. There is no salvation apart from Christ (Acts 4: 10, 12). Christianity, furthermore. he says, is bound to the literary testimony of this fact of Christ. The New Testament bears its own witness, but, at the same time, it brings its proof for Christ from the Old Testament. Vischer does not believe it possible to reject the Old Testament and keep the New Testament. They hang together inseparably. With Calvin and Barth, he holds to the basic identity of the two Testaments.

The chief ground of objection to the authority of the Old Testament, Vischer asserts, is to be found in the fact that there is so much in the Old Testament that is low and immoral. But those who read the Bible as a document of human piety are not reading it aright. The theme of that book is—as Barth has said —the piety of God, not that of man; the morality of God, not the morals of man. The modern individual is motivated at every turn by the Greek ideal—he is looking for the glorification of man; but the Bible seeks only the glorification of God (I Peter 2: 9). God's condescension to sinners, His acts of grace whereby He chooses sinful men for His ends—these are the things of which the Bible speaks.

The Church, Vischer asserts, (and it is a most debatable assertion), *rests on Holy Scripture*, which is composed of two halves—an Old Testament and a New Testament. It is the task of an Old Testament study carried on by the Church to inquire into this given relationship. This task prevents Old Testament scholarship from becoming a mere branch of the study of Semitic languages and literatures. That the latter fields of study also have a legitimate interest in the Old Testament is fully conceded. The Semitists may tear the Old Testament down and build it up again to suit themselves; they may evolve a "history of the Hebrew religion" on the basis of such critical study. But that sort of thing does not do justice to the needs of the Church with respect to the Old Testament.

The task of an ecclesiastical study of the Old Testament is to understand the Old Testament as a whole (as we now have it) and the relation of every part of which it is composed to the whole. This task is not merely an æsthetic one—as for instance the appreciation of the artistic character of a composite building like San Marco in Venice—but a theological one. Every generation anew must make a fresh attempt to understand the Old Testament and New Testament as a unified structure.

For Vischer the Old Testament is like an arch of which the keystone is the Messiah—a thing which he infers from the testimony of the New Testament. If it were not for this inclusion of the witness of the apostles into the arch of prophecy, the Old Testament would still be an open question concerning one yet to come (John 1: 41, 45; Acts 4: 11). One can deny this, but then one does not read the Old Testament as Old Testament—part of the sacred book of the Christian Church. On a purely historical basis, such as a non-ecclesiastical scholarship may pursue, only hypothetical judgments are attainable concerning this matter. Highly important Old Testament passages like Is. 53 cannot be understood at all, or only hypothetically, without the New Testament. The Old Testament as a whole becomes fully clear only when it is related to Christ, and critical scholarship without wishing to do so has made that increasingly apparent.

The Old Testament could not be authoritative witness of Christ for the Church of all times if the Messiah had not been actually present as head of the Church of the Old Testament and if the saints had not seized upon salvation through hope and faith in him (cf. John 8: 56-8, 12: 41, 1: 30; I Cor. 10). Vischer thus stresses the pre-existence of Christ as the thing that makes the continuity reasonable. But the fact of historical progression has a full reality. The incarnation of the *logos* was the event through which the Old Testament became the *Old* Testament. "He came unto his own, and his own received him not" (John 1: 11). If that had not occurred, the Old Testament would not have become *old*. In that it became *old*, it must now bear witness that this unheard-of thing (the crucifixion of the Messiah) took place, and that this turning-point from the Old Testament to the New Testament is also the turning-point of the world and of the individual life.

Real history does not repeat itself. The genuine Christian message based on the Old Testament summons us to let ourselves be drawn by that which the Bible tells of the people of the Old Testament, into the presence of the same God who commands and promises, and not to harden our hearts (Heb.

4: 7). In order to become servants of the same master, we must hear Moses and the prophets (Luke 16: 29).

Vischer then proceeds to inquire into the meaning that "the Law", i.e., the Pentateuch, has for us.[4] The absolute claim that God has on us comes to us in the Bible through relative, historically and individually conditioned commands. Every word of the Torah draws us into the presence of this sovereign God, who is the same to-day as He was for Moses or Habakkuk. The question, then, is whether a particular commandment also applies to me in every concrete situation.

Here Vischer is highly modern; he asserts every commandment was spoken in and for a concrete situation of its own which may by no means be identical with mine. As such they all testify to concrete commandments which Israel received. They concern us only as witness of what God once commanded. He quotes Barth to the effect that no Biblical commandment or prohibition is a rule or moral generality, but that it comes to us rather as a testimony of the absolute, concrete, real commandment, that is behind and above all recorded commandments.

Vischer then tries to define more closely what "law" really means. He considers it to be the most definite expression of the deity's will for the right. It is an expression of the fact that the address and claim of the gospel are meant existentially. "I am the Lord thy God" (Ex. 20: 2)—that is not only the presupposition but also the content of the divine legislation; it is that which expresses itself in its totality as well as in its particular decrees.

The self-revelation of God is the source of this law. God only says "thou shalt" to him to whom He has said "thou art mine". I cannot existentially hear the gospel "thou art mine" if I do not in the obedience of faith also hear the commandment "then be mine". Vischer thinks it a mistake to believe that the law was given as a preparatory condition for entering into the covenant relation. The law flows out of the covenant. "You are my people—therefore really be my people." The indicative is turned into an imperative. Man's obedience to the law is man's answer in the obedience of faith to the promise of the gospel; it is gratitude for grace shown, not an attempt to earn grace.

Judaism, Vischer finds, misunderstood this basic theological situation. How was that possible? Did not the cultic law even show in what sense it was meant? In rather speculative fashion Vischer then presents a teleology of the law of sacrifice, explaining what the purpose of God was in establishing such an arrangement. How was it possible for the Holy One to dwell in Israel's midst when His requirement was "You shall be holy, for I am holy" (Lev. 19: 2) without the dispensing of daily forgiveness through daily sacrifice? Since knowledge of the moral law could produce nothing but consciousness of sin (Rom. 3: 20) and resultant despair, God gave His people the cultic law as a sign that they might live before Him and with Him, in spite of their sin. Every sacrifice points beyond itself. It would be nothing if it were not for that one sacrifice of which all other sacrifices are but the symbol and prophecy. Here Vischer avails himself of a thought of Luther: the *obtaining* of forgiveness took place only once, but the *distribution* of it took place often, both before Christ and after Christ. For since God had decided upon forgiveness, it mattered not whether He dispensed it previously or subsequently through His Word: as He subsequently dispensed it in the sacrament through the Word, so He previously dispensed it in the Old Testament sacrifices through the Word.

At this point the reader will have his doubts. The manner in which Vischer explains "sacrifice" shows him as understanding the cultic law of the Old Testament in the light of the Epistle to the Hebrews. But the thought of the author of Hebrews hangs together at that point with an ancient philosophy of typology that is in itself of debatable value. Can we, furthermore, naïvely assume that the sacrificial law was revealed by God, as the Jews did, when we know that its whole procedure and terminology are closely related to what we find among Israel's heathen neighbours?[4] Surely there is no use in resolutely ignoring what modern knowledge teaches us and proceeding along an orthodox line as though nothing had happened in the last hundred years. Fine religious dicta of Calvin or Luther, valuable as utterances of their piety, but "pre-scientific" in their use of the Old Testament, can only becloud the situation.

Vischer's view of the prophets[5] and of the prophecy element in the Old Testament is similarly governed by New Testament viewpoints. God has elected Israel to a living history in order that His will may be done on earth and in heaven. His will, however, is never a fully revealed entity, but only present in the history of revelation, as it unfolds. "I shall be that I shall be"—that, rather than "I am that I am", as the familiar translations render, is the real meaning of the divine name of Ex. 3 and it expresses perfectly how God reveals Himself in different moments. Again and again we hear in the Old Testament that "the Word of the Lord came". God does not reign as rigid law but as a free sovereign. Hence, in the Old Testament the law is woven together with history, and bound to the books of the prophets.

God is present in the word of the prophets, and His Word given through them makes history. Prophets and history belong together—that is why (a purely speculative assertion) the historical books Joshua—II Kings are called the "former prophets". The Old Testament history, furthermore, is written in prophetic spirit, with an eye to the eschatologically oriented chronological scheme of the Priestly writer. It is evident, too, in the way in which contemporary history is interpreted in the prophets. If we say that all this prophecy is fulfilled in the New Testament, then that is true in the sense that it is confirmed. All promises of God find their confirmation in Jesus Christ, but not necessarily their complete realization. The goal of prophecy is not yet attained at the stage of the Incarnation. We, too, live in faith in the promise like the Old Testament saints, except that we see more clearly than they.

As for the third part of the Hebrew Canon, the Writings,[6] Vischer looks on this division as "the congregational echo" to the speaking of God in law and prophets. They cover the whole breadth of human life—health and sickness, love and hate, prosperity and adversity. This would seem to imply a lower rank for this portion of the canon—unless one regards the Old Testament congregation as so fully inspired by the Holy Ghost that the "echo" is given back in absolute purity.

In his elaboration of his programme in his *Witness of the Old Testament to Christ*, Vol. I, Vischer argues that Christianity must regard as normative for its reading and understanding of the Old Testament the New Testament assertion John 5: 39. "Ye search the Scripture because ye think that in them ye have eternal life; and these are they which bear witness of me." Christological exegesis of the Old Testament is the slogan.

The very humanity of the Scripture is seen as comparable to our Lord's humanity in the Incarnation. God willed that these imperfect human and fallible words should testify concerning his Son, the incarnate Word, and be attested to by the Holy Spirit. Vischer finds the Old Testament fully on a par with the New in principle—Jesus is only the Christ if the unity of the Bible is preserved. The Christian Church, he declares, stands and falls with the acceptance or rejection of the Old Testament. He spurns the idea of a "pneumatic" exegesis—thinks of it as leading over to a theosophy. But he then has recourse to the Holy Spirit as the one that gives us proof out of the Old Testament that Jesus is the Christ. He quotes Augustine's saying: "Read the prophetic books without reading of Christ and what can you find that is more insipid and flat? But read Christ here, then that which thou readest not only tastes good but will intoxicate thee."

Writing of the literature on the Old Testament from the period of the German church struggle, a reviewer who was not inexperienced in biblical criticism, Abramowski, described Vischer's book as "both necessary and correct".[7] It is "necessary" because the theological and political situation of the hour required a Christian witness on the basis of the Old Testament— not merely an opinion about the Old Testament—and it was impossible to wait until modern Old Testament science should arrive at the point where it would produce it. The book is "correct", furthermore, because the New Testament and the Protestant Reformers declare in unison that the Old Testament gives witness to Christ. He agrees with Vischer that no mere humanistic approach, augmented with æsthetic and religious considerations, will find Christ in the Old Testament. Since, furthermore, the attack is being carried forward by the anti-Christian forces to Christ Himself, it is necessary to hold the Old Testament from the vantage point of Christ and for Him.

Such an utterance highlights the fact that Vischer's book arose out of a special situation and met the acclaim it did on that account. There is a definite principle behind Vischer's thought—it was heard much earlier from the lips of the great liberal, Stade (p. 267)—that for Christian use the Old Testament must be Christianized. But Stade conceived of that task as part of the preacher's role. Vischer's exegesis is essentially a preacher's and that of one sharing the dogma that is basic for all Calvinism, viz., that the whole Bible is sole authority. From this doctrine flows the need of fusing the Testaments to create unity, and the view of Messianic prophecy found in the New Testament provides the means of mastering the Old. Vischer manages in this way to give the Old Testament a present significance, just as the apocalyptically minded are able to do in their way for both Old and New Testament prophecy.

The advantages of this are clear. But have we a moral right to attempt to read the mind of God and assert that something about Christ is foretold or foreshadowed in the Old Testament, when that is only our own guesswork? For Vischer indulges in typological interpretations beyond those found in the New Testament. And do we have the obligation to accept New Testament assertions of a similar nature about this or that Old Testament passage? The assumption that we have that obligation governs Vischer and all who are of his colour. Behind this attitude stands the fear that without such Christianization the Old Testament loses all living importance. That explains much, but it can hardly justify the approach taken. For to force oneself to believe something that is contrary to reason is hardly the evangelical idea of faith. To take such a view is to lose sight of the great lesson taught by Ritschl (p. 99). The Old Testament, furthermore, is too rich to be compressed into the prophecy and fulfilment formula. Some better way must be found to make it meaningful than Vischer's, whatever may be the benefits that have accrued from his approach.[8]

Chapter Fourteen

THE OLD TESTAMENT AND THE EXISTENTIAL QUESTION

A LINE of Dialectic theology differing considerably from Karl Barth's is that represented by Gogarten and Bultmann. Instead of assuming a direct relationship of man and God, they hold that our relation to God is indirect and is only realized in our relation to our fellow man or the world.[1] For these theologians, therefore, a theological anthropology was of basic importance. Necessarily, then, they had to seek a link with contemporary philosophical thought—the approach of Gogarten being influenced by E. Grisebach,[2] and that of Bultmann by Heidegger.[3]

These philosophies attempted a new ontology, describing human existence in its fatefulness, its bondage and contradictoriness, and in particular stressed the idea that this life is not to be regarded in a neutral manner as from the outside, but is to be understood only by actively participating in it. Our responsibility is not to the individual self, as Idealism presupposes, but to *being* as such, which we did not create and over which we have no control. Therein these philosophies provide a startingpoint for thought about revelation as an existential reality that claims us.

We may now inquire how this affects the standing of the Old Testament.

For Gogarten, then, our fellow man is the decisive existential reality, and it is toward him that our responsible action is directed.[4] Where the relation of man to man is fully realized it is as the work of the creating and redeeming God. Speech or word being the channel of contact between the self and the other, revelation must take place through "Word". There being no direct relation between us and God, revelation can only come to us in this roundabout manner. But Gogarten does not limit the "other" to our contemporary. He sees us holding a relation also to men of the past. History is decision and can only be understood in participating action. While history, therefore, is something that happens in the present, it is incessant contact of a past with the present. Where this contact is not experienced there is no real history. From this angle Gogarten accepts the idea that God has also revealed Himself to men of the past, in other words, he posits a history of revelation. This history occurs within total-history, it is the history of the people of God, through which God desires to show Himself as Creator and through which He would accomplish His history of redemption. But to believe in this history is to participate in it. The history of revelation consists in this—that the word of men of the past speaks to me as present "thou", exercising a divine claim upon me. Christian faith confesses this of the men of biblical history, and that includes also the Word of the Old Testament.

But the Old Testament, according to Gogarten, only speaks to us of God as Creator and of His order of Creation. It is revelation of the law, not as a timeless idea, but rather as a concrete claim. It is but the requirement of a responsible "I-and-thou-relation", not its fulfilment; but at the same time it is a prediction of fulfilment. The implication is that in this history of the people of God, with which we become associated through our hearing the Old Testament Word, the relation will be fulfilled. Contact with the Word of the Old Testament is thus not yet revelation in the full sense. The latter is experienced only in contact with the Word of the New Testament— the message of Jesus Christ, who vicariously fulfilled the law and gives Himself to man in His Word. In so far as Christ's love of man is the work of God and obedience to God, His love is revelation of the love of God and His Word the Word of God.

It is thus apparent that for Gogarten, as for Luther, the Old Testament is primarily "law". In later essays he dealt in more detail with this supposed primary aspect of it.[5] The only revealed commandment of the decalogue, he declares, is the first "that we permit God really to be our God as He, in revealing Himself to us, wishes to be our God".[6] The legal materials of the Old Testament, or in other words, the whole law apart from this one commandment, he takes to be derived from reason and experience.

Bultmann, to whom we must now turn, is impressed by the

fact of our mortality, which would make life meaningless if it were the ultimate thing.[7] Revelation, he holds, can only consist in the gift from on high of a life that overcomes death. As such it is not a phenomenon of the present order, but a future entity that is ever drawing near and to that extent is already present. This "life", however, is not revealed to us as something objective, but as a mode of being that we comprehend only in faith. Revelation is the new understanding of the self and the boundaries fixed for us, as ordained by the Creator and opening the way from death to life.

History is another important category for Bultmann. He regards it as involving decision. The decision is a choice between oncoming possibilities: death or life, God or the world. The possibility of life or God is not a tangible actuality but something potential. I can only know it if I know the possibilities of being, and I can know these only when I seize one of them and in the moment of seizing it. But the past, too, reaches into the present situation, because in the latter a possibility that occurred in the past is merely being repeated. Only in the present existential encounter with the claim that the past places on us is there any history. This is true of all history, including the history mirrored in the Bible.

For Bultmann the person of the historical Jesus is of no particular concern. He stresses the Christ who is God's Word to man as bringer of divine forgiveness. The Word is bound to its bearer and does not count except as spoken by him who is its authorized messenger. On the other hand, Jesus has no revelatory authority apart from his central "Word" and mission. Like Kaehler, Bultmann hands the "historical" Jesus over to the critics (of whom he himself was one of the most radical) to do with Him as they please, and stresses the Christ of faith. For we encounter the revelatory Word only through the biblical testimony, as it is brought home to us in the living preaching of the Church.

The problem of the Old Testament engaged Bultmann in a special essay.

He first of all rejects certain ways of approaching the problem of the relation of the Old Testament to Christianity as outside of the pale of specifically theological interest. These other ways are legitimate in themselves on neutral or more or less anti-Christian standpoints, but must be ruled out where the discussion is truly theological. He even discards an approach that would ask in a detached manner whether the Old Testament has a significance for a faith that sees in Christ the revelation of God; this mode of questioning, he asserts, is still an asking from the *outside*—in which one surveys everything from the historical perspective. Theological questioning can only be from *within*—from the vantage point of faith. Can the Old Testament Word of God be heard by me as intended for myself? That he says, is how the question must be formulated.

In dealing with the Old Testament, Bultmann asserts, one must ask what basic possibility of understanding human existence finds expression in it? And this is not to be regarded as an inquiry out of idle curiosity; it is to be undertaken from the point of view of one who is convinced in faith that the Christian understanding of existence is the only correct one, but who is compelled to measure it and compare it with other possible views of existence. It takes the Old Testament seriously, not asking what it had to say to the men of 2000 years ago, but what, if anything, it continues to say to us here and now.

Bultmann finds that in the days when men really were aware of the understanding of existence that speaks forth from the Old Testament and sought to contrast or relate it to that which is truly Christian, they expressed it in the antithesis "law and gospel". For Paul, as for Luther, the Old Testament as a whole was an expression of the law, or the requiring will of God. In the new order, represented by the New Testament, man stands under the grace of God that accepts him, though a sinner. But only he who is aware of the law and of his inability ever to fulfil its requirements can understand the message of the gospel. Hence the law remains the presupposition of the gospel. Man must continue to hear what God requires of him, for though the Christian is free from the law and stands under the Spirit, his status in that respect must be a constant experience of the renewal of such a liberation. Yea more, the Christian may be free from the law as a "must" for the sake of obtaining grace, but not in so far as it is reconstituted through grace.

But the question arises: If the Old Testament remains the presupposition of the New—namely, as expression of the requirement of God that constantly encompasses man—does it retain its specifically Old Testament character? This Bultmann denies. The concrete legislation of the Old Testament, in so far as it is cultic or ritualistic, had a significance only for particular stages of Hebrew history. The ethical requirements of the Old Testament, however (as well as those of Jesus), in so far as they grow out of the basic relationships of life and not merely some concrete, transient form of such life, have not fallen to the ground. But for that very reason they are not specifically Old Testament requirements—even if they had by any chance first been formulated there. Their validity depends on their universal acceptability, and actually they were not first or exclusively laid down in the Old Testament. One can see how even Paul recognizes this. For he assumes that Gentiles who have not had Old Testament indoctrination know of themselves what God requires of them (Rom. 1: 32). Their consciences testify that the Word of God is written in their hearts (Rom. 2: 14 f.).

Thus, while the gospel presupposes the law, the latter is not necessarily identical with the concrete legislation of the Old Testament. Some other historical embodiment of the law may conceivably serve equally well for such a presupposition. The zeal for God that Paul concedes Israel possesses but calls a zeal "not according to knowledge" (Rom. 10: 2), and to which the message of the Cross is particularly addressed, is possible in principle everywhere. Hence the reasons for using the Old Testament in the Christian Church are purely pedagogical. It is a useful instrument to bring home to man that he is under the requirements of God. Bultmann thinks that in the Decalogue and in the words of the prophets these requirements are expressed with a force and a clarity found nowhere else except in the preaching of Jesus. But the law of the Old Testament, he concedes, is not actually addressed to us but to a definite people, living a definite history that is not ours. If we understand it as an expression of the law of God as such, we simply do so by virtue of the fact that in the Christian history out of which we have come this Old Testament element has happened to have played a considerable role.

Bultmann then takes up the Old Testament understanding of existence in direct approach. He points out that we are subject to a variety of influences, not only collectively but individually, so that various possibilities of understanding of the self are intermingled in our present situation. In striving to obtain clarity and to appropriate the fruits of our own history, we are forced to give consideration also to the Old Testament and its distinctive view of existence. For here a very important human possibility becomes clarified in all its consequences.

Bultmann, thereupon, tries to set forth the peculiarities of this Old Testament view in contrast to that which comes to us from the Greeks and likewise forms so potent a factor in our heritage. In the Old Testament, he asserts, the divine imperative governs man's entire existence in the most radical fashion. It makes no concession to an idealistic or utilitarian interpretation of the moral requirement. When you read the Old Testament you have to be conscious of the fact that there is a parting of the ways between the striving to attain some ideal of excellence or perfection, and that of serving one's neighbour in obedience to God and in perpetual consciousness of inadequacy and guilt. The real Old Testament understanding of man finds expression notably in the consciousness that we have been created by a higher power. It implies that man cannot in his thinking deal arbitrarily with the world, but in his capacity as a creature is delivered up to the Lord of the world. And since man primarily has his destiny in history, the Old Testament understands history not as the result of human activity but as the work of God, which assigns to man his fate and comforts him with tasks conferred. Man knows himself to be put in a definite place by the divine will and facing the possibility of judgment or grace, according as he does that which God demands of him.

This peculiar understanding of existence found in the Old Testament is basically identical with that of the New Testament and stands in sharp contrast to the idealistic or humanistic view of the Greeks. Only in a fundamental, critical grappling with this Old Testament position, whether its result be negative or positive, can we attain clarity for the understanding of existence that we would make our own. Only in such grappling can the question whether Christianity has any significance for the present be clarified. In view of this similarity of the Old Testament and New Testament view of existence it would appear senseless, Bultmann says, for anyone to want to hold fast to Christianity and discard the Old Testament! Such a one can be sure that the Christianity he wants to hold fast to is no longer

Christianity. The alternative is neither or both. Our whole history gives the Old Testament a claim on us—the claim to be heard and to make us come to grips with its idea of existence and thereby to grasp our own present situation.

But after thus insisting on the place of the Old Testament in a manner that seems almost too strong in the light of what he said previously and develops subsequently, Bultmann hastens to point out that what he means is something very different from that which the New Testament and the Christian Church mean, when they describe the Old Testament as revelation or Word of God. The critical consideration that he has just characterized is no listening to the Word of God, and not faith. The question whether Christian preaching can refer to the Old Testament as the revelation of God, and if so, to what extent, is one yet to be considered. He approaches it via a further discussion of the relation of the Old Testament to the New Testament. If the understanding of existence is the same in the New Testament as in the Old Testament, if faith, righteousness and grace, sin and forgiveness are essentially the same in the Old Testament and New Testament, as already stated, where, then, is the difference? What is the new in the New Testament over against the Old?

Bultmann now inquires whether the difference between Old Testament and New Testament is correctly described as that between law and gospel. Just as existence under grace always refers back to that under the law, so likewise the Old Testament knows no existence under the law that is not at the same time an existence under grace. He then tries to show how the grace of God underlies the entire Old Testament order. The prevenient grace of God establishes the Old Testament relation of God and man, and provides the basis for man's obedience.[8] It was an act of divine grace that God chose Israel and bestowed His law upon it and gave His people a task to be realized in a definite history. Furthermore, in the Old Testament the grace of God is understood as forgiveness. Amid all the unfaithfulness of His people, God's faithfulness remains unchanged: He is the God who forgives and has mercy upon His children (Ps. 103: 8–13). Hence the Christian Church can directly take over sayings in the Psalms and Prophets which pray for forgiveness or which promise God's grace.

In so far as gospel is the preaching of the grace of God for the sinner, one cannot assert that the gospel element is lacking in the Old Testament. One can, of course, say that this gospel is not found everywhere in its purity, and that the ideas of sin and the forgiveness of God are not always understood radically. A symptom of this, for instance, is the manner in which a Psalmist appeals for God's grace by pointing to the frailty of man as a mere mortal creature (103: 14–16); so long as man thinks there is something about himself that is deserving of grace, even though it be only his own frailty, he has not yet understood God's grace radically. But in Psalm 90: 8 f. this human frailty itself is considered the result of God's wrath, whereby it is put in a different light. Sometimes the appeal for divine mercy is uttered in absolute humility, as in Psalms 51 and 130. In the Old Testament the typical idea of sin is not one of moral transgression, but of injury done the divine honour, of distrust of God's grace, of human rebellion—in short, of unbelief. For the thing required of man above all is faith, waiting on God (Ps. 147: 10 f.). It is finding one's help in the Lord and boasting only of Him. It is hoping and experiencing the grace of God in the vicissitudes of collective and individual life. In all this the men of Israel experienced the forgiveness of their God. And if the Old Testament saints did not always experience it, they looked forward to it. Here lie the roots of the eschatological hope. On the basis of the radical knowledge of collective sin that has deserved nothing but judgment, prophecy reaches out to the last things. The future of hope that looms up behind the judgment is purely one of grace (Is. 48: 11; cf. Ezek. 36: 22). There is no continuity between past and present; Israel may be dead but God's grace can and will restore it (Ezek. 36: 26 f.; 37: 1–14). He will make a new covenant with the people thus re-established (Jer. 31: 33 f.).

In so far as both the idea of God and the ideas of sin and grace are radically understood in the Old Testament, its faith is at the same time a hope. Over against it there stands the faith of the New Testament, as the faith that has the fulfilment. For this is the decisive thing in the New Testament and in Christian faith, that God has carried out an eschatological act in Jesus Christ; that in Christ he has forgiven sin, called the new Israel and given it His Spirit. If in Christianity our relation to God is bound to the person of Jesus, this means that we believe in a God who has reconciled the world with Himself through Christ (II Cor. 5: 19). Such an assertion is no mere supplementing of Jewish belief in the one God by a belief in a second divine person. Nor is faith asked to assent to speculation about the deity of Christ and His alleged two natures. Faith in Christ is faith in what God does through Christ.

If in Christ we have the eschatological act of God's forgiveness, then the idea of the grace of God is understood radically. This means that knowledge of forgiveness is not tied to the experience of external, collective or individual destinies. God's grace is pure forgiveness, and this alone makes man new and strong (II Cor. 12: 9). The judgment has transpired, the new æon has begun, all speculation concerning future final events is cut off in principle. God's grace and forgiveness are present exclusively in the message that God has established in the world through Jesus Christ (II Cor. 5: 18 f.). The Word is the light that has come into the world and Jesus is the Word (John 1: 1 f.).

If Jesus is understood in this manner then the demonstration of God's grace given in Him is quite different from the proofs of such grace of which the Old Testament speaks. The latter expects that this grace is to be manifested in the destinies of the Jewish nation. In the grace shown to the nation of the past the individual shares because this history lives on in the present life of the people. Similarly in the future, the individual will share as a member of the nation. But the act of God in Christ is not to be understood as similar to an historical event of Hebrew history from which succeeding generations derive profit. One cannot think of Jesus as of Abraham or Moses, or as the passage through the Red Sea or the Sinaitic legislation. For He is the eschatological act of God which makes an end to all national history as the sphere of God's dealing with man. The message of the forgiving grace of God in Jesus Christ is not a historical report about an event of a distant past, but is the Word of the Church spoken now to each one as God's Word, in which Jesus Christ is present. In this Word God and His forgiving grace encounter man directly. Man is not asked to look at the proofs of God's grace in a past history and then draw the inference that God is gracious and hence will probably also be gracious to him now, but rather God's grace comes to him directly in the Word that is preached. The Church of Christ is not a mere sociological entity that has a history like any other group. It is constituted through the Word of God's forgiveness in Christ and is the fellowship of those who receive the message in faith. It is the eschatological congregation that stands at the end of history, for Jesus Christ is the end of the old æon—He is the final word that God has spoken and speaks. The preaching of the Word is not just another link in the process of universal history, but proceeds, as it were, on a plane outside of or above it. "Old things are passed away; behold, all things are become new" (II Cor. 5 : 17).

This means that for the Christian faith the Old Testament no longer is revelation in the sense that it was and still is for the Jews; and the history of Israel is not for us the history of revelation. The events that had a significance for Israel and were a Word of God to Israel cannot be that to us. Of course, one can say that certain happenings like the Exodus, or the giving of the Sinaitic law, or the building of the temple of Solomon, are of some interest to historical reflection, since they have had an influence on our Occidental history. But in the same sense one can say that the Spartans who fell at Thermopylae fell for us, or that Socrates drank the cup for us. Furthermore, whatever is discernible in any effort to grapple with history, in so far as it shows us the possibilities of human self-understanding, can be seen by the eye of unbelief as well as by that of faith. It therefore does not belong exclusively to the province of faith.

If Israel's history is not a history of revelation for Christian faith we may still ask, however, whether the Old Testament entirely divorced from its history—not as it spoke to Israel but as it speaks immediately to us—can be revelation for Christian faith. It is true that Christian faith can appropriate the Old Testament and can assert that that which is said there, though it was originally only said in a preliminary and limited sense, now has a much fuller and clearer meaning. But this in itself implies that, in so far as the Church proclaims the Old Testament as Word of God, it is merely finding in it what it already knows from the fuller revelation in Christ. This was, indeed, the procedure of the New Testament and primitive Christianity.

It interprets the Old Testament from the eschatological consciousness that all that has gone before was preliminary and limited, and only now receives its deepest meaning.

The form in which the New Testament and early Christianity used the Old Testament was that of Scripture-proof. The understanding of the significance of the fate of Jesus was based on the assertion that it was prophesied and interpreted in advance in the Old Testament. Such Scripture-proof, however, is actually impossible. The supposed prophecies of the Old Testament are partly no prophecies at all and partly contain merely expressions of the Hebrew hope of the future. Most of the relevant passages were understood by the early Christians in a way contrary to their real meaning, in an allegorical manner, to provide the supposed predictions. This shows that faith existed before and without the Scripture-proof: it only discovered and seized upon such proof secondarily. This Scripture-proof played its historical role in the first and second centuries, but it cannot and should not convince anybody to-day. A faith resting on such proofs is no true faith at all.

But is there any other sense in which the Old Testament can be understood as Word of God? One thing is clear: the Old Testament must not be interpreted contrary to its original sense, as historical research can alone determine it. For then it would no longer be the Old Testament that is speaking. All allegorization is mere trifling and nonsense.

If Jesus Christ is God's Word to man, as the eschatological act of forgiveness, then one can say that all words that help to make this Word understandable (in that they bring man into the situation in which he can understand it and unfold the understanding of existence contained therein) are God's Word in an intermediate fashion. In this sense one can still consider the Old Testament, too, to be the Word of God. In it is found the understanding of the law and gospel in their correlation, that is normative for the Christian understanding of existence. In it we have the understanding of man as a lord of creation, as well as the consciousness of sinfulness and the hope of God's grace—all of which are highly important elements of the Christian consciousness as well. We therefore can see ourselves reflected in the Old Testament, just as Paul (I Cor. 10: 11) holds up the generation of the desert wanderings for our instruction.

Faith thus dares to take words not spoken for us and to address them to ourselves in order that we may get an understanding of our own situation and of the Word of Christ that is addressed to it. In this sense one can call the Old Testament "prophecy" and the New Testament "fulfilment".

This *may* be done and is, perhaps, the normal thing to do. But it does not *have* to be done. Even in the New Testament there are differences in this respect. Some writings utilize the Old Testament prominently and others do not. It depends on the particular situation of teacher and hearer. Similarly to-day, the use of the Old Testament cannot be regarded as absolutely essential. But if the Old Testament is still to be given a place in the preaching of the Church as Word of God, then two conditions must be laid down for its use. First, the Old Testament must be taken in its original sense, without any allegorization, though it is permissible to detach it from its original exclusive pertinence to the Hebrew people and its history. Second, the Old Testament must be utilized only in so far as it really prepares the way for the Christian understanding of existence. To the extent that it can be made to do this, one may say that Christ speaks already in the Old Testament.

It seems clear that this approach has enabled Bultmann to discern the human situation in the Old Testament and to compare it with the Christian situation in a more fundamental way than has ever been done. The result is that one realizes both the similarities and the differences in the Hebrew and Christian religion more clearly. In spite of the statements already noted pointing in the conservative direction, his main line of argument is negative in its consequences. The value of the Old Testament lies in the sphere of the intellect—in the insight it gives us into existence, but what insight we really need we can have without it. From the angle of making the Old Testament essential for the Church this view is not as effective as Vischer's. But it has the virtue of requiring no *credo quia absurdum*.

Chapter Fifteen

THE OLD TESTAMENT AS ANTITHESIS TO CHRISTIANITY

IF Vischer, carrying Barth's approach further, attempted to give the Old Testament the immediate value and authority of Word of God that it had for the early Christians; if Bultmann sought to make it meaningful by pointing out that its understanding of human existence was substantially the same as that of the New Testament and that, with proper allowance for the transitory elements, it was still valuable (though not absolutely essential) for Christianity; Hirsch, basically following the radical line in Paul's thinking, views the Old Testament as the very antithesis of Christianity, but instead of rejecting it on that ground holds it to be of value for us because we can only appreciate the meaning of the gospel fully in the light of the contrast it provides.[1] And Hirsch does not merely present this as historical enlightenment but in terms of individual human experience.

For the better understanding of Hirsch's position it should be said that like Herrmann he regards revelation as a thing of the present, not of the past.[2] It is God's speaking to us as apprehended by faith and is in principle of twofold character—law and gospel. The revelation of law confronts us in the reality of human-historical existence. There is an external law and also a deeper law,[3] of the existence of which man is not at first aware. Divine revelation by means of the law is experienced in our passing through both of these spheres. *Per se* the deeper law is present in the external law, but man in his rebellion against God seeks to use the power and responsibility given him by the external law for his own vain purposes, therewith making this law a wall shutting man off from God. But in so doing he gets out of harmony with the deeper law. God in His goodness then reveals the latter to man and forces him to perceive the reality of his life before God. The passage from the one sphere to the other has a negative result in that it leads to the realization that we are under the divine wrath, and can only be considered "revelation" in conjunction with the gospel-revelation, for which it prepares the way. The aforesaid transition is the ultimate secret of all non-Christian religions and at the same time the abiding part of the Christian's sharing in human-historical existence. The Old Testament revelation does not concern us in so far as it is external law (for the latter differs in its expression according to national character and historical circumstances) except in so far as there is a kinship and similarity above all differences between all such legislations. The relation of the Christian to the Old Testament rests on this, that since it also preaches the deeper law it is an instrument endowed with effectiveness by God and operative in Christian history.

In frank fashion Hirsch describes how he arrived at his position on the Old Testament. As a theological student he came in contact with modern critical scholarship and realized to what extent the Old Testament is an Oriental book. He found Old Testament science a rather chaotic thing. It seemed doubtful to him whether it deserved to be included in theology at all. In the instruction he received at the hands of such scholars as Gunkel, Gressmann and von Baudissin he felt that the one thing lacking, from a theological point of view, was any real grappling with the significance of the Old Testament for the Christian. Old Testament study had therefore left him disappointed. It came as a shock to him when, following German graduation requirements, he was directed to prepare for the ecclesiastical authorities a thesis on the question whether one could justly accuse certain Psalmists of self-righteousness and carnal vindictiveness. In investigating this theme he realized that the relevant utterances of the Psalmists were not mere individual aberrations, but flowed from the central idea of the religion of the Old Testament as such. His conclusions opened his eyes all the more to the basic difference existing between Christianity and Judaism on the one hand, and Judaism and the pagan religions on the other hand. Subsequently, incidents of pastoral experience and homiletical exercises conducted with theological students forced him to come to grips with the matter of the Christian religious use of the Old Testament. He found some of Luther's thinking along these lines particularly suggestive. In a controversy with advocates of Bible revision he defended Luther's occasionally Christianizing translation of the Old Testament over against all modern attempts at correction for the purpose of rendering the Hebrew more accurately; such activity, he warned, would bring about either a Judaizing of Christianity or the casting out of the Old Testament from the Christian Bible.[4] Subsequently he was driven to even more extreme conclusions by certain utterances of Kierkegaard, which we shall cite later.[5]

Finally, in the fierce anti-Semitic agitation that arose in the Third Reich after 1933, Hirsch saw that the Old Testament was a serious liability for Christianity and took that situation for an indication that the Church must clarify its position concerning that book. He set forth his views first in a rather incidental manner in a commentary on the Gospel of John,[6] and then more elaborately in the treatise already mentioned.

Hirsch points out that the Old Testament owes its place in the Bible of the Christian Church to three presuppositions: (1) False Christianizing understanding of the Old Testament by the Church; (2) Infiltration of Jewish and pagan ideas into Christianity, corrupting the original purity of the gospel and thus making the toleration of the Old Testament easier; (3) The belief in the permissibility of symbolic, spiritualizing interpretation of such a mysterious book. All of these presuppositions, he asserts, have fallen to the ground to-day. Biblical scholarship makes it impossible for us to read the Old Testament in Christianizing or spiritualizing fashion. Read in its full Hebrew realism, as it must be, the book no longer seems close to us at all.

According to Hirsch, the early Christians really took away the sacred book from the Jews and turned it into a witness for Jesus against Judaism. A worse injury could hardly have been inflicted on the Jews than that. But no honest person to-day can accept the evangelists' proof from prophecy for the Messiahship of Jesus as carrying any weight, or regard the allegories of Old Testament stories which a Paul develops as having any validity. The anti-Semitic agitators sometimes represent Christianity as having perpetrated a fraud in such matters. But that inference is doing the early Christians an injustice. They used the Old Testament as it was customary to use ancient writings in their time—reading more profound meaning into sayings than the context warranted. The Greeks did this with Homer and other writings, and the Jews themselves did it with their canon. If the Christians outdid all others in this procedure, they acted simply as children of their time. But now that we recognize it as false and untenable, we cannot allow it to be continued. Should we not rather give this book back to the Jews and let them keep it exclusively for their own use?

Hirsch then sets forth that the Old Testament can be understood in four different ways. *First*, there is the plain historical meaning. Read in this manner the Old Testament is not a unity, but a book containing a considerable diversity of viewpoints. It is a compilation of a variety of documents from a thousand years of Hebrew history, in which minds great and small, narrow and broad, have left some record of their faith. Even the underlying religion is not a unity but exhibits a process of struggle in which various ways of serving God remain in constant clash. *Secondly*, there is the sense in which it was understood by the Jewish Church from Ezra to the destruction of the second temple in A.D. 70. Here the whole Hebrew religion is conceived of as built on the Mosaic law, though a certain open-mindedness for the elements of divine grace and the humane viewpoints inherent in the Old Testament faith, as well as for the prophetic and apocalyptic possibilities, still remains. This Jewish view of the Old Testament religion is really the only unified one—and, be it noted, it is that of the period that created the Old Testament canon, and hence has a special importance.

The *third* meaning is that which early Christianity gave the Old Testament in its polemic against Judaizing influences. It does not accept the view that the five books of Moses, understood as "law", are the heart and soul of the Old Testament. It takes chiefly three books, Genesis, Isaiah and Psalms, and understands them, in accordance with the artificial scheme of prophecy and fulfilment, as pointing to something above and beyond the religion of the law. So far as the other elements of the Old Testament religion are concerned, there is a vacillation between two different attitudes. In part, there is a rejection of them as belonging to a strange order and mode of worship— an old covenant abrogated by Jesus—and in part acceptance of them as symbols of something not yet realized in the Old Testament, but attained in Jesus. *Fourthly*, there is the meaning given to the Old Testament by late Judaism which has lost its temple and has rejected Jesus. It represents a deterioration of the earlier Jewish viewpoint (the second described above)—a hardening of the legalistic outlook together with a polemical attitude toward all the elements in the Old Testament heritage that rise above and beyond the national and legalistic. "It is the Jewish religion debased toward the demonic[7] by the negation of Christ." The fourth interpretation may be dismissed as decadent, but the first and the second seem legitimate in their sphere. The third, or Christian interpretation, has ceased to be the solely valid one —in fact it has become extremely difficult to maintain it at all. Wherever the Christian Church fails to admit this and gives the Old Testament out as a Christian book, this amounts to a lack of honesty which rightly draws wrath down upon its own head.

The impossibility of holding to the Christian interpretation of the Old Testament has become clear not only because of the destruction of the early Christian proof of the correspondence between prophecy and fulfilment, but also because of a better historical understanding of the Old Testament hope. We discern quite clearly what elements were included in this hope and though we see that a Christian continuity with it is quite possible at some points, we realize that Judaism of the time of Christ could well take the position that Jesus was not the Messiah whom its sacred books had foretold, and that the kingdom He brought was not that for which Israel was waiting. The Christian "fulfilment" of the Old Testament expectations is in reality their disappointment. Christianity has not been able to take over a single word or thought from the Old Testament religion without filling it with a different meaning. We can no longer read the Old Testament to-day without becoming conscious of this essential remodelling, of this constant doing of violence to the Old Testament, of this destruction of the religion of the law by the freedom of the gospel, this steady breaking down of a faith and worship basically bound to racialism by a religion which recognizes only those as God's children that are His in spirit and in truth. We are therefore forced to ask ourselves whether the Old Testament is revelation for us at all. In the Yahweh of the Old Testament there is as yet an unclarified fusion of a Jewish national God who grants His people a kingdom, and the Creator of heaven and earth whose living voice comes to all men. The Jewish national God is as much a thing of the past for us as Odin and other Nordic gods. Only when we understand the Old Testament out of an idea of God that is not really the one meant in its own pages does it speak to us of *our* God.

The right of the early Church to use the Old Testament in a Christian re-interpretation that is not in accord with its real meaning rested on the fact that the Old Testament religion is something unclarified, contradictory in itself and having no possibility of further vitality after Jesus had come. In its ultimate aspect, as faith in the living God, it either had to burst through the historical shell to which it was bound (Judaism)— or die and be mummified in those fetters. The former possibility was realized where the first and second type of interpretation were dissolved or metamorphosed into the third—the Christianizing one—while the latter eventuality occurred where the first two types of interpretation passed over into the fourth— the late Jewish. It was Jesus who ushered in this fateful crisis for the Old Testament religion by partly adopting and partly rejecting it. He adopted it in so far as He regarded Himself as the promised Messiah and found the eternal life that the children of God have through Him expressed in the Old Testament hope of the kingdom. He rejected it in so far as He denied the political Jewish Messianism and divorced the kingdom of God from all national hopes of the Jewish people. In other words, Jesus brought the inner contradiction that was inherent in the Old Testament religion out into the open. With the authority of the Son who knows the Father, He took the ultimate, hidden idea of God that was contained in that religion and revitalized it, and thereby turned it against the whole historical shell that held it. Thus He liberated the grace that lies in man's encounter with the living God from the bonds of servitude to Mosaic Yahwism, when He reached beyond the Jewish national and religious community with His gospel. And this received absolute finality by the cross to which the Jews delivered Him.

The coming of Christianity is thus a revolutionary event within the Jewish religion. And when the Church, in the light of its faith in Jesus, re-interpreted the Old Testament in Christian fashion, it only did again in the sphere of theological reflection what Jesus had already done in the living historical process: it burst through the historical limitations of the Old Testament by availing itself of an eternal and transcendent element that was in it. Nothing remained now for the Jews who had rejected Jesus but to destroy or abandon this eternal and transcendent element of the Old Testament that had been turned against them, and hold fast to the dismal remnants. Of their own volition they thus condemned themselves to a miserable existence as a community that has really died off to the hidden Holy that was theirs.

For a constructive attitude toward the Old Testament, Hirsch thinks that we must have a picture of the Old Testament religion as a whole from another of the aforementioned standpoints.[8] He considers it impossible to create such a picture purely on the basis of the Old Testament understood as modern criticism reads it, or the first standpoint; he believes that it can only be done from the second standpoint, i.e., that of the Jewish community of the Persian and Hellenistic eras, for it was this community that created the canon and thus had a standpoint into which all these books could fit. Neither the presence in the Old Testament of barbaric elements which this community rejected, nor the greater possibilities of earlier prophetic religion which it did not wish to realize, can be decisive when we seek to establish a relation between the Old Testament and the New. Only when we regard the Old Testament as a whole from that Jewish standpoint are these demonic trends and these nobler possibilities seen in their correct perspective.

Hirsch then sketches the main characteristics of this Old Testament Jewish religion as follows. Its most obvious earmark is the fact of its being bound to a cult in which laws of clean and unclean, sacrifice and other observances, and emphasis on a specific holy place are dominant. In this respect this religion does not basically differ from any pagan religion of the old world. Through the cross of Christ this whole cultic theory of religion has been cancelled. There is only one way in which God manifests His presence: in Jesus Christ, raised to be Lord through the cross, and there is only one thing with which God is pleased: with the faith in a gospel that makes us free. There is only one service of God: the living realization of this faith in the service of one's neighbour, out of the strength of the Holy Spirit. We are thus radically cut off from the entire range of religious experience of the people of the Old Testament, and are simply unable, if we are clear as to the implications, to share the outlook of even Isaiah 6 or Psalm 23 or Psalms 42 and 43 without subtracting much of what is basic there.

The second earmark of the Old Testament Jewish religion, according to Hirsch, is the fact that its very heart and soul is an indissoluble relation between the God Yahweh and the Hebrew people. This people is the chosen, and God's glory is manifested in its destiny. Congregation and nation are a unity. This belief is cancelled in the New Testament idea of the kingdom and redeemer. Nation and congregation, civil law and will of God have become separated; the relation of the individual to God is based only on faith. This really makes a large part of the Old Testament entirely useless for us. We cannot identify nationality and kingdom of God, as the Jew could, without becoming unfaithful to the gospel. To apply the Old Testament promises given to Israel to the Church involves spiritualizing and allegorizing them in a manner doing violence to their real meaning. It is obvious, therefore, that the New Testament history is fulfilment of the Old Testament order only in a paradoxical sense really involving the disappointment of the actual expectations.

A third earmark of the Old Testament Jewish religion is its lack of knowledge of the Christian belief in eternal life. It is purely a religion of this life, even though at some high points it does get beyond a mere eudaemonistic approach. The thought of a resurrection which comes to the surface in a few late passages does not change this in principle, but is only a fantastic broadening of the Old Testament position—even the dead are to share in the glory promised Israel. It signified a radical change of outlook when Christianity, by virtue of the death and resurrection of Christ, saw the goal of man in an eternal life that comes to us through death and that transcends this earthly existence. At once the idea of God, as well as the idea of human life, and every thought connected with the divine-human relationship completely changed their meaning. The more fully we appreciate this, the more clearly must we realize how radically different, how unsatisfactory the Old Testament religion really is, but the more we will also see how in some of its utterances this religion is vainly seeking to break through the bars of its cage.

The fourth main trait of the Old Testament Jewish religion is that it is the religion of the law. This does not mean that it has no knowledge of grace and forgiveness, but rather that grace and forgiveness are legally conditioned. Forgiveness is granted the sinner who purifies himself and returns to the state of obedience through penitence; the grace of God is a grace that is zealous to reinstate man in the legal relation. In Christianity this is totally changed. God freely gives the sinner sonship and eternal life. Repentance is simply the reception of forgiveness in faith and is not the work of man but of God. The relation to God in which we are placed by forgiveness, faith and repentance is not that of being bound under a law, but one of freedom from the law in that love which faith begets in the heart. According to the Old Testament, the law and the divine judgments reveal the glory and holiness of God, and forgiveness and grace are related to this glory and holiness; according to the New Testament, the law and the divine judgments are the "strange work" of God (Isa. 28: 21) in which He is concealed, while He is truly revealed in that work which is clearly expressive of Him, in grace and love. Under the influence of Old Testament ideas this true Christian idea of God is usually corrupted and distorted in Christian preaching.

In view of this situation, it is by no means self-evident that the Old Testament should continue to be used by Christianity. If at every point along the line we must be conscious of the sharp divergence of that religion from all we hold dear, why plague ourselves with it at all? Protestant theology has only two reasons to offer for the continuance of the use of the Old Testament. The first is that the Old Testament has not its equal as a document of the History of religion as such, that nowhere in any literature outside of Christianity do we find such clear and powerful expression of the belief in a deity. It is thus held to be useful for religious training, as an auxiliary source. Secondly, the historical connection between the Old Testament and the New Testament is such that the latter cannot really be understood without the former. Hirsch concedes that both of these points rest on correct observation, but holds that they must be brought into relation with the insights previously emphasized. When this is done, it is realized that nowhere is there an alternative to Christianity.

The proper Christian use of the Old Testament, Hirsch thinks, depends on a full realization of the revolutionary character of the situation involved in the coming of Christianity. In the first place, there must be constant and conscious renewal of this grappling with the Old Testament, appropriation of that which is eternal in it, and polemic against that which is intolerable. We must realize that a Christian faith which does not maintain a polemical attitude toward the Old Testament religion actually is unfaithful to Jesus and is drawn into Judaism—putting grace captive beneath the law. In the second place, Christianity must cease putting the Old Testament on a level with the New. For us, the former is definitely of a lower order. The Old Testament has no message for the disciples of Jesus; there is merely a Christian freedom on the part of the disciple of Jesus to illuminate with the word of the New Testament the difficult and mysterious history whereby God prepared the way for the coming of His Son. Of that history the Old Testament is indeed a witness. But there is no possibility for us to proceed from the Old Testament basis to faith in Jesus. From the basis of faith in Jesus, however, we can have a Christian glimpse into the dark mystery of the Old Testament that is both opponent and preparer of the way for the gospel.

In this final line of thought a stimulation by Kierkegaard's viewpoints, of which Hirsch had made mention in connection with the narrative of his own development, becomes apparent. Kierkegaard had experienced a crisis in July 1843 in which his faith in a divine justice in life, as based on the Bible stories of Abraham and Job, broke down completely; from that time on he had had no use for the Old Testament. Hirsch quotes the following:

It cannot be made sufficiently clear or be repeated often enough that Christianity, indeed, does have a relation to Judaism, but, be it noted, of this sort, viz., that Judaism is for Christianity the thing with the help of which the latter makes itself negatively recognizable—that it is its absolute opposite. . . .

This cannot be emphasized enough. For one will find in Christendom, that almost all (if you will) of the 'more pious' aberrations hang together with the circumstance that the Old Testament has been put on the same level with the New Testament instead of this, that the New Testament constantly presupposes the Old in such a way as to make that which is truly its own negatively known. In this sense the New Testament can not be rightly understood without the Old, for this, its absolute opposite, is its (the New Testament's) dialectic criterion and the indication of its spiritual altitude. . . .

But people would much rather be Jews, and sensually cleave to this life—and that, furthermore, with (apparent) divine sanction—than be Christians, that is to say, spirit. . . .[9]

Christianity could not have had any other religion as foreground, for no other makes so definitely, so decisively known by means of negation, what Christianity is, as does Judaism.[10]

Only when it is understood in this fashion, Hirsch claims, does the Old Testament have anything to say to the followers of Jesus Christ. But that is still important enough. For the history of the struggle between a religion of the law and the sonship of God according to the gospel is an everlasting history that is repeated in every life. The moment we think of it as closed, the gospel becomes a new law and the relapse into Judaism is complete. The history of Jesus is the coming of the truth and freedom of the gospel in the destruction of the Old Testament religion and of every other religion of the law, through which the expectation of God on the part of the human heart that cannot live or die out of captive grace, is fulfilled.

Hirsch concerns himself in particular with the use of the Old Testament in preaching, and a large part of his book is devoted to showing what theological reflections should occupy the mind of the preacher in dealing with the Old Testament. He discusses three selected biblical stories: the Sacrifice of Isaac, David and Goliath, and the tale of Jonah, to illustrate how this should be done. In each case the divergence of the Old Testament religious ideas and ideals from Christian ideas and ideals is carefully considered.

Hirsch's points did not find much favour, though they elicited a considerable amount of critical discussion, for his view was too moderate for those who wanted to get rid of the Old Testament and too radical for those who were determined to hold the Old Testament as present Word of God to the Church. His position is a half-way station on the road from Paul to Marcion and can hardly be put outside of the pale of Christian possibilities. If it fails to appeal, Kierkegaard's remark that people would rather be Jews than Christians could well occasion some searching of soul. One must concede to Hirsch, as to Harnack and Delitzsch, a sincere desire to see Christianity attain the full purity inherent in its nature.

From the angle of Old Testament scholarship Hirsch's position is unsatisfactory, of course, in that he views the Old Testament in terms of the Judaism that set up the canon. We prefer to interpret the documents in their full historical reality. If one follows the high-water mark line in the Old Testament there is no such sharp contrast between it and Christianity as is established by Hirsch.[11] But one must concede that on this basis the entire Old Testament cannot be given immediate importance for us. For Hirsch the whole of it has the abiding significance of total contrast.

Chapter Sixteen

RECENT DISCUSSIONS

DURING the years of the Second World War German discussion of our subject was limited by the internal situation and was sealed off from the attention of those in other lands. The desire to use the Old Testament, and therewith also the necessity of justifying its use, came forward prominently in England and in America in this period, as was but natural, since cataclysmic events always make people turn to a book so full of that sort of thing.

Two notable works by American scholars that appeared at the beginning of the fourth decade are not only significant for their learned material, but also because they reveal the urge to bring into focus some sort of positive relationship to the Old Testament. This is the more surprising since both authors are primarily identified with Semitic philology and historical inquiry. Yet W. F. Albright[1] injects into an account of Biblical and Oriental research, as that illuminates Hebrew history, a chapter of discussion of Philosophy of History and dignifies the succeeding chapters with such religious titles as: *"Praeparatio"*, "When Israel was a Child", "Charisma and Catharsis", "In the Fulness of Time". He sees civilization at an impasse similar to that the world had reached in the time of Christ and calls for "a reawakening of faith in the God of the majestic theophany on Mount Sinai, in the God of Elijah's vision at Horeb, in the God of the Jewish exiles in Babylonia, in the God of the Agony at Gethsemane . . ." But his basic categories are sociological.

R. H. Pfeiffer, though he has a long journey through Old Testament literary criticism,[2] devotes separate preliminary chapters to the religious, literary and historical-critical interest in the Old Testament. He puts the religious interest first. He finds that for us moderns the Old Testament is religiously significant in three ways; as inspired Scripture it continues to be norm of faith and conduct for Church and Synagogue; it is the ultimate source of their basic doctrines; it is a unique record of religious progress. The first two points, however, are merely empirical statements concerning the situation created in the past, without investigation of their validity, and the third operates only with one of the "values" provided by the Old Testament.

The year 1944 saw the appearance of a number of works directly concerned with our theme. A distinctly liberal approach marks the discussion of H. F. D. Sparks.[3] He holds that Criticism has shown that the traditional Christian attitude towards the Old Testament stands in need of drastic modification. The phrase "Word of God" as applied to it can no longer mean what it did. Historical investigation has not only demonstrated numerous errors in the Old Testament, but has shown that its writers differed little from their Gentile contemporaries. Science has demonstrated that the Old Testament ideas of cosmology and earth history are "ancient" in their character and unable to give us any enlightenment and that in the light of anthropology Old Testament custom, morality and religion are but part and parcel of a general process; the distinction between "revealed" and "natural" has, therefore, broken down. Thus, although the Old Testament may be the record of a Divine revelation, it cannot be equated with it. We may say if we will that the Old Testament not *is* but *contains* the Word of God, though we should remember as we do so that such a statement is very far from representing what the Church has for centuries maintained.

Sparks then proceeds to ask what value the Old Testament has to-day. Here he turns first to such matters as the literary excellence of the Old Testament and its importance for historians and anthropologists, but he realizes that that is only peripheral. The question is what is its Christian value both for me individually and for the Church. He points to the quandary of the cleric who at ordination is required to state that he "unfeignedly believes all the canonical Scriptures of the Old Testament", when, if he has been properly educated, he cannot possibly believe them in anything like the traditional sense. He expresses the feeling that the Church must come out into the open and declare itself. The three possibilities he sees are: (1) The Church may simply give up the Christian use of the Old

Testament; (2) It may discriminate between different parts and direct the attention of its members to some parts, rather than to others; or (3) It may retain the use of the Old Testament whole and entire, although it will certainly find itself compelled to advance reasons for doing so which are other than traditional.

Sparks rejects the radical solution and finds sentiment largely in favour of the second or moderate solution. He himself, however, espouses the third. He thinks that the bond of union between the Old Testament and the New Testament is so close that it cannot be broken and that Christian people should be taught to appreciate the entire Old Testament historically. Even the Old Testament lessons in the Anglican service must be chosen not particularly, so as to fit in with private or popular religious prejudice, but impartially, so as to illustrate the Old Testament as a whole. A rather heavy yoke of historicism!

A new slant on our subject came in that same year through H. H. Rowley, who introduced the term "relevance" to describe the relation of the Old Testament to ourselves.[4] He notes the change that has recently come over biblical studies—that of attempting to transcend the previous critical approach by seeking the abiding significance of the Bible and in particular its significance for this generation. Thereupon he undertakes to do some theological or religious undergirding by discussing such matters as revelation and inspiration. He finds revelation coming through the organ of human personality and depending for its character not merely on God but on the organ through which it comes. The writers of the Bible were real men with all the imperfections and the individuality that this implies. But God can only reveal Himself perfectly in perfect personality. That is why the Incarnation was necessary for the full revelation of God. It is not just something wholly other than the revelation of God in the Old Testament, but rather its climax and crown.

In setting forth how the failings of some writers of the Old Testament era and their false ideas and false hopes affected their writing, Rowley elaborates on Old Testament passages in which the will or purpose of God was wrongly interpreted. He rejects the accusation that this is taking away from the objective character of revelation and instituting a purely sub-

jective test for what is of God and what is not. He insists
that if God's actions or demands are ever portrayed in the Bible
in a manner inconsistent with His character as revealed in
Christ they are unworthy of Him, and the portrayal is due to
misunderstanding of Him by sincere men whose view was distorted by the eyes through which they looked upon Him. If this
elicits the suggestion that it would be better to discard the Old
Testament, Rowley replies that the latter is necessary for the
appreciation of the New Testament and that rightly understood
it is a great asset to our spiritual life. He rejects the idea of
progress in revelation so far as God is concerned; the progress
was merely in man's ability to understand and receive it. On
the other hand, the formula that the Old Testament is the
record of man's search for God is declared insufficient. Man's
search for God and God's reaching out to man are two sides of a
single process. Even man's capacity to receive Him is itself His
gift.

There are thus divine and human factors woven together in
the Old Testament. It is the record of man's growing experience
of God and progressive response to God. But Rowley feels that
such recognition of the inspiration of the Bible does not make it
final and unchallengeable authority for men. He criticizes the
Protestant Reformers for that view, and thinks the Church
should be vested with authority too. But neither can be the
ultimate authority, which is Christ Himself. "Neither Bible nor
Church can take His place, though both may lead us to Him,
for God is Spirit, and through Spirit He speaks His final Word to
us. Our desire for something lower than Spirit, something more
tangible and certain as we imagine, does not honour Christ, in
whom, and not through whom, is God to be seen."

In subsequent studies Rowley has sought to delineate the
deeper message of the Old Testament, or the Word of God in it.[5]
He sees the Old Testament not merely as preparatory to the
New, but rather the New as supplementary to the Old. Into the
making of the latter went human and divine factors that interpenetrate one another. The message of the Old Testament is
essentially religious, and that in a broad sense, affecting belief,
conduct and worship, in all of which it makes contributions of
enduring worth.

In a lecture of 1949 Rowley discussed the authority of the

Bible.[6] It is his aim here to offer evidence, "valid at the bar
of reason", to support that authority. He rejects such a procedure as mere acceptance of the authority of the Bible on the
authority of the Church. While he concedes that man is not
only reason, and that since he is also guided by instinct and
emotion there is almost certainly a non-rational factor in any
man's belief in the authority of the Bible, he insists it cannot be
wholly non-rational. He then seeks to adduce the arguments
that will approve it to reason. He rejects equating the authority
of the Bible either with inspiration or with the appeal to the
inner witness of the Spirit. "Bibliolatry" is abhorrent to him—
the ultimate authority is in God alone. There were other media
of revelation beside the written word, and none of these is
infallible; hence their authority is never absolute. Even God is
limited by the spiritual maturity and sensitiveness of those He
uses. It is not surprising, therefore, that in the Bible there are
different levels of grandeur and loftiness. Two things are
required of him who would maintain the authority of the Bible:
(1) He must establish a test whereby these levels may be judged.
(2) He must produce evidence that the Bible is the Word of God
even if not all in the same degree.

For the test of the level of inspiration he adduces Christ, who
is the supreme medium of divine revelation (essentially Luther's
famous principle). So far as the Old Testament accords with
the revelation in Christ, it is enduringly valid, but so far as it
falls short of that it is superseded. But that does not mean that
the Old Testament as such is superseded. In developing the
second point, the adducing of evidence that the Bible is the
Word of God, Rowley stresses the idea that the two Testaments
belong together and neither is complete without the other.
However, the hand of God is to be found not so much in the
Bible as in the revelation of which the Bible contains the record.
In that history itself, in the complex of person and event,
promise and fulfilment, he discerns the guidance of God, who
was active in a whole great process that culminated in the death
and resurrection of Christ. The Bible itself is a unity because
reflecting this unified process to which it testifies. He rejects
the idea that by the same type of argument one can also prove
the divine authority of Buddhism. While he finds the latter
religion vindicating Paul's idea that God did not leave Himself

without witness among heathen peoples (Acts 14: 17), he sees here no parallel to the complex of event and personality to which he has drawn attention in the process of divine revelation, but merely the natural spread of the influence of a teacher. It is evident, then, that Rowley's primary support for the authority of the Bible, including the Old Testament, rests on a philosophy of history.

In a recent book Rowley tries to show the dynamic unity of the Bible,[7] and this leads him to make clear that he is not thinking in terms of a purely human development that leaves God out of account, nor yet reverting to traditional dogma leaving reason out of account. He thinks it can be demonstrated, e.g., that the belief of Israel that Moses was called by God and effected the deliverance of Israel through divine aid is a more reasonable hypothesis than any other which discounts the divine element, and he shows in connection therewith what unreasonable assumptions all rival explanations of the Exodus tradition are forced to make. In speaking of the dynamic unity of the Bible Rowley does not mean that everything is on a flat level of authority. He seeks rather the continuity of religious life found in the Biblical record, mirroring as that does a long religious history. As in a personality the ideas of youth and of advancing age are not the same and yet not unrelated, so it is also with the Bible. (Cf. further, p. 280.)

In a study limited to the Prophets the Canadian scholar, R. B. Y. Scott, also pursues the relevance theme.[8] He undertakes "to state in positive terms the meaning and worth of the Hebrew prophetic writings and to indicate their profound importance, as a feature of our religious heritage having the constant freshness of a perennial stream". If the prophets do not speak of our age (and Scott—like Fullerton in 1919—is quite concerned about refuting those who seek in prophecy clairvoyant predictions of events of our own time) "they speak *to* our age because they were faced with crises and thereby can disclose the reality and nature of our crisis when speaking of their own". They are contemporaries of every generation because the truth they declare is permanently valid. What they say has the timeless quality and compelling power of authentic spiritual utterance. No explanation of them is sufficient that does not recognize that through them the Eternal God was carrying out His purpose for the redemption of mankind. Scott describes the prophets as men who had given themselves whole-heartedly to God's service, who were tremendously concerned with social conditions and public issues as marking a spiritual crisis, as having a vivid awareness of God's presence and activities in the turmoil of men's ordinary social life, as showing how their religion and ethic by its effect on the community demonstrates how a religion may become the dynamic and its ethic the directive of social transformation, as declaring the truth that God is a living God and not bound within the tradition of the past.

Scott then undertakes to show that the prophets have relevance to certain areas of life to-day. He quails a little at this assignment because he realizes that "the meaning and the moral imperative of religion for each person is for himself to recognize". But since he finds the prophets speaking largely to the *collective* mind of society and social groups, he is willing to say where he individually thinks he finds them speaking to our time.

The prophets first of all have a great deal to tell us about the nature and meaning of religion. What we learn from them on this score is not superseded (though it is illuminated) by the self-revelation of God in Jesus Christ. It is an essential element in the total Christian understanding of God and His ways. The Bible is *one* literature, and we know more about the God of Christian faith than is found in the pages of the New Testament when, like the evangelists and apostles, we read the prophetic writings with eyes opened by Jesus Christ. The relation between the Testaments, he asserts, is not simply one of succession and development, but one of interrelationship and vital continuity. The prophets, Scott then shows, make it plain that religion and ethical behaviour must form a unity. They enunciate man's social responsibility before God. They instruct us in the right evaluation of organized religious life, protecting us against its corruption and abuse and suggesting that the ends of worship are more important than the forms. They teach us that religion is not a specialized activity but a quality and attitude in all activities. Their relevance for religion in its personal aspects is to be found in what they *were*, rather than in what they said; the witness of such authentic saints carries stimulus.

In the second place, Scott finds the prophets having an importance for theology both because their thought is necessary to the understanding of certain major terms of New Testament theology and because the peculiar intensity of their apprehension of the ways of God demands the direct attention of the modern theologian. When we think of God in personal terms, when we speak of sin and evil, of the meaning of history, and of eschatology, we cannot ignore the thoughts of the Hebrew prophets. In connection with revelation, Scott mentions deposits "remaining from moments of it, to be added to the sum total of the knowledge of God and man".

In discussing the significance of the prophets for the work of the preacher Scott stresses their suggestiveness for messages on social justice, national responsibility, religious interpretation of historic events and on evangelism. Then he speaks of the relevance of the prophets for the cultural crisis of to-day. What Israel's prophets said long ago, as they condemned the manner of this world and pointed men to the city of God, is directly and profoundly relevant for us. The democratic struggle—the prophet's part in the spiritual ancestry of democracy—is especially singled out. They contributed the concept of a society where all had an equal right to justice and where authority was subject to a divine law of righteousness. They proclaimed the covenant society where God's way would be realized, and set before men's eyes the hope of a better day when all men would be delivered from want and fear and war. Scott gives up the idea that what the prophets say is directly applicable:

> One cannot simply summarize and catalogue their insights and consider them disposed of when their relevance to one set of circumstances has been suggested. The dynamic of their message is not so easily exhausted, nor can its intrinsic authority be claimed for all that seems to follow from the attempt to apply it at one particular point. What really counts is a first-hand knowledge of the prophetic records, the recognition of their formative influence in our religious tradition, and their potential spiritual power over men's minds to-day. Finally we need the capacity constantly to discern afresh their relevance to the human situation of this and every age.

Since it takes an especial capacity to see this relevance it obviously cannot be made generally valid, but is a matter of faith.

A further and even more resolute bringing forward of the Old Testament came from another American quarter in that same 1944.[9] Here G. E. Wright saw not so much a relevance in the Old Testament as a challenge, placing on us a demand of decision (therein revealing an impact of modern existentialism). In accord with old Calvinistic tradition he conceives of the (Protestant) Bible as one book, and holds that there is such a thing as a "biblical religion", and that the Old Testament contributes much to it that is not duplicated in the New. He complains, furthermore, that in the last century the Protestant Church has become increasingly a New Testament Church. One reason is that the New Testament is more accessible—it takes time, study and much concentration to discover the Old Testament revelation. But even more to blame, he thinks, is the modern theology since Schleiermacher and Ritschl. They have stressed the importance of ideas. "This belief misses the really essential point about biblical revelation: that is, that God has made himself known not primarily in ideas, but in events."

Wright takes the message of the first chapter of Isaiah, giving a transposition of it into the contemporary situation of World War Two. In analysing the effect of Isaiah's message on the modern reader, Wright accuses him of evading the issue— whether there is in Isaiah an actual word for us from the Lord, the Creator and ruler of the Universe. By pointing to the faults and foibles of the past we avoid those disturbing claims which the words of the prophet might have if taken seriously as spoken by God to us. But there is something within us, he asserts, that tells us Isaiah is right in his basic assertions. Where, however, is the line to be drawn between what is man's word and God's Word? Wright turns for suggestions to Jesus' use of the Old Testament—taking it as authoritative and yet feeling free to criticize it—and the similar attitude of Luther. Quoting the latter's dictum that we ourselves must decide as to whether something is God's Word and that God must confirm it to our heart, he says, "in other words conscience is between us and the Bible." He also invokes Calvin's thought that the Word must be confirmed by the internal testimony of the Holy Spirit. He infers from all this that there is an actual claim of God on us through the Old Testament. But we have to find the Word behind the words. The Word behind the words, however, is discerned only by those who are conscious of the human predicament and examine the facts of life as did the prophets, and are brought to such an attitude of prayer as Jer. 14: 7–9. But he finds it necessary to reject the view of those who, in dealing with the Old Testament, want to leave the historical situation aside entirely. The Word behind the words, he reiterates, is one that is made concrete and vivid in historical events.

In surveying the Old Testament literature Wright discovers that everything was written in states of crisis, not unlike those facing us. History, he says, is no mere story of human activity to be viewed and dissected, but the arena of the creative activity of the living, righteous, holy God. He asserts that the prophets were not interested in saying anything novel, but in confronting the people with the will of God for that particular moment of crisis. He lays down two conditions for understanding them: (1) That we be willing to stand with them at their point of vantage and experience the challenge and immediacy of God's will for that moment; (2) That we endeavour to stand in our own history and strive to find the Word of the Lord for us now. For we too are in a situation of crisis and our task is to find the Word of the Lord. There is thus a kinship between us and the Old Testament (cf. further, p. 279 f.).

Our theme has also been of particularly vital concern to several scholars approaching it from a New Testament angle. Thus M. Burrows in a recent book[10] on Biblico-theological topics sets forth his views on the problem of Scripture authority at the very outset. In general he adheres to the liberal position. He finds that the modern mind cannot accept any external compulsion in matters of belief. We cannot return to the Catholic principle of religious authority, but dogmatic assertion that the Bible is the Word of God is beset with so many difficulties that to assert it without reasonable explanation can only drive people away from the Church, even though winning fanatical approval from narrow-minded groups. He sees the solution in a properly qualified acceptance of the Bible as authority. He grants that it may seem to make the matter too involved to be worth the trouble, but answers the objection by asserting that to set up any other principle of authority,

whether in philosophy, science or in immediate spiritual experience or intuition, also requires explanation and justification.

In proceeding along this line Burrows first points out that in
the Bible itself authority is more a matter of what must be *done*
than of what must be *believed*, and that man is judged in it
according to his obedience or disobedience to the revealed will of
God. God's authority resides in His superior knowledge. We
accept the authority of superior knowledge everywhere in
human relations. The authority of what is revealed resides in
the fact of revelation itself, if only we can recognize it as such
and be sure of its authenticity. But how can we do that?
Burrows infers that the authority of the Bible depends upon
inspiration. But he then is at pains to show that inspiration is
not the divine origin of what is revealed or the process by which
it is communicated. Rejecting the claims of that nature made
by older theologies, he asserts that the only tenable ground of
assurance for the authenticity of the revelation given in the
Bible is its own inherent truth and worth. By and large, he
finds, it is not the wording of the final record (which has suffered
corruption and change) that is inspired; the men behind it were
inspired. This leads him to examine the way in which revelation
was received and here he distinguishes between "general" and
"special" revelation. In the end, however, this raises the
anxious question whether the inspiration given such individuals
in the past is true. He does not hold that it would be fatal to
Christian faith if it could be shown that all revelation came
through the same means and processes as other knowledge, so
that there were no such thing as direct inspiration. The only
final proof is the test of experience. Since we cannot wait for a
conclusive demonstration, we must commit ourselves by an act
of faith without such knowledge. This is tantamount to saying
that the only basis of assurance is the witness of the Spirit with
the believer's own spirit.

Fully aware of all the change and diversity in the Old and
New Testaments, Burrows yet perceives a unity in the Hebrew
Christian tradition. The focus and principle of that unity for
Christians is faith in Christ; everything is to be judged by its
relation to the truth as it is in Him. Essentially, therefore,
Burrows grants only a partial authority to the Old Testament in
line with Luther's principle (cf. further, p. 276).

From the New Testament angle, too, A. G. Hebert has taken a particular interest in our subject. He returned to it in 1947 after dealing with it in 1941.[11] In the earlier book he already showed a fondness for mystical ideas. No one, he held, can interpret the Old Testament aright unless he takes seriously the two dogmas on which it rests: (1) that Yahweh the God of Israel is real in a sense in which none of the other gods is real; (2) That He has chosen Israel to be His people. The consequences of this would seem to be that we must all become Jews and pray only to the God of Israel. But here mysticism provides a ladder of escape. In the light of the fact of Christ's coming the Old Testament texts have taken on a fuller and richer meaning. In Christian use, for instance, the Psalms must be understood in the light of their fulfilment in Jesus the Messiah. Zion and Jerusalem, the temple and the throne of David, are all to be mystically interpreted. Hebert likes to think of the Old Testament as a whole and yet not by itself but with the New Testament as its continuation. "While the Old Testament is divine it is incomplete; the several writers are incomplete when taken as individuals and separated from the whole which is Israel; and Israel as a whole is incomplete, apart from its fulfilment in the Messiah and His Ecclesia." For the Old Testament he claims inspiration though not inerrancy. "The Old Testament scriptures are imperfect because the writers can only apprehend in diverse ways various judgments of his truth; they are true because they nevertheless apprehend it."

The newer work of Hebert maintains this same position, but gives more room to the thought of a History of revelation. The Bible is the book of the divine kingdom. Through it there runs the theme of God's conflict with all that militates against His glory—an obvious echo of Calvin's emphasis on this attribute. Hebert sees the clash between the Church and secular forces going on in Israel of old as in Christendom to-day. The Old Testament is authoritative because of its relation to the divine kingdom (*a*) as historical record of its establishment; (*b*) as giving teaching about God and the way of His spiritual service which His people learned in the course of its history; (*c*) as declaring the end to which the divine purpose was and is moving. The book is viewed as having a function in the history of revelation, and mystical interpretation, which he would differentiate from the more arbitrary allegorical exegesis, enables us to use it as authority. Imperfections in the record are acknowledged, but these are believed to lie on the cultural level; behind and below this there is a deeper level on which its teachings are profoundly right. On the whole God has spoken in and through the record. We thus find continuing here the substance of the views of a Rothe or Hofmann.

In the same year another New Testament scholar, C. H. Dodd, writing of the biblical problem in general, was likewise compelled to think of the place of the Old Testament.[12] He differentiates between an Old Covenant and a New Covenant. The New Covenant is prior to the Church, but the Church is prior to Scripture, and of course, the same thing applies in the case of the Old Covenant: the Jewish Church is prior to Old Testament Scripture. Essentially he restates Rothe's famous definition of the Bible as "record of revelation". He holds that some of the Old Testament writings suggest that the earlier covenant was inconclusive, but he shies away from admitting that the New Covenant supplements, modifies or supersedes it; he asserts rather that it fulfils it. This means that the Old Testament is to be read in view of that for which it prepared the way, and that the New is not to be understood apart from the Old. In considering the Biblical history he finds it related at every point to the fundamental reality which lies behind all history and human experience—the living God and His Kingdom. There is furthermore a supra-historical factor entering history and directing it—revelation or the Word of God. God makes an approach to man in a way commanding his attention and elicits a response of some kind, positive or negative. In proportion as man responds the Word proves a creative factor in history. Dodd finds that the inspiration of prophets is essentially a power of insight into a situation as expressing a meaning which is God's meaning for His people. In the Old Covenant the principle of particularism works itself out to a logical conclusion; in the New Covenant Christ represents a fresh, universalistic approach of God to man. The perfect meeting of God and man toward which the whole course of the earlier history was tending is at last realized in the unity of a single personality—Jesus Christ.

This account of the views of representative professionals of biblical scholarship on both sides of the water will suffice to characterize the main lines of thought. There have been, of course, some with much more secularized standpoints, such as S. A. Cook[13] in England, or I. G. Matthews[14] in America, on whose approach we need not elaborate here. We likewise can mention only in passing such books as those of Cunliffe Jones, G. E. Phillips, J. Woods, and the volume edited by A. Richardson and W. Schweitzer.[15] Taken together they reveal impressively the degree to which the English-speaking religious world is being agitated by this topic.

A final glance at the German scene is in order. The destruction of National Socialism through the outcome of the war liberated the German Church from threatened domination by elements opposed to the Old Testament, and again allowed the free operation of all shades of opinion. In continuation of the trend existing before and during the war, there has been a pronounced effort to hold the Old Testament for Christianity as source of a living message by means of Christianizing interpretation. While the extreme devices of Vischer find no favour among leading scholars, some are, nevertheless, utilizing typology in their search for ways of expressing the unity of faith that binds us to the Old Testament saints, and a commentary series dedicated to that viewpoint is being contemplated.[16] Several significant studies from that quarter will receive attention in the next chapter.[17]

Chapter Seventeen

TOWARD A BIBLICAL THEOLOGY?

THE modern search for the meaning of the Old Testament lent a fresh importance to the discipline known as Old Testament theology.[1] For it is in this field, if anywhere, that such a meaning must be vindicated and set forth. It had frequently been noted—we fear not without some irony—that it has chiefly been a subject for posthumous publications. The German books on it by Hävernick (1848), Schultz (1869, 5th edn. 1896, E.T. by J. A. Paterson, 1892), Oehler (1873–74, 3rd edn. 1891, E.T. by G. E. Day, 1883), Kayser (1886), Riehm (1889), Dillmann (1895), and the English one of A. B. Davidson (1904), all appeared when their authors could no longer be called to account.

Before the last but one of this series of voices from the grave was heard, one of the leaders of the great critical school, B. Stade, gave a circumspect discussion of this discipline.[2] Much of what he said he repeated more briefly and sought to apply in his great book of 1905.[3]

He views Christianity as standing in historical continuity with Judaism. The appearance of Christ presupposed the existence of a set of religious and ethical ideas that had been formed in Hebrew history. Jesus connected up His own attitude with the religious faith and ethical ideals of His time and claimed to be the fulfilment of the earlier development. His message deepened the Jewish faith and ideals and remoulded them—partly even turning them into their very opposite—so that they became filled with new content; but He did not create a fresh set of religious and ethical concepts. The new thing in Christianity is the significance of Jesus Himself as perfect revelation of the Father and as abiding mediator. Jesus could set up His own authority over against that of the law, and therewith His message steps forth out of the framework of the Old Testament. New also is the life in God that He demonstrated to His followers and the valuation placed on service to one's neighbour. The Jewish Messianic conceptions do not exhaust the range of His consciousness of self. But since they formed the starting-point for it they may be viewed as the historically conditioned form in which the new thing represented by Christianity had to appear in order to become effective.

For Stade, "Biblical theology of the Old Testament" is the discipline dealing with the intellectual and spiritual history leading up to Christianity. He rejects speaking of "theology of the Old Testament" or of "History of the Old Testament Religion", because this leaves the New Testament out of consideration, while "Biblical theology of the Old Testament" preserves consciousness of the fact that theology is interested in this subject from the angle of New Testament Christianity. For while an interest in the preparatory history of Christianity can be assumed for all Christians and thinking men in general, that fact only vindicates the subject as a branch of general study and does not yet prove it to be a necessary part of *theology*. The justification for its inclusion in this department arises from the needs of the Church. The latter requires that the task envisioned above be carried out. For it has at all times, since it rejected Marcionism, held that the revelation of God which appeared fully in Jesus Christ was in some sense already present in germinal form in the Old Testament. The presupposition that the Old and New Testament revelations belong together and are of a similar nature has never been given up, nor has the claim of the earliest Church that the Old Testament revelation concerns the Church and was divinely intended for it been abandoned. It is a desideratum for the Church that this be justified theologic-ally. At the same time it is also necessary that the uniqueness of Christ and His revelation, which the Gnostics had emphasized to the point of rejecting the Old Testament, be affirmed and safeguarded, lest the higher nature of the New Testament revelation and the new element in Christianity, as well as the Christian insight into the nature of the objectives of salvation, be dimmed. Both needs are met by a "Biblical theology of the Old Testament" when it proceeds to discover the germs of Christian thinking in the Old Testament and follows their evolu-tion, and yet at the same time sets forth also the relative distance separating the Old Testament revelation from that of the New.

The value of a Christian theological discipline, says Stade, is measured by the extent to which it can be used for the nurture of the new life that has gone forth from Jesus Christ. Only the revelation of the Father in and through Him can be law and doctrine for Christianity. That alone, therefore, is strictly speaking the subject of instruction in the Church. But ever since the beginning of Christianity—indeed before there was a New Testament—the Church has used the Old Testament, and no sensible person would want it to stop doing so, the more since it excellently suits the religious-educational purpose through the manifold nature of its insights and its vividness of language.

But while the fact that the Old Testament was preparatory to Christianity justifies its use in the Church, a prerequisite for such use is its Christianization; it must be understood from the angle of the New, its contents must be raised to the level of the religious and ethical ideals of the New Testament. Whatever cannot endure this process of Christianization must be left aside. For the historical understanding of the Old Testament is not the object of the Church's religious instruction, but rather its Christian understanding. Conversely, however, the historical interpretation is dominant for Biblical theology of the Old Testament as a subject of scholarly study, and the first prerequisite for a successful performance of its task is rigid adherence thereto. Thus the results of Biblico-theological study of the Old Testament would seem to be meaningless for the Church! But that is only seemingly the case. The Christian minister or teacher cannot successfully raise the Old Testament up to the Christian level and use it as means of religious instruction without damage to the Church's religious and ethical ideals, unless he is aware of the gulf that separates the two Testaments and is able to gauge its breadth properly. This is what the subject of Biblical theology of the Old Testament teaches us. By accurately portraying the development of religion under the Old Covenant it sharpens our perception of the higher religious and ethical level attained in Christianity. Whoever is not yet conscious of the fact that the contents of the Old Testament are not immediately applicable in the instruction of the Church, but only in so far as they can be interpreted on the Christian level, will become so through this study, and thus will be enabled to avoid spreading sub-Christian thinking in the Church through the medium of the Old Testament.

Stade has here put his finger on the crux of the problem. But if he thought that the individual equipped with "historical" Old Testament knowledge was able to Christianize the Old Testament by himself without some guidance he was pre-supposing a greater capacity than most human beings have. The question is: how can it be done? Here Stade leaves us without help, presumably considering that to be the concern of "Practical Theology". In his own book he produced what essentially was a history of the Hebrew religion. The title of Kautzsch's work, which echoes Stade's, was more properly given in its English translation *The Religion of Israel*; for it was hardly a Biblical Theology.[4] Indeed, under the impact of the history of religions the subject of that name virtually expired and Gunkel pronounced a death sentence upon it.[5]

The problem came to life again, however, in the 'twenties. Symptomatic of this was Steuernagel's plea for the usefulness of Old Testament theology as a purely historical subject, supple-mentary to the History of the Hebrew religion.[6] But there were deeper forces at work than that. An awareness of them prompted a new discussion of the matter by Eissfeldt.[7] He declared that it was futile to attempt to mix the historical study of the Hebrew religion with treatment of it from the angle of a subjective, living faith, as the advocates of "spiritual exegesis" and of the Dialectic theology were demanding. The historical study of this religion can never get beyond relativity and immanence, while faith, impressed with the absolute and transcendent, has not the means of comprehending the Old Testament religion as a historical entity. A theological approach artificially contracts the manifold nature of the historical phenomena, while the historical approach makes shallow the depth of the revelation which faith finds there by setting it side by side with similar religious phenomena. The two ways of looking at the subject belong to different planes and correspond to two different functions—knowledge and faith. Knowledge in the sense of historical inquiry is active; faith on the other hand knows itself seized by an eternal. Both of these approaches have to be kept separate.

The Old Testament was formed by factors of faith, and our

present faith ever and anon finds some aspect of the Old Testament religion replete with new meaning; currently the irrational and "demonic" (see p. 176) elements in it strike us most forcefully and so the historical approach, too, turns to explore them in its objective way. Faith thus stimulates knowledge and presents it with fresh themes. On the other hand knowledge, on its part, can aid and unburden faith. The life of a single generation can only find a relationship to a portion of the religion of the Old Testament. That book is too rich for it to be otherwise. Thus the prophets were unappreciated for 1800 years; then in the nineteenth century their greatness dawned on us and latterly has been very much appreciated. Who can deny that it was historical research that brought this insight? On the other hand, historical study has unburdened faith by pointing out to it the elements of the Old Testament that are below the average spiritual and moral level. These elements at the same time are not just criticized or condemned by us but are understood in the light of historical conditions.

Eissfeldt then points out how dangerous it is to make faith the criterion of history. The Old Testament gives us examples of interpretations of history governed by faith—the Deuteronomistic, with its attempt to construe history after a pattern of retribution, or that of the Chronicler who sees retribution governed by the conduct of the Hebrew kings in cultic matters. These were illusory beliefs. Historical study shows how better and deeper insights overcame these errors in the course of the Hebrew religious development.

The historical study of the Hebrew religion, Eissfeldt holds, must be carried on objectively in the interest of faith itself. It must confine itself to the Old Testament and not look over into the New. If in some situations the Old Testament religion points beyond itself, one must leave the matter open whether the New Testament and Christianity represent the fulfilment. The discipline of the History of the Old Testament Religion can thus be dealt with by men of all faiths. The theological approach, on the other hand, portrays what in the Old Testament is God's Word for the observer and for the Confession in which he stands (for one's judgment will always be conditioned by one's Confession). Such a presentation is thus limited in its usefulness to the author's own group. Little inter-confessional co-operation is possible here; only the one view or the other can finally prevail "in demonstration of Spirit and power".

Since the subject of Old Testament theology must describe the revelation faith has found and finds ever anew in the Old Testament, Eissfeldt says, it cannot take on the form of a historical presentation, for faith is concerned with the present. Revelation is above the category of time. Hence the presentation must be systematic, but not in the sense of methodically developing the material from central positions, but rather in a loci type of arrangement. Eissfeldt sees an author of such a work dealing with those matters in the Old Testament that to him are living truth. The execution will therefore be influenced by the central religious standpoint. That need not mean, however, that the Christian must seek for every Old Testament belief a fulfilment in the New Testament. There are numerous thoughts in the Old Testament that can stand by themselves and be revelation for us, the more since there often is no equivalent for them in the New Testament. In such cases the Old Testament takes on a co-equal role of authority rather than its usual subordinate one. While the History of the Hebrew religion and Old Testament theology move on different planes, the lines converge in infinity; here and now they can only form a unity in that one and the same person can treat of both.

A friendlier attitude toward the appeal for a more "theological" viewpoint in Old Testament theology was shown in W. Eichrodt's reflections on this subject.[8] But he keeps both feet planted in the historical sphere, saying that Old Testament scholarship should not be burdened with considerations of true or false—that being the prerogative of philosophy or of Dogmatic theology. Staerk had already quite a number of years before tried to place the waif Biblical theology on the doorstep of Dogmatic theology.[9] But Eichrodt saw a legitimate objective for Old Testament scholarship in trying to determine the real nature of the Old Testament religion, setting forth its structure and the inter-relationship of its component elements, and held that to be a systematic task (the term seemingly not used normatively, but rather in reference to arrangement). In the fulfilment of it the permeation of the approach by a philosophically influenced refinement of method is necessary. One must be fully conscious of the extent to which subjective factors are operative, not only in the choice of object, but in the selection the historian is forced to make in arranging the phenomena, and in the pragmatism according to which he construes. There is, too, the matter of the individual's inner predisposition to stress or favour one element or another for which he has an appreciation that some other individual does not have. On the other hand there is a rising awareness among all historians of the fact that the only possibility of bringing history to life lies in our appropriating it from some definite standpoint. Actually there is no historical science without a Philosophy of history. He finds that for the Christian Old Testament scholar the goal lies in the New Testament, and therefore it must be the task of Old Testament theology to select and arrange its material in a manner serving the end of understanding the latter. Therewith he, partly at least, confirms the objective already marked out, though not carried through, by Stade.

The impact of Comparative Religion on Old Testament science increased with the revival of Phenomenology of Religion —the study of the different types of religion and of religious ideas; a subject originally developed by Hegel. It was possible now to deal with it in the light of a far greater factual knowledge than was available in Hegel's time and in a modern realistic manner.[10]

Such study raised the question of what is distinctive or different about a given religion, and of the structure of its piety. For the case of the religion of the Old Testament the matter was taken up by F. Baumgärtel in 1932.[11] He is interested in grasping the distinctive nature of this religion as a whole. He sees it as a living relationship between man and God that is progressively purified with the march of time and relieved of those limitations which adhered to it—the process of course only finding completion in Christianity. The theme was also dealt with briefly by J. Lindblom in 1936 in a symposium devoted to the Old Testament.[12] In his opinion not every religion can be examined by the same method. For determining the nature of the Old Testament religion he recommends finding in it a certain idea of such importance that everything else can be made to depend on it, and which then will characterize the religion and differentiate it from all others. Hänel had, indeed, attempted to do this by means of the Holiness concept (p. 194). But Lindblom thinks that this idea is too widespread and too variable to suffice. He would choose the idea of God as such. He favours a systematic treatment (and thus is basically thinking of Old Testament theology). But he rules out any discussion of values or of the normative nature of the ideas from such a treatment. The Old Testament scholar should leave that to Dogmatic theology and content himself with preparing the historical materials that can be of service to the latter discipline. That one's personal religious convictions can give one a better appreciation for this or that is conceded, but that fact must remain in the background.

Lindblom finds that the proper systematization of the Old Testament ideas in a manner doing justice to reality and under organic viewpoints (in other words Old Testament theology) is the crowning task of Old Testament study. He develops in brief manner the Old Testament idea of God with due consciousness of existing similar concepts in other ancient religions. He then compares the Old Testament idea of God with the New Testament idea. Their organic connection and unity cannot be dissolved, but at the same time there are marked differences. He illustrates that from the divine love. In the New Testament God's love is turned toward the sinner; in the Old Testament the object of the divine love is Israel. This hangs together with the fact that in the Old Testament God is primarily King while in the New He is Father. But in spite of such differences many elements in the Old Testament idea of God continue to have significance for the Church. That He is the Creator protects us against dualism. That He is the God of history shields us against all forms of false mysticism. That He is transcendent, personal Will is a bulwark against pantheism. That He is holy love and holy anger prevents the abuse of the divine grace and patience. That He is leading the world to a goal preserves us from any static conception of history or any view leaving Him out of consideration in this process.

The theological task of Old Testament study was discussed by A. Weiser in the same 1936 symposium.[13] He links up with the widespread and growing consciousness that all theological disciplines must form a living unity and that true theology is only possible within the Church. One can approach the matter either from the broader angle, assigning to Old Testament study its place and objectives in the light of the whole sphere of theology, or one can start out from the Old Testament field itself and see what tasks present themselves. The second course is that chosen by him.

He sees exegesis as the basic task. It must make the Old Testament speak as it was understood (or ought to have been understood) by its contemporaries. One can only talk about an Old Testament scholarship if this historical-critical work is conscientiously done. But in which direction is the original meaning of the Old Testament to be sought? What goal does the determination of that give to exegesis? Direction and objective must flow forth from the object itself; there must be no employment of extraneous principles, such as was the case in orthodoxy when the Old Testament was looked on as a repository of proof-texts for Christian doctrines, or as prevailed in nineteenth-century liberal thought when that book was construed according to evolutionistic principles. The question is: what in any given section is the real viewpoint and spirit of the writer, his "understanding of self"? One has not yet adequately understood the Song of Deborah, for example, when one derives from it information about Hebrew tribal history and archæological matters; the real life of the thing lies in its religion and its distinctive character in this respect must be discerned. Out of the study of the whole Old Testament in such a manner there will arise an insight into what is generally characteristic of the totality. Weiser finds that two things can be singled out in describing the general understanding of existence prevailing in the Old Testament: (1) There is a dynamic view of reality running through it; (2) There is a theological way of looking at men and events—everything is regarded as from God and unto God. The Old Testament understanding of truth and reality is not a knowledge of what exists somewhere and is discerned by reason, but knowledge of reality gained in the moment of action or of some happening. It is a decision of faith in which man is confronted with ultimate reality through the act of God. It is thus that the Old Testament understands reality and it is this understanding of it that makes the preservation of that literature as Holy Scripture comprehensible. It testifies to the ages that God is present in history; it speaks of the divine reality confronting man and of human reality before God.

Old Testament study, Weiser asserts, must lead to this kind of an understanding of the Old Testament. As a theological task its concern is with man's relation to God and therein it differs from every other kind of anthropology. We are not mere spectators, facing what we see in a neutral manner, but are somehow drawn in and affected by what we read. In the dimension of divine-human relations there is no other possibility of real knowledge—in other words knowledge and faith are correlates. Since in the Old Testament the dynamic understanding of reality and the theological angle interpenetrate each other, a theological understanding of the Old Testament of the sort indicated is alone adequate to the situation and therewith also becomes the true scholarly approach.

In differentiating his position from others, Weiser discusses historicism such as that represented by Gunkel on the one hand and the idea of a systematic Biblical theology on the other. He insists that there is a subjective element operative in the so-called objective historical approach and that, since it evades the divine claim the Old Testament places on us, it really fails to be objective. For to be objective is to let the object confront us with its own understanding of being. Faith thus plays a decisive role in understanding. And he adds: only as our own existence is involved, as our own fate is in process of decision, do we understand the concerns of the Old Testament. But we are by no means to take the historical concreteness out of the ancient situations. Our task is merely to see in the situation in which we ourselves stand those relations between man and God which are the same for us as they were for the men of the Old Testament. It is not in our power, however, to achieve this for every Old Testament passage. At different times we get a better understanding of different portions of that book.

A subject of "History of the Hebrew Religion", by ruling out the question of valid truth, cannot meet the theological need. Can biblical theology do it? Weiser then asks. He believes that in this discipline a systematic treatment of Old Testament ideas is foisted on the Old Testament in accordance with Greek thought. The Old Testament knows no "doctrine" of God; the reality of God is experienced here in ever new and concrete happenings. It is contrary to the dynamic understanding of reality found in the Old Testament to systematize this subject-matter, though he concedes that there may be a certain peda-gogical value in such a marshalling of scattered facts. The Old Testament, however, puts the systematizer to shame or else is put to shame by him. Weiser's thought is that the theological task should be borne by exegesis. It is interesting to recall in passing that Barth was able to convey his original message through that channel.

In a more recent paper[14] Weiser has reaffirmed and amplified these views. He concedes that the full revelation of God does not come to us in our grappling with the Old Testament. The more deeply we look into its truths the more riddles and open questions remain. We can suffer with the men of the Old Testament and feel that like them we are *en route* to a goal still not attained. But at the same time we have an advantage over them—a source of added life and light that they do not have: the knowledge of Jesus Christ. One thing that the Old Testa-ment shows us is our sinfulness and need of redemption; the New Testament gives us the certainty of redemption through the cross.

As though to prove that scholars could publish on the subject of Old Testament theology ere they die, no less than three books of this nature appeared on the scene[15] in 1933–39.

The first was that of E. Sellin,[16] who resolutely divested the subject of all those antiquarian elements in the Old Testament that no longer have any importance for us and concentrated on the line that found its consummation in the gospel of the New Testament. This narrowing of scope makes it understandable that he felt the need of prefacing the systematic treatment with a separate account of the history of the Hebrew Religion. In his systematic part he speaks of the "teachings" of the Old Testa-ment on various topics.

L. Köhler, whose work is noteworthy for its penetrating detail, attempts to bring together the ideas of the Old Testa-ment which are, or could be, of theological importance and puts them under the heads of Theology, Anthropology and Soteri-ology.[17] The cult of Israel is treated at the end of the anthro-pology under the rather artificial construction "the self-redemption of man". He, too, thus basically follows an intellectualistic approach. For Köhler the Old Testament material is authoritative revelation wherever it fits organically into the whole Christian picture. To him the central position of the Old Testament is the assertion of God's majesty—His absolute supremacy over the world and man; he finds that viewpoint operative everywhere.

W. Eichrodt, whose attempt is on the largest scale of the three, sees a constant element in the Old Testament religion undergirding all its variations.[18] His purpose is to understand the structural unity of this Religion and interpret its deepest meaning both with consideration of its ancient environment and its connectedness with the New Testament. No extraneous scheme is thrust on the Old Testament material; the substance is developed out of the Old Testament consciousness of the God of Israel who shows Himself to be the God of the world and of the individual as well. The Covenant idea is made central—a point open to criticism. In presenting the materials the historical principle is utilized, and the book basically remains within the sphere of historicism.

A fourth major attempt to produce an Old Testament Theology—that of O. Procksch—did not appear in print until 1950, but is of earlier origin.[19] His general approach has already been set forth (p. 193 f.). He begins with a "Theology of History", taking a Christocentric view of history and of the Old Testament in the spirit of von Hofmann, and in this way tries to make the Hebrew canon relevant for the Christian. In the systematized part of the book, which follows a historical sketch of the religious development, he attempts to group the materials on each topic as far as possible around the prophetic personality chiefly associated with it.

A novel treatment of the Old Testament material in conjunction with and prefatory to New Testament concepts came from the pen of the American scholar M. Burrows.[20] The procedure necessitates selection, of course, and does not permit giving a compact and vital picture of the Old Testament religion such as can be hoped for from a book concentrating its attention on the earlier part of the canon. The attempt brings to mind the somewhat related objective of a "theology of both Testaments" suggested by G. Bertram.[21] This scholar has set forth the degree to which the Greek translation, the authoritative Old Testament for the Church of the days when our canon was formed, had been influenced by Hellenic viewpoints. He finds that the unity of the two Testaments can best be established by a Christological interpretation of the Septuagint, linking it with the Passion of Christ, after the manner of the early Christians.

One book devoted to the theology of the Old Testament has appeared in America in recent years—that of O. J. Baab.[22] He sees a fundamental unity in the Old Testament religion and finds it provided by the religious experience of the Hebrew community which continued the same through all vicissitudes of history. This religion is unique, and its main tenets have an abiding significance for us. The author deals with the more important topics in the order familiar from dogmatic theology.[23]

Turning once more from practice to theory we find another American, R. C. Dentan, discussing the history of Old Testament theology and the principles according to which it has been and should be written up.[24] He gives a preliminary definition of the subject as "that Christian theological discipline which treats of the religious ideas of the Old Testament systematically, i.e., not from the point of view of historical development, but from that of structural unity of the Old Testament religion, and which gives due regard to the historical and ideological relationship of that religion to the religion of the New Testament." Later he revises this and holds that "the scope of the subject is the normative or distinctive religion thought or assumed by the canonical books of the Old Testament, all of which have their centre on a distinctive doctrine of God"; it should include ethics and cultus, and give a picture of Old Testament piety. The first definition is more intellectualistic than the second, but it brings in the relation to the Christian order; the second could be subscribed to by a Jewish scholar. In any case Dentan remains in the sphere of the historical approach in the spirit of Eichrodt.

Soon afterward N. W. Porteous gave a discussion of the subject of Old Testament theology in a valuable British symposium.[25] He leaves it uncertain just where the line should be drawn between Old Testament theology and Dogmatic theology, but he approves of the emphasis on a historical revelation "when through the divine-human encounter, a word is spoken to which a response is made". He holds that man's response is what the Bible means by knowledge of God and that Old Testament theology is the critique of this knowledge. If this means that there must be an existential element in Old Testament theology we shall just have to bear the consequences of that. A treatment of that discipline, he declares, must keep close to life. In seeking to understand the structure of the Old Testament, not as strangers but as heirs, we shall not lose sight of the fact that Christ is its fulfilment.

During the war years the problem of a Biblical theology of the Old Testament was discussed in Germany by G. von Rad.[26] He finds the proper unifying principle in the idea of history to which that faith constantly has recourse. The Old Testament, he maintains, shows the way that God went with Israel. If one takes its teachings out of the historical frame of reference the primary peculiarity is lost sight of. A theology of the Old Testament to qualify as *heilsgeschichtlich* will have the task of setting forth the correspondence of Word of God and History in the various ways in which the former reacts on the latter. He notes that in the Old Testament the events are set in motion by a Word of God and are continuously fashioned and led to a goal by ever new Word of God. The Old Testament is thus a witness of God's continuous action in History.

Von Rad thinks that even books that do not fit in with this principle (Job, Ecclesiastes!) must be given their niche in relationship to it. He assigns an important role to the prophecy and fulfilment idea and thinks it is one of the main tasks of Old Testament theology to sketch this dialectic interplay, though he urges that it be done without any leaning on philosophies of history of modern vintage. In this connection he would even permit the use of typology to a certain degree. He also stresses the importance of the *kerygma* or the "message" aspect of the Old Testament prophetic religion. The unity of the Testaments, he claims, is provided by the concept of the Word of God; for He speaks in both.

We may note in passing that von Rad in one of his recent historical studies has tried to set forth that the Hebrew "creed" was a confession of the acts of God in past history, notably at the Exodus. The Old Testament faith is basically soteriological;

the idea of God as Creator is taken by him as completely subordinate to the belief in Him as Redeemer.[27]

Close in some respects to this scholar's viewpoint is the fresh approach undertaken by Wright. In his earlier book he had already stressed the idea that the Word behind the words of the Old Testament is one that is made concrete and vivid in historical events.[28] But that Word behind the words is discerned only by those who are willing to stand with the prophets at their point of vantage and experience the challenge and immediacy of God's will for that particular moment of crisis which concerned them, and who at the same time are ready to stand in the history of the present and seek the Word of the Lord for us now. Apparently Wright at that time imagined the message of the Old Testament as best presented in the form of biblical exegesis or exposition, as also favoured by Weiser.

But in his new book,[29] under the impact of von Rad's idea of a Hebrew confessional declaration (*heilsgeschichtliches Credo*), Wright has gone beyond this. His announced purpose is "to describe the special and characteristic nature of the biblical presentation of faith and to use the word theology for it". Whatever one may think of the idea of reviving Biblical Dogmatics (which Wright seems to have in mind), one may concede that the Old Testament writers are governed by theologies; since they are members of the same religious group these theologies will certainly have a great deal in common; ascending upwards in the scale of generalization to include the New Testament writers, one may perhaps describe an overarching element of agreement as the biblical theology in the higher sense. The question can only be: what is this *communis opinio*?

For Wright it is History, or "a God who acts" in History. The biblical presentation of faith consists of a recital of the deity's past acts. For the Old Testament these acts are the election of Israel, allegedly an inference from the Exodus deliverance, and the confirmation and clarification of it in the covenant ceremony at Sinai. He shows how this faith is made meaningful for Christians in the New Testament by typology and goes so far as to assert that it is impossible for us to discard typology without separating ourselves from biblical faith. Still, in view of the criticism incurred on that score by Vischer, he dreads typological innovations and would not go beyond what is written in the New Testament in that particular. He then turns to the confessional element in the New Testament. Following Dodd,[30] he stresses the idea that acts of God were the primary content of the Faith of the early Christians also. He finds in Paul's address at Antioch in Pisidia (Acts 13: 16 f.) a combination of the Old Testament and New Testament Creeds and presumably the sum-total then of the Biblical Faith.

In his opinion, therefore, the subject matter of Biblical theology and Dogmatic theology as well is the confessional recital of the unique events of biblical history, together with the inferences and interpretations which the Word in biblical faith by historian, prophet, psalmist or apostle and evangelist drew from them or associated with them. Wright is aware, of course, of the great variety of thought found in the Bible, but he maintains that it is never of such a nature as to constitute a totally different series of theologies because the central and especial concern with the meaning of historical events and life within history holds the whole together.

Wright, who is fond of assailing the theology of ideas of Greek derivation, here himself resorts to the Greek concept of History and the religious-phenomenological category of a "God who acts" (i.e., a voluntaristic divinity) to string together very dissimilar things in an external, unorganic manner. Some of his readers may feel that if a theology of the saving acts of God (another *Theologie der Heilstatsachen*) is in order it would be preferable to limit those acts to the ones that spell salvation for the Christian—Christ's Incarnation, Cross and Resurrection—and to have the Old Testament development construed as prophetic of the redemption in Christ, after the example of von Hofmann, Delitzsch, Orelli, Briggs and others.

A unity of the Old Testament religion, yea of the Bible and biblical religion as such, but based rather on biblical thought than on divine acts has been emphasized recently by Rowley.[31] His discussion seriously impairs the claims of those who since Kuenen and Wellhausen have been stressing the supposed anti-cultic or anti-sacrificial attitude of the prophets, and who have been finding the continuity between the New Testament and the Old in a progression from that alleged prophetic standpoint. Rowley sees the prophets merely criticizing a cult that was made a mockery by evil men. He holds that the law and the prophets are not in conflict and that the use of the Psalms was designed to make the practices of the law the organ of the spirit the prophets called for. From Old Testament sacrifice he can pass over to the New Testament sacrifice of the Cross and its celebration in the Sacraments, and therein find an underlying unity of teaching as to the supreme observances of both Old and New Testament religion.

Perhaps the most significant contributions to the theological theme to come from post-war Germany are those of F. Baumgärtel.[32] In his approach there is a resolute attempt to integrate the Old Testament heritage with that of the New (but with frank acceptance of all truth brought forward by historical research), and to focus it existentially on ourselves.

His presupposition—and he states it at the outset with commendable directness—is the Pauline Gospel of salvation: it is my being saved through Christ, my encounter with God through this Christian message, that matters. And the question for him is: do we also meet our God in the Old Testament? The affirmative to the latter question necessitates showing how this God of the Old Testament is related to the God of the New. The Christian gospel, he holds, is the yardstick wherewith the contents of the Old Testament are to be judged. But the latter are not to be taken in any other sense than that arrived at by objective historical interpretation. Baumgärtel is particularly concerned with finding some better formulation for the relationship of Old and New Testaments than that which the early Christian writings employ so prominently: the prophecy and fulfilment principle. He sees clearly that this was an ancient thought-pattern and that, however useful it may have been once, it can carry no persuasion to-day. He substitutes for it the special formulation of Eph. 3: 6, that the Christian is partaker of the promise through the gospel. Differentiating sharply between promise and prophecy he asserts that the Old Testament is promissory, not prophesying, in character. Its prophecies are not relevant for us, though they were to the contemporaries for whom they were intended. The basic thing in the Old Testament, he holds with others, is the divine assurance "I am the Lord thy God". This puts the generations of Israel under the necessity of deciding for or against God and so experiencing either the implied promise by being loyal to Him or the threat and punishment connected with defiance. The consequences of this become ever clearer in the course of Old Testament history. The Christian finds the continuity with the old order in this: that the promissory aspect of that assurance is realized in Jesus Christ.

It is apparent, then, that for the subject of Theology of the Old Testament Baumgärtel will wish to make use of the history of redemption principle (*Heilsgeschichte*), but not so much with an eye to external history as to inner development.[33] This is indeed the nub of his project as recently set forth in a fresh methodical discussion of the discipline.[34] It must be shown here, he says, that the Old Testament development is part of the self-revelation of God in Christ. For the forgiveness brought by Christ to sinful man presupposes the Old Testament judgments of God, without which that which Christ required would not have been comprehensible; and also God's promise (see above), without which Christ's appearance among this people as the One who fulfils would be incomprehensible. Repentance under the impact of the Word of God in the Old Testament order likewise is to be viewed as in organic relation with the future coming of Christ. So for the Christian the Old Testament history is from God and leading to God in Christ. Running in the form of divine promise and human response, it brings humanity to a situation where the *De profundis* cry is answered and the fulfilling and redeeming Word, Jesus Christ, is given to it by God.

The *Heilsgeschichte* of the Old Testament is a thing of the past, but for Christian faith the historical fact of Christ is at the same time one of the present, and so the things concerning Him (the events leading to His coming) also share in this characteristic. Like the witness concerning Christ, that of the *Heilsgeschichte* preceding Him awakens faith. In hearing it I realize that it concerns me both in its aspects of judgment and promise. It confronts me with the question whether I will join the true Israel in bowing before the divine majesty in confession of guilt, or remain amid the Israel that hardened its heart and go down into the judgment of God. To set this forth is a normative theological function, but unless it is undertaken one is forced to remain in the area of historicism. It is this existential approach alone, however, this present experience of the Old Testament

witness, that makes the Old Testament development meaningful for me, instead of leaving it a mere historical development
that may have touched the men of New Testament times but no
longer need trouble me.

Heilsgeschichte as seen by us from the angle of faith in Christ,
Baumgärtel claims, is not identical with the self-understanding
of the Old Testament. Only the Jew can read the Old Testament
in disregard of the New. Jesus Christ shattered the Jewish
understanding of this sacred literature for us, so that we have
to see it in a new, a Christian light. But our understanding of the
Old Testament cannot be that of the early Christians either.
While they no longer read their Old Testament as Jews read it,
but as Christians, we are far removed from their place and
situation. We cannot honestly avail ourselves, as these early
Christians did, of typology to bring the Old Testament history
to have direct relevance for us. We must from where we stand
relate ourselves to Christ and so also to the *Heilsgeschichte*
leading up to Him in a direct Christian approach. This preliminary normative manner of dealing with the Old Testament
religion, however, Baumgärtel would distinguish from Dogmatic
theological discussion, since the former must leave out of consideration the light that the ecclesiastical kerygma and the
history of Christian thought throw upon the subject. He gives
the last word on the normative position to Dogmatic theology.
But how, he asks, shall the latter have the proper discernment
in Old Testament matters unless the Old Testament scholar
points the way and by normative statements of his own shows
with what principles he operates in relating the Old Testament
to his Christian standpoint?

Baumgärtel's programme thus tries to lead beyond the
historicism in which all previous Old Testament theologies
remain bound, and goes far toward realizing Eissfeldt's ideal of
the subject and the existential approach indicated by Vischer,
Bultmann and Hirsch. The laudable purpose of all these men
was to give the Old Testament a present meaning; Vischer does
it in terms of a revival of the understanding of the Old Testament writers by the New Testament writers—through their
kind of Messianic prophecy and typology—and with the aid of a
doctrine of a pre-existent Christ who was operative in the Old
Testament period. Bultmann seeks the Old Testament under-

standing of existence on its higher levels and therein finds the Old Testament of present value for us. Hirsch takes it as the Jews of the time of Christ understood it and finds it the great antithesis to Christianity, but of permanent importance on that account. Baumgärtel's position seems closest to that of Bultmann.

We observe, then, on all sides a drift toward the normative. It is doubtful, however, whether two kinds of normative theology can be admitted—a Biblical and a Dogmatic. The task of appraising the abiding substance and worth of the historical records is hardly a halfway station on the road from a historical Biblical theology to Dogmatic theology, but is a function of the latter. If the Biblical scholar, weary of struggling with rocks and underbrush, wants to get out of the narrow ravine up which he has been toiling and gain the high plateau, where the Systematic theologian paces about, scanning broad horizons, he is free to do so. Theological history gives him ample precedent. But the Biblico-theological task itself can be greatly enriched by legitimate historical means. The photography has largely been "flat" rather than third-dimensional. To achieve the latter effect requires an improvement in our ability of seeing the reality before us, some appreciation of foreground as well as background, some power to go to the very essence of phenomena and to discern their transitional function in the vast historical process. There is room, furthermore, for two standpoints—one establishing distance and another proximity. Only the peaceful rivalry of the productions themselves can demonstrate which is the most instructive, the most useful way of dealing with the Old Testament order.

In his survey of modern theology Stephan observed that there is no happy ending to this development.[35] And this is true also of that segment of theological history we have been reviewing. The current goes on and on. But at each moment there is in the onrushing flood the desire to be merged with the river of water of life that proceeds from under the throne of God. That lends the whole course of this current an interest and significance.

NOTES

Introduction

[1] J. Orr, *The Problem of the Old Testament*, 1906. See p. 144 f.

[2] See the various "Introductions", such as R. H. Pfeiffer, *The Books of the Old Testament*, 1957, or the same author's massive *Introduction to the Old Testament*, 1941. Of German works, O. Eissfeldt, *Einleitung in das Alte Testament*, 3rd edn., 1963, is available in an English translation by P. R. Ackroyd: *The Old Testament—An Introduction*, 1965. The literary–historical rather than the book-by-book approach was followed in the inspiring book of J. A. Bewer, *The Literature of the Old Testament*, 3rd edn., 1962, completely revised by E. G. Kraeling.

[3] The great repository of such information is L. Diestel, *Geschichte des Alten Testaments in der Christlichen Kirche*, 1869. See further A Duff, *History of Old Testament Criticism*, 1910; E. M. Gray, *Old Testament Criticism, its Rise and Progress*, 1923.

[4] *The Old Testament in Early Christianity.* For the approach from the customary angles see R. V. G. Tasker, *The Old Testament in the New Testament*, 1947; C. H. Dodd, *According to the Scriptures*, 1953; J. Coppens, *Les harmonies des deux Testaments*, revised edn., 1949.

Chapter One
Luther and the Old Testament

[1] See T. Zahn, *Die bleibende Bedeutung des neutestamentlichen Kanons für die Kirche*, 1903, 12 f. For mediaeval matters see B. Smalley, *The Study of the Bible in the Middle Ages*, 1952.

[2] Cf. E. von Dobschütz, "Die Lehre vom vierfachen Schriftsinn", in *Harnack-Ehrung*, 1921, 1 f.

[3] K. Holl, *Gesammelte Aufsätze zur Kirchengeschichte*, vol. I, *Luther*, 6th edn., 1932, 419. This important study contains many valuable observations for the matter that here concerns us. Useful, too, is O. Scheel, *Luthers Stellung zur Heiligen Schrift*, 1902 (*Sammlung gemeinverständlicher Vorträge*, no. 29). See further, H. Bornkamm, *Luther und das Alte Testament*, 1948 (the most recent study by an authority on Luther).

[4] Holl, *loc. cit.*

[5] Holl, *op. cit.*, 420.

[6] *Ibid.*, 402.

[7] *Ibid.*, 429 f.

[8] Scheel, *op. cit.*, 43.

[9] Holl, *op. cit.*, 431.

[10] Scheel, *op. cit.*, 45.

[11] *Ibid.*, 44.

[12] *Loc. cit.*

[13] See the summary in J. Köstlin, *Luthers Theologie*, II, (1883), 257, 269 f., 273. On Semler, see p. 55 f.

[14] Scheel, *op. cit.*, 44.

[15] Compare the discussion of this in E. Troeltsch, *Vernunft und Offenbarung bei J. Gerhard und Melanchthon*, 1891, 139 f.

[16] Weimar Edition L, 643.

[17] Luther's Preface to the Old Testament, as quoted by J. Hempel, *Zeitschrift für die alttestamentliche Wissenschaft*, LIV, 1936, 298.

[18] Scheel, *op. cit.*, 43.

[19] The consequences are drawn by Hirsch (see ch. 15).

[20] W. Herrmann, *Gesammelte Schriften*, 1923, 250 f.

[21] See Scheel, *op. cit.*, 42. For the items that follow see Köstlin, *op. cit.*, 266.

[22] H. Schmidt, *Luther und das Buch der Psalmen*, 1933 (*Sammlung gemeinverständlicher Vorträge*, no. 167).

[23] *Tischreden*, ed. J. G. Walch, V, 5518.

[24] See Köstlin, *op. cit.*, 266 f. for the references to the quotations that follow.

[25] Carlstadt, *De Canonicis Scripturis* (1520), reprinted in K. A. Credner, *Zur Geschichte des Kanons*, 1847, 291 ff. He not only accepted the Jewish idea of three divisions of different degrees of authority in the Old Testament but even applied a similar principle to the New Testament, ascribing highest authority to the four gospels, second degree authority to a group comprising the Pauline epistles, 1 Peter and 1 John, but third degree authority to Hebrews, James, 2 Peter, 3 John, Jude and Revelation.

[26] A. von Harnack, *Marcion, das Evangelium vom fremden Gott*, 1924, 250 ff. (*Texte und Untersuchungen zur Geschichte der altchristlichen Literatur* vol. XLV.)

[27] The appraisal of Luther's position from a modern-conservative angle by L. Ihmels, *Die Christliche Wahrheitsgewissheit*, 2nd edn., 1908, 11 f. is well worth reading.

Chapter Two

Zwingli and Calvin and the Old Testament

[1] See P. Wernle, *Der Evangelische Glaube nach den Hauptschriften der Reformatoren*, III, *Calvin*, 1919, 268 f. His interpretative summaries are helpful.

[2] Cf. C. Sigwart, *Ulrich Zwingli. Der Charakter seiner Theologie mit besonderer Rücksicht auf Picus von Mirandula dargestellt*, 1855, 45 f. An early work of the well-known logician, and still useful.

[3] Wernle, *op. cit.*, 267.

[4] When Calvin published the second *Institutes* in 1539, he had

written a commentary on Romans and drew on his new insight for expanding his main work. See Wernle, 268.

⁵ See A. H. Hays, "The Authority of Scripture", in *From the Pyramids to Paul*, ed. by L. G. Leary, 1935, 80.

⁶ Wernle, *op. cit.*, 5.

⁷ Here Calvin was much influenced by Luther's *De servo arbitrio*.

⁸ A. Tholuck, "Calvin als Exeget", in his *Vermischte Schriften*, II, 1839, is the fullest study. Cf. K. Fullerton, *Prophecy and Authority*, 1919, 133 f. For a special theme see L. P. Smith, "Calvin as Interpreter of Ezekiel", in *From the Pyramids to Paul*, 267 f.

⁹ See Wernle, *op. cit.*, 3 f.

¹⁰ In the final edition of *The Institutes* this is found in II, 8, 16.

¹¹ = II, 10 f. in the final edition.

¹² See H. W. Wolff, *Die Einheit des Bundes. Das Verhältnis von Altem und Neuem Testament bei Calvin*, 1942.

¹³ Calvin's view of existence is of course extremely pessimistic.

¹⁴ Cf. II, 11, in the final edition of *The Institutes*.

¹⁵ Cf. M. Schulze, *Meditatio futurae vitae. Ihr Begriff und ihre herrschende Stellung im System Calvins*, 1901.

¹⁶ M. Albertz, *Die Botschaft des Neuen Testaments*, I, pt. 1, 1947, 12.

¹⁷ The Authorized Version in the title given the Epistle to the Hebrews asserts authorship by Paul, therein following the Alexandrian claims; it puts the Epistle after the other Pauline writings. Luther did not accept the Pauline authorship and in his Bible put Hebrews with the Catholic Epistles. That Luther's position was not unique may be seen from the fact that his contemporary, the Catholic theologian Cajetan, could deny Paul's authorship of Hebrews, hold its canonicity to be doubtful and declare that it had no authority in doctrinal matters; see Zahn, *Die bleibende Bedeutung*, 10. At Trent, however, Catholicism accepted the Pauline authorship of Hebrews.

Chapter Three

The Old Testament from the Reformation to the Middle of the Seventeenth Century

¹ This formulation, however, did not come up until early in the nineteenth century, as was shown by A. Ritschl, "Über die beiden Prinzipien des Protestantismus", *Gesammelte Aufsätze*, I, 1893, 234 f.

² See *Dogmatic Canons and Decrees of the Council of Trent*, New York, 1912, 7 f.; P. Schaff, *The Creeds of Christendom*, II, 1887, 79 f.

³ Cf. the *Confessio Dosithei*, Schaff, *Creeds*, II, 401 f.

⁴ Zahn, *Die bleibende Bedeutung*, 27 f.

⁵ Schaff, *Creeds*, III, 233 f. A. Niemeyer, *Collectio confessionum in ecclesiis reformatarum publicatarum*, 1840, 467.

⁶ Niemeyer, *op. cit.*, 361 f.

⁷ Zahn, *op. cit.*, 46.

[8] Schaff, *op. cit.*, 491.

[9] Schaff, *op. cit.*, 93; Die *Bekenntnisschriften der Evangelisch Lutherischen Kirche*, Berlin, 1930, 767 f.

[10] L. Ihmels, *Die Christliche Wahrheitsgewissheit*, 53 f.

[11] *Ibid.*, 54.

[12] Schaff, *op. cit.*, 600 f.

[13] Niemeyer, *op. cit.*, 730.   This was directed against Capellus (p. 43).

[14] Cf. Ihmels, *op. cit.*, 55 f.

[15] G. Oehler, *Prolegomena zur Theologie des Alten Testaments*, 1845, 21.

[16] *Ibid.*, 23.

[17] H. Schöffler, *Abendland und Altes Testament*, 1937, 36 f.

[18] *Ibid.*, 73 f., 114 f.

[19] A. von Harnack, *Über den privaten Gebrauch der Heiligen Schriften in der alten Kirche*, 1912, 6 f.

[20] See A. D. White, *A History of the Warfare of Science with Theology*, 2 vols., 1910.   The work takes up the sciences separately.

Chapter Four

The Reaction Against the Orthodox View of the Old Testament

[1] L. Capellus, *Arcanum punctationis revelatum*, 1624. *Critica sacra*, 1650.

[2] J. Morinus, *Exercitationes Biblicae*, 1633.

[3] R. Simon, *Histoire Critique de Vieux Testament*, 1685.

[4] J. Spencer, *De legibus Hebraeorum ritualibus*, 1685.

[5] J. Clericus, *Ars sacra*, 1697.

[6] Cf. H. P. Smith, *Essays in Biblical Interpretation*, 1921, 94 f.; J. Cocceius, *Summa doctrinae de foedere et testamento Dei*, 1648.

[7] See G. Schrenk, *Gottesreich und Bund im älteren Protestantismus*, 1923 (*Beiträge zur Förderung christlicher Theologie*, 2nd series, V).

[8] H. Grotius, *De veritate religionis Christianae*, 1627: *Adnotationes ad vetus et novum testamentum*, 1641–47.   See the essay on him in A. Kuenen, *Gesammelte Abhandlungen*, tr. by K. Budde, 1894.

[9] T. Hobbes, *Leviathan, or the matter, form and authority of Government*, 1651.

[10] Spinoza, *Tractatus theologico-politicus*, 1670.   For his general view of religion and its impact on his critical ideas see L. Strauss, *Die Religionskritik Spinozas als Grund seiner Bibelwissenschaft*, 1930.

[11] Cf. K. Fischer, *Geschichte der neueren Philosophie*, vol. II, (5th edn., 1909), 320, 326.

[12] His *Dictionnaire historique et critique* (1645–47) had a great influence on the 18th century mind.

[13] T. Morgan, *The Moral Philosopher*, 1737–40.

[14] W. Warburton, *Divine Legation of Moses*, 2 vols., 1737–41.

[15] Facts about the still extant manuscript in the edition of

Lessing's works edited by Petersen and Olshausen, XXII, 24. A detailed summary of this 2000-page opus was given by D. F. Strauss, *Hermann Samuel Reimarus und seine Schutzschrift*, 1862.

[16] *Beweis des Geistes und der Kraft*, 1777.

[17] See reprint in E. Schmidt, *Goezes Streitschrift gegen Lessing*, 1893.

[18] K. Fischer, *Geschichte der neueren Philosophie*, III, 648.

[19] Harnack, *Über den privaten Gebrauch der Heiligen Schriften*, 6 f.

[20] *Transzendentale Dialektik*, II, 2, para. 3.

[21] See Fischer, *Geschichte*, V, 371 f. On the incident mentioned, *ibid.*, IV, 93 f., 100.

[22] *Kants Gesammelte Schriften*, VIII, 1912, 255 f. See my *Book of the Ways of God*, 1938, 242 f.

[23] Fichte, *Versuch einer Kritik aller Offenbarung*, 1792. Cf. Fischer, *Geschichte*, VI, 221 f.

[24] See Fischer, *Geschichte*, VII, 14 f.

[25] His *Conjectures* appeared anonymously in Brussels, 1753. The work was set before the American public by Theodore Parker's translation of 1835.

[26] H. B. Witter's precedence over Astruc was forgotten until it was ferreted out by A. Lods, *Jean Astruc et la critique biblique au XVIIIe siècle*, 1924. Witter's book was *Jura Israelitarum in Palaestinam*, 1711. Cf. J. Hempel's book (chapter 12 n. 11), p. 3 f.

[27] J. A. Ernesti, *Institutio interpretis Novi Testamenti*, 1761.

[28] J. S. Semler, *Abhandlung von freier Untersuchung des Kanons*, 4 vols., 1771–75.

[29] G. T. Zachariae, *Biblische Theologie oder Untersuchung des biblischen Grundes der vornehmsten theologischen Lehren*, 5 vols., 1772–86.

[30] L. Bauer, *Theologie des Alten Testaments*, 1796.

[31] J. P. Gabler, *De justo discrimine theologiae Biblicae et dogmaticae*, 1787.

[32] J. G. Eichhorn, *Einleitung in das Alte Testament*, 5 vols., 1780–1783, 4th edn., 1823–24.

[33] W. M. L. De Wette, *Beiträge zur Einleitung in das Alte Testament*, 2 vols., 1806–7; a work really marking the beginning of the higher critical movement.

[34] See A. Ritschl, *Geschichte des Pietismus*, III, 1886, 62 f.

[35] F. Delitzsch, *Die biblisch-prophetische Theologie, ihre Fortbildung durch Chr. A. Crusius und ihre neueste Entwicklung seit der Christologie Hengstenbergs*, 1845, showed a great enthusiasm for this school's literal acceptance of biblical prophecy.

[36] On him see H. Stephan, "Hamanns Christentum und Theologie", *Zeitschrift für Theologie und Kirche*, XII, 1902, 345 f. W. Vischer frequently quotes Hamann.

[37] Cf. Fischer, *ibid.*, 666 f. Herder, *Vom Geist der ebräischen Poesie*, 1782–83 and his *Älteste Urkunde des Menschengeschlechts*, 1774, were particularly significant here.

[38] See K. Galling, "Goethe als theologischer Schriftsteller", *Evangelische Theologie*, 1949, 529 f.; H. H. Schaeder, *Goethes Erlebnis des Ostens*, 1938, 24 f. It should be mentioned that Schiller, too, took an interest in Old Testament matters in several short papers.

[39] Cf. J. Pedersen, "Die Auffassung vom Alten Testament", *Zeitschrift für die alttestamentliche Wissenschaft*, XLIX, 1931, 161 f.

Chapter Five

Schleiermacher and the Old Testament

[1] *Der Christliche Glaube nach den Grundsätzen der Evangelischen Kirche*, 2 vols., 1821 f. E.T. by H. R. Mackintosh and J. S. Stewart, *The Christian Faith*, 1928.

[2] See W. Wiesner, *Das Offenbarungsproblem in der dialektischen Theologie*, 1930, 4 f.

[3] § 3–5. In the *Reden* Schleiermacher held that the important thing was how one experiences reality; when one discerns a single living power behind all events that concern us (*individuell bestimmte Anschauung des Universums*) one has religion. Cf. W. Herrmann, *Dogmatik*, 1925, 10.

[4] § 10. He says: "Die Ursprünglichkeit der einer religiösen Gemeinschaft zu Grunde liegenden Tatsache", etc. I have worded his meaning in a free manner. It should be noted that this position implies a new beginning also for the Christian religion; the latter is not just a continuation of the Hebrew religion.

[5] § 128 f.

[6] § 12.

[7] In the light of modern studies such as have been carried on by Bousset and Reitzenstein his statement takes on fresh meaning.

[8] Bertram's studies in the Septuagint are a case in point. See Chapter 17, n. 21.

[9] He quotes Clement, *Stromata*, VI.

[10] He is thinking notably of the fourth Eclogue of Virgil.

[11] The term heathenism of course is used here in the nuance of heathenism at its best and finest, as in Plato, Epictetus, etc.

[12] § 132.

[13] This is Luther's secular view of Old Testament law.

[14] In § 14, he discusses proofs from Messianic prophecy.

[15] B. Stade, *Biblische Theologie des alten Testaments*, I, 1905, 5, considers it briefly but rejects it.

[16] Cf. W. Bousset, *Kyrios Christos. Geschichte des Christusglaubens von den Anfängen bis Irenäus*, 1913, Paul's powerful presentation of Christianity is with tools of Greek thought; no contemporary teacher of purely Semitic training could have carried through a trend of reasoning as Paul does. See H. Leisegang, *Der Apostel Paulus als Denker*, 1923, on the intellectual background presupposed. The

greatly Hellenized Septuagint, the authoritative Scripture for Gentile Christianity, must also be recalled; (cf. Bertram, "Septuaginta und Urchristentum", *Theologische Blätter*, 1925, 208 f.)

Chapter Six
The Old Testament in Nineteenth-Century
Theological Thought Before Ritschl

[1] So K. I. Nitzsch, prominent exponent of the Prussian Union, in his *System der Christlichen Lehre*, 1829. Cf. K. Schwarz, *Zur Geschichte der neuesten Theologie*, 1856, 41, a writer who stood close to the time and the events.

[2] W. M. L. De Wette, *Lehrbuch der Christlichen Dogmatik*, I. *Biblische Dogmatik*, 1813.

[3] J. F. Fries, *Wissen, Glaube, Ahndung*, 1805 (re-issued by the Neo-Friesian L. Nelson, 1905). Rudolf Otto was also profoundly influenced by Fries and De Wette. See his *Kantisch-Friesische Religionsphilosophie und ihre Anwendung für die Theologie*, 1921; E. T. by E. B. Dicker, *Philosophy of Religion*, 1931.

[4] *Das Wesen des Christlichen Glaubens vom Standpunkt des Glaubens*, 1846.

[5] E. W. Hengstenberg, *Christologie des Alten Testaments*, 3 vols., 1829–35. E.T. by R. Keith, *Christology of the Old Testament*, 1836–39.

[6] See Schwarz, op. cit., 88, for the quotations given here.

[7] See Fischer, *Geschichte der neueren Philosophie*, VII, 627 f.

[8] See especially P. Tillich, *Mystik und Schuldbewusstsein in Schellings philosophischer Entwicklung*, 1912, 16 f., 131 f. (*Beiträge zur Förderung Christlicher Theologie*, XVI, 1).

[9] For analysis and discussion see Fischer *op. cit.*, VII, 794 ff.

[10] Fischer, *op. cit.*, VIII, pt. 2, 985 f.

[11] *Ibid.*, 997 f.

[12] *Ibid.*, 1171 f.

[13] See Fischer, *op. cit.*, IX, *Schopenhauer*, 488 f. Cf. also A. Schlatter, *Die Philosophische Arbeit seit Cartesius nach ihrem ethischen und religiösen Ertrag*, 2nd edn., 1910, 231 f.

[14] W. Vatke, *Die Biblische Theologie wissenschaftlich dargestellt*, I, *Die Religion des Alten Testaments*, 1835.

[15] B. Bauer, *Kritik der Geschichte der Offenbarung*, I, *Die Religion des Alten Testaments*, 1838. On his later apostasy see A. Schweitzer, *The Quest of the Historical Jesus*, 1910, 137 f.

[16] D. F. Strauss, *Leben Jesu*, 1835.

[17] His *Christentum der ersten drei Jahrhunderte*, 1853, unrolls the full panorama of his results.

[18] J. T. Beck, *Die Christliche Lehrwissenschaft*, 1838 f. On him see A. Schlatter, *J. T. Becks theologische Arbeit*, 1904 (*Beiträge zur Förderung Christlicher Theologie*, VII, 4). Beck, too, taught at Tübingen. Great, too, was the influence of A. Tholuck of Halle,

likewise a pietist, but no distinctive line of theological thought went forth from him.   An interesting figure is C. A. Auberlen, whose *Die göttliche Offenbarung*, I, 1861 (not completed because of his early demise) is a model of irenic discussion.

[19] J. C. K. von Hofmann, *Weissagungen und Erfüllungen im Alten Testament und Neuen Testament*, 2 vols., 1841–44.

[20] *Schriftbeweis*, 1852–55.

[21] *Die Heilige Schrift zusammenhängend untersucht*, 13 vols., 1862–86.

[22] A. Vilmar, *Die Theologie der Tatsachen wider die Theologie der Rhetorik*, 1856.   Professor at Marburg, he wielded a strong ecclesiastical and political influence and protested against the Prussian absorption of the principality and the Prussian Union enforced on the Churches.

[23] R. Rothe, *Zur Dogmatik*, 1863.   Rothe was perhaps the most important Systematic-theological thinker in the period from Schleiermacher to Ritschl.

[24] *Ibid.*, 330 f.

[25] R. H. von Frank, *Die Lehre von der Christlichen Gewissheit*, 1872, § 41.

[26] G. Oehler, *Prolegomena zur Theologie des Alten Testaments*, 1845.

[27] See Introduction, n. 3.

[28] K. H. Graf, *Die geschichtlichen Bücher des Alten Testaments. Zwei geschichtliche Untersuchungen*, 1866.

[29] A. Kuenen, *De Godsdienst van Israel*, 2 vols, 1869 f.

[30] H. Ewald, *Geschichte des Volkes Israel bis auf Christus*, 5 vols., 1843–55 (2nd edn. 1851–59).   E.T. by R. Martineau, *The History of Israel*, 8 vols., 1869–86.

[31] J. H. Kurtz, *Geschichte des Alten Bundes*, 2 vols., 1848 and 1855. His widely used *Lehrbuch der heiligen Geschichte*, 1843, is an abridgement of it, with extension to cover the New Testament period (E.T. by C. T. Schaeffer, *Manual of Sacred History*, 1856).   Like K. Bähr, *Symbolik des Mosaischen Kultus*, 2 vols., 1837–39, he can find symbolism and typology in the Hebrew worship; in the main he applies von Hofmann's principle.

[32] *Die Lehre der Bibel von Gott oder Theologie des Alten und Neuen Bundes*, 4 vols., 1871–76.   See Vol. I, *Die Lehre vom Wort Gottes*, 472 f.

[33] E. B. Pusey, *Daniel the Prophet*, 1868, p. xi f.   Pusey virtually insisted that Christianity must stand or fall with the early date of Daniel.

[34] J. H. Newman, *Arians of the Fourth Century*, 1876, 153 f.

[35] Newman, *Discussions and Arguments on Various Subjects*, 1872, 246 f.

[36] Newman, *Lectures on the Doctrine of Justification*, 1874, 36 f., 145 f.   I am indebted to Prof. John E. Smith for aid on Pusey and Newman.

[37] T. Parker, *A Critical and Historical Introduction to the Canonical*

Scripture of the Old Testament. Translated and enlarged from W. M. L. De Wette, 2 vols., 1843.

[38] See his *Critical History and Defense of the Old Testament*, 1845.

Chapter Seven

The Transition to the Modern Situation

[1] See especially White, *History of the Warfare of Science with Theology*, I, 232 f.

[2] *Ibid.*, II, 394 f.

[3] *Ibid.*, II, 342 f.

[4] *The Pentateuch and Joshua critically examined*, 1862 f. Cf. White, *op. cit.*, II, 350 f.; H. P. Smith, *Essays in Biblical Interpretation*, 1921, 128 f.

[5] Out of these lectures came his *The Old Testament in the Jewish Church*, 1881. On him see J. B. Pritchard, "W. Robertson Smith, Heretic", *Crozer Quarterly*, XXIV, 1947, 146 f.; T. K. Cheyne, *Founders of Old Testament Criticism*, 1893, 211 f.

[6] *Deutsche Schriften. Gesammtausgabe*, 1892, 217 f. Cf. L. Schmid, *Paul de Lagardes Kritik an Kirche, Theologie und Christentum*, 1935, 110 f.

[7] J. Wellhausen, *Geschichte Israels*, I, 1878 (in the later editions the title became *Prolegomena zur Geschichte Israels*, 1883, 1886). Wellhausen, who was Professor in the conservative Greifswald, was forced to relinquish his post and became Professor of Semitic Languages, first at Marburg then at Göttingen. He contributed greatly to the study of Islam and later also to Gospel criticism.

[8] See W. Baumgartner, "Wellhausen und der heutige Stand der alttestamentlichen Wissenschaft," *Theologische Rundschau*, 1930, 287 f.

[9] Franz Delitzsch, many of whose books were translated into English, was Professor in Leipzig. His distrust of the modern movement was expressed in his *Der tiefe Graben zwischen alter und moderner Theologie*, 1888. Cf. chapter 4, n. 35.

[10] White, II, 357 and 359. On Driver cf. Cheyne, *op. cit.*, 248 f. He was one of the foremost in scholarship, and his *Introduction to the Old Testament*, 1891, created the first really modern work of this kind in English. It was translated into German by Rothstein, 1896. Driver's contributions to Hebrew studies, to Kittel's *Biblia Hebraica* and his commentaries, are part of the heritage we all enjoy. W. Sanday was Professor in Oxford and contributed notably to New Testament scholarship. His Bampton lectures were on *Inspiration*, 1893.

[11] E. Robinson, pupil of Moses Stuart (cf. Chapter 6, n. 38) translated Gesenius' Hebrew Lexicon. Professor at Andover and later at Union Theological Seminary he won enduring scholarly fame as the father of Palestinian geography through his *Biblical*

Researches in Palestine, 3 vols., 1841–42. Cf. J. A. Bewer, "Edward Robinson as Biblical Scholar", *Journal of Biblical Literature*, LVIII, 1939, 355 f. In criticism he leaned toward Hengstenberg.

[12] C. H. Toy became Professor at Andover. His commentary on Proverbs in the *International Critical Commentary*, 1899, was noteworthy. He also wrote *Quotations in the New Testament*, 1884.

[13] C. A. Briggs had only gradually become a convert to higher criticism in spite of four years in Berlin. At his trial he argued that the Westminster Confession did not require belief in the inerrancy of Scripture, but he was suspended, nevertheless, by a vote of 298 to 116 from the Presbytery of New York. His scholarly output was considerable. For his theological position his *The Bible the Church and the Reason*, 1892, is instructive; his *Messianic Prophecy*, 1886, still operates seriously with Adamic and Noachic periods in the history of Messianic prediction. His most abiding achievements are his co-editorship of the *International Critical Commentary* (to which he contributed *The Psalms*, 2 vols., a work vitiated somewhat by his metrical theories) and his co-editorship of the great Hebrew Lexicon.

[14] F. Brown became President of Union Theological Seminary. The Hebrew Lexicon of which he was co-editor is his chief scholarly monument. At the time his defence of the young science of Assyriology in *Assyriology, its Use and Abuse*, 1885, was significant.

[15] H. P. Smith after leaving Lane Theological Seminary in consequence of his support of Dr. Briggs eventually became Professor in Meadville (later Librarian at Union Theological Seminary). He wrote some excellent books in the Old Testament field, notably a Commentary on *Samuel* in the I.C.C. series. His *Inspiration and Inerrancy*, 1893, deserves mention here; in old age he wrote his reminiscences, *The Heretic's Defence*, 1926.

[16] W. H. Green, *The Higher Criticism of the Pentateuch*, 1895; *The Unity of the Book of Genesis*, 1895. He had already taken the field against Colenso in his *The Pentateuch vindicated from the Aspersions of Bishop Colenso*, 1863. Princeton Theological Seminary long remained a seat of anti-critical attitude.

[17] W. R. Harper had a great impact on Hebrew studies in America. His Commentary on Amos and Hosea in the I.C.C. Series, 1905, was excellent. As first President of the University of Chicago he still maintained his interest in Hebrew Studies.

[18] B. W. Bacon, *The Genesis of Genesis*, 1893. Son of a noted New Haven divine, he became Professor at the Yale Divinity School and contributed notably to New Testament study.

[19] G. F. Moore, *Judges*, 1898, in the I.C.C. was an important contribution. Professor at Andover, he later transferred to Harvard. His pupil C. C. Torrey made a lasting contribution with his *Composition and Historical Value of Ezra-Nehemiah*, 1896. Professor at Yale, he became the most original biblical critic produced by America.

[20] In England A. H. Sayce, *The Higher Criticism and the Monu-*

ments, 3rd edn., 1894, was a pioneering publication along the line of archæology's "confirming" the Bible, but was not anti-critical enough to suit conservatives. Sayce, Professor at Oxford, was a man of great learning and wrote many books. The large literature of this type cannot be reviewed here. E. Schrader in Berlin did more than any contemporary to further sound use of the cuneiform sources. His *Die Keilinschriften und das Alte Testament*, 1872, was most valuable; the 3rd edn. by H. Winckler and H. Zimmern, 1901, has been one of the books most frequently cited by Old Testament scholars and though antiquated in many particulars is still useful. H. Gunkel, *Schöpfung und Chaos in Urzeit und Endzeit*, 1895, was a great eye-opener.

[21] F. Delitzsch, the son of Franz Delitzsch and Professor at Berlin, was Schrader's pupil and became the teacher of numerous Assyriologists and Old Testament scholars who delved into Assyriology. He also contributed to Hebrew lexicography and to Biblical geography. The lectures mentioned were translated as *Babel and Bible*, ed. by C. H. W. Johns, 1903.

[22] A new and revised edition was issued in 1921. There was a great outpouring of Apologetic by Old Testament scholars on this subject. E. Koenig, *Bibel und Babel*, 1902, is a good example; he re-published it in an 11th edition (re-written) as *Die moderne Babylonisirung der Bibel*, 1921.

[23] H. Winckler, who taught at Berlin, had important achievements to his credit, notably publication of the Tell el Amarna letters and his rediscovery of the capital of the Hittite Empire in Anatolia. A. Jeremias, *Das Alte Testament im Lichte des Alten Orients*, 1904, 4th edn., 1930 (E.T. *The Old Testament in the Light of the Ancient East*, 1911), became increasingly devoted to Pan-Babylonism. His *Handbuch der altorientalischen Geisteskultur*, 1913, then developed the Babylonian world-view. Both books are useful for their material. Jeremias, clergyman and *Privatdozent* at Leipzig, was a conservative theologically. In the end he was influenced by Theosophy.

[24] P. Jensen, *Das Gilgameschepos in der Weltliteratur*, I, 1906, II, 1928–29. Professor at Marburg, he contributed greatly to Assyriological studies. See H. Gunkel, "Jensens Gilgameschepos", in his *Reden und Aufsätze*, 1913.

[25] The question: what is new or original in Israel's religion? can hardly be answered yet. New texts, like those from Ras Shamra, bring increasing demonstration of Hebrew dependence.

Chapter Eight
The Old Testament in Systematic Theology since Ritschl

[1] See W. Herrmann, "Der evangelische Glaube und die Theologie Albrecht Ritschls", *Gesammelte Schriften*, 1923, 1 f. Ritschl was Professor at Göttingen.

[2] W. Wiesner, *Das Offenbarungsproblem in der dialektischen Theologie*, 18.

[3] A. Ritschl, *Die Christliche Lehre von der Rechtfertigung und Versöhnung*, II, 1874, 9 f.

[4] H. H. Wendt, *System der Christlichen Lehre*, 1907, belongs here; see also his *Idea and Reality of Revelation*, 1904. He was Professor at Jena and a noted New Testament scholar. A. Harnack's celebrated lectures, *Das Wesen des Christentums*, 1900, E.T. by T. B. Saunders. *What is Christianity?* reflect a similar position. J. Kaftan, *Grundriss der Dogmatik*, 1897 (8th edn., 1920), the most representative Ritschlian, veered more toward the conservative line; he was Professor in Berlin.

[5] W. Herrmann, *Der Verkehr des Christen mit Gott*, 1886, (7th edn., 1921). E.T. by J. S. Stanyon and R. W. Stewart, *The Communion of the Christian with God*, 1895. Herrmann was Professor in Marburg. His influence was world-wide, for in the face of historical criticism he provided a theology that men could preach, and his personality added weight to his message. For an appreciative study of his theology, see F. W. Schmidt, *Wilhelm Herrmann, Ein Bekenntnis zu seiner Theologie*, 1922.

[6] He has a fine passage on Hebrew monotheism in *Die Wirklichkeit Gottes*, 1914, 39 f.

[7] See *Gesammelte Aufsätze*, 19.

[8] See his posthumously-published lectures, *Dogmatik*, 1925, 34 f. E.T. by N. Micklem and K. Saunders, *Systematic Theology*, 1927.

[9] *Ibid.*, 56.

[10] M. Kaehler, *Wissenschaft der Christlichen Lehre*, 1883, (3rd edn., 1905). He was Professor at Halle-Wittenberg. Pietistic influences stemming from Tholuck and Beck here were fused with confessional Lutheran inclinations.

[11] Kaehler, *Dogmatische Zeitfragen* I, *Zur Bibelfrage*, 1907, 126, 130.

[12] *Ibid.*, 127.

[13] *Ibid.*, 140.

[14] *Ibid.*, 266 f.; cf. 410 f.

[15] The thought of Kaehler on the Biblical problem strongly influenced E. Weber, *Bibelglaube und historisch-kritische Schriftforschung*, 1913 (2nd edn., 1914), one of the most worth-while discussions from the conservative side.

[16] L. Ihmels, *Die Christliche Wahrheitsgewissheit, ihr letzter Grund und ihre Entstehung*, 1901, 2nd edn. 1908. In his valuable *Centralfragen der Dogmatik*, 2nd edn., 1912, 55 f., he shows himself primarily an adherent of Rothe's Scripture doctrine. Ihmels was Professor in Leipzig, later bishop of Saxony, and exercised a great influence as Lutheran churchman and preacher.

[17] A. Schlatter, *Das Christliche Dogma*, 1911. Primarily a New Testament scholar and an expert on the Judaism of the time of Christ, he was Professor at Tübingen. His scholarly output was

enormous. But he did not debate the N.T. issues of the day and in N.T. literary criticism was a singleton, as A. Klostermann was in the Old Testament field. His reflective-speculative approach, which makes him peculiarly difficult to read, suited the role of *Dogmatiker* better than that of exegete or historian.

[18] E. Schaeder, *Theozentrische Theologie*, 2 vols., 1909–15. He was Professor in Greifswald.

[19] Schaeder, *Das Wort Gottes. Eine systematische Untersuchung*, 1930. W. Caspari, "Das alttestamentliche Wort", *Neue Kirchliche Zeitschrift*, 1931, 752 f., is a discussion of Schaeder.

[20] E. Troeltsch, *Die Absolutheit des Christentums und die Religionsgeschichte*, 1901. See also his article *Offenbarung* in the first edition of *Die Religion in Geschichte und Gegenwart*, IV, 1913, 918 f. Troeltsch as theologian was primarily associated with Heidelberg. Transferring to Berlin he became "Kulturphilosoph". His influence was great, but his thought was viewed as destructive by churchmen. Cf. also his *Soziallehren der Christlichen Kirchen und Gruppen*, in *Gesammelte Schriften*, I, 1912, 848 f. (E.T. by O. Wyon, *Social Teaching of the Christian Churches*, 1931).

[21] I here follow his *Glaubenslehre*, 1925 (posthumous; lectures of 1911–12), p. 97 f.

[22] "Glaube und Ethos der Hebräischen Propheten", *Gesammelte Schriften*, IV, 53.

[23] *Ibid.*, 61.

[24] *Ibid.*, 820.

[25] He is thinking of the Jewish influence—Maimonides, Spinoza.

[26] Meaning Harnack, *Das Wesen des Christentums*; see note 4.

Chapter Nine

The Apologetic of Biblical Scholars

[1] Professor in Bonn and a man of tremendous industry. His own survey of his position and labours is found in *Der doppelte Wellhausenianismus im Lichte meiner Quellenforschungen*, 1927. He tried to demonstrate the reality of revelation in his *Der Offenbarungsbegriff im Alten Testament*, 2 vols., 1882. On his foray into Dogmatic theology see L. Ihmels, *Christliche Wahrheitsgewissheit*, 78 f. See also chapter 17, n. 15.

[2] W. Lotz, *Geschichte und Offenbarung im Alten Testament*, 1891, 43 f., showing also some impact from the philosophy of Lotze. The author was Professor in Erlangen and also made a worth-while contribution to Assyriology. His *Das Alte Testament und die Wissenschaft*, 1905, was one of the best books of its kind. W. Volck, *Die Bibel als Kanon*, 1885, contains excellent thought on the canonicity of the Old Testament. His *Heilige Schrift und Kritik*,1897, is also deserving of mention. The author was Professor in Dorpat.

[3] K. Marti, *Der Einfluss der Ergebnisse der neuesten alttestamentlichen Forschungen auf Religionsgeschichte und Glaubenslehre*, 1894.

Marti became Professor in Bern and deserves to be remembered for his editorship of the *Zeitschrift für die alttestamentliche Wissenschaft* (founded by Stade) and of one of the two great German series of critical Commentaries, the *Kurzer Handcommentar zum Alten Testament*.

⁴ G. Dalman, *Das Alte Testament ein Wort Gottes*, 1896. Dalman, Professor in Greifswald and long Director of the Deutsches Evangelisches Institut für Altertumswissenschaft des Heiligen Landes zu Jerusalem, and editor of its valuable *Palästinajahrbuch*, 1905–26, was widely known for his expertness in *Judaica* and his Palestine research. Books translated into English include his *Words of Jesus*, 1902; *Jesus: Jeshua*, 1939; *Sacred Sites and Ways*, 1935. He did not venture much into Biblical criticism, but the lecture here summarized reveals his attitude.

⁵ R. Kittel, *Zur Theologie des Alten Testaments*, 1899. As Professor at Leipzig he played an important role. His *Biblia Hebraica*, 1906, 3rd edn., 1937, (carried through by P. Kahle, A. Alt and O. Eissfeldt) has been a great boon to all students of the Old Testament. His great opus, *Geschichte des Volkes Israel*, 3 vols., (vol. I and II, 6th edn., 1923–25), is still valuable (notably vol. III, 1927–29). An early form of his work, *Geschichte der Hebräer*, 2 vols., 1888–92, was translated as *History of the Hebrews*, 1895. His *Great Men and Movements in Israel*, 1929, tr. by C. A. Knoch and C. D. Wright, is a noble book. His *Die alttestamentliche Wissenschaft in ihren wichtigsten Ergebnissen*, 1910, 4th edn., 1921, was a useful popularization. His commentary on the Psalms (1914) is one of the best.

⁶ E. Kautzsch, *Die bleibende Bedeutung des Alten Testaments*, 1902. Professor at Halle, he did yeoman service through his continued revisions of Gesenius' Hebrew grammar (the 28th edn., 1909, was translated by A. E. Cowley, 1910). The great annotated Old Testament that he edited, *Die Heilige Schrift des Alten Testaments*, 2 vols., 3rd edn., 1909; 4th edn. by A. Bertholet, 1923, has been one of the most useful tools available for the study of the Old Testament.

⁷ J. Koeberle, *Die alttestamentliche Offenbarung*, 1908. While not so widely known he contributed in an able manner to the study of Old Testament theology in special monographs. On our theme see further his *Heilsgeschichtliche und religionsgeschichtliche Betrachtungsweise des Alten Testaments*, 1906.

⁸ S. Oettli, conservative Swiss scholar, Professor at Greifswald and author of numerous commentaries and monographs, wrote on our subject: *Die Autorität des Alten Testaments*, 1906, (*Biblische Zeit und Streitfragen*, II, 2). F. Wilke, *Das Alte Testament und der Christliche Glaube*, 1911, likewise deserves mention. The author was Professor in Vienna.

⁹ H. Gunkel, "Was bleibt vom Alten Testament?" in *Reden und Aufsätze*, (E.T. by A. K. Dallas, *What Remains of the Old Testament?* 1928.) The author, Professor in Giessen, was doubtless the most important Old Testament scholar since Wellhausen. He taught us how

to analyse and classify both Hebrew prose and poetry from the angle of the life-situations producing the varied forms of material and to discern the stylistic peculiarities. His commentaries on Genesis and on the Psalms were masterpieces.

[10] E. von Dobschütz, "The Abandonment of the Canonical Idea", *American Journal of Theology*, XIX, 1915, 416 f. Professor at Halle, he was one of the best of New Testament exegetes.

[11] G. Adam Smith, *The Higher Criticism and The Preaching of the Old Testament*, 1901. No one since Ewald has been able to make the Old Testament as inspiring as did Smith. His books on the prophets, in particular, have been invaluable to students. His *Historical Geography of the Holy Land*, 1901, and his *Historical Atlas of the Geography of the Holy Land*, 1915, were great contributions to biblical study. He was Professor in the Free Church College at Glasgow.

[12] J. E. McFadyen, *Old Testament Criticism and the Christian Church*, 1903. He was Professor in Trinity College, Glasgow; his book on *The Message of Israel*, 1931, deserves mention here.

[13] J. Orr, *The Problem of the Old Testament*, 1906. Professor in Glasgow, his field was Systematic theology, particularly Apologetics. He introduced Ritschl's theology into the English scene.

[14] C. F. Kent, *Origin and Permanent Value of the Old Testament*, 1912. Professor at the Yale Divinity School and an indefatigable worker in disseminating modern Old Testament knowledge. His most ambitious undertaking was *The Historical Bible*, 6 vols., 1908–16.

[15] K. Fullerton, *Prophecy and Authority*, 1919. Fullerton was Professor at Oberlin, Ohio. His exegetical papers in various Journals are monuments of painstaking thoroughness and critical acumen.

[16] W. Rauschenbusch, *Christianity and the Social Crisis*, 1907. His ministry among working people in New York City gave him an insight into this crisis. He became Professor in the Rochester Theological Seminary and attained a large influence.

Chapter Ten

Harnack and Delitzsch

[1] A. von Harnack, *Entstehung und Entwicklung der Kirchenverfassung und des Kirchenrechts in den zwei ersten Jahrhunderten*, 1910, 3. In speaking of a boyhood incident he recalls a quotation from the Apocrypha (Wisdom of Sol. 1:7) that influenced his whole life (*ibid.*, 4); testimony of the Holy Spirit for the Catholic Bible?

[2] A. von Harnack, *Marcion*, 253 f. See also his paper, "Die Neuheit des Evangeliums nach Marcion", *Reden und Aufsätze*, V, 1930, 128 f.

[3] F. Delitzsch, *Die grosse Täuschung*, 2 vols., 1920–21. The foreword of vol. I is dated 1914.

[4] I, 70 f.

[5] II, 18 f.

[6] II, 21, 38 f.

[7] II, 52.

[8] II, 53 f. Not all will agree with this. See W. F. Albright, "The Biblical Period", in *The Jews; their History, Culture and Religion*, ed. L. Finkelstein, 1950, 61.

[7] Josephus, *Antiquities*, XII, 318. Cf. Delitzsch, II, 62.

[10] II Macc. 12: 29–31.

[11] II, 67.

[12] I, 94.

[13] There was thus poetic justice in the fact that his Hebrew lexicon, which (as one of his American students told me) was complete to the last dot on the i, remained unpublished. His *Prolegomena eines neuen Hebräisch-aramäischen Wörterbuchs zum Alten Testament*, 1886, shows that its preparation was the work of many years.

[14] In effect this has meanwhile come to be the situation in most American theological schools, largely because Greek (which has dropped out of general education), is still insisted on, and because of all the new subjects now held more useful.

Chapter Eleven

Systematic Theology and the Old Testament after 1918

[1] See H. R. Mackintosh, *Types of Theology*, 1937, 218 f. on Kierkegaard.

[2] Barth, a Swiss clergyman, burst on the scene with his *Der Römerbrief*, 1919 (E.T. by E. C. Hoskyns, *The Epistle to the Romans*, 1933). Here again was a theologizing exegesis such as had hardly been seen since Luther's *Galaterbrief*. From the standpoint of historical exegesis it was vulnerable; cf. E. von Dobschütz, *Vom Auslegen des Neuen Testaments*, 1927, 50. But the new generation wanted something different from the husks of philology and historicism. Hence the wide acclaim it received. Barth became Professor at Basel. His subsequent theological works show the metamorphosis of a prophet into a theologian of the Church (more particularly of the Reformed Church).

[3] See Barth, *Das Wort Gottes und die Theologie*, 1924, 167 f.

[4] W. Wiesner, *Das Offenbarungsproblem in der dialektischen Theologie*, 1930, 45, a most helpful and clarifying discussion of Dialectical theology from an angle close to our present concern.

[5] Barth, *Die Lehre vom Wort Gottes. Prolegomena zur Christlichen Dogmatik*, 1927, 236. (E.T. by G. T. Thomson, *The Doctrine of the Word of God*, 1936.)

[6] Wiesner, *op. cit.*, 45.

[7] Barth, *op. cit.*, 39.

[8] *Ibid.*, 334 f.

[9] *Ibid.*, 339.

[10] *Ibid.*, 355.

[11] *Ibid.*, 361.

[12] Wiesner, *op. cit.*, 107 f.

[13] We need only mention here his *Der evangelische Glaube und das Denken der Gegenwart*, 3 vols., 1931 f.

[14] Heim, *Die Weltanschauung der Bibel*, 1920.

[15] R. Otto, *Das Heilige*, 1917 (21–22 edn., 1932). E.T. by J. W. Harvey, *The Idea of the Holy*, 1936. See also his *Religious Essays. A Supplement to The Idea of the Holy*, tr. by B. Lunn, 1931, and *The Kingdom of God and the Son of Man*, E. T. Lutterworth Press, 1938. Otto was Professor in Marburg.

[16] We mention only G. Wobbermin, *Systematische Theologie nach religionspsychologischer Methode*, 3 vols., 1913–25.

[17] Compare K. Girgensohn, *Grundriss der Dogmatik*, 1924. He was Professor at Leipzig; an early death cut short his career. His brochure *Die geschichtliche Offenbarung* in *Biblische Zeit und Streitfragen*, V, 12, 1910, is well worth reading.

[18] In *Greifswalder Reformgedanken zum theologischen Studium*, 1922, 88 f. A large literature was elicited thereby. A very full report will be found in A. Wendel, *Religionswissenschaftliche und theologische Auslegung des Alten Testaments*, 1938.

[19] See H. Gunkel, *Ausgewählte Psalmen*, 4th edn., 1917, and A. Weiser, *Die Psalmen ausgewählt, übersetzt und erklärt*, 1935.

[20] P. Tillich, "Die Idee der Offenbarung", *Zeitschrift für Theologie und Kirche*, 1927, 27 f. Tillich became Professor in Frankfurt in the philosophical field and later came to the United States, to Union Theological Seminary. His current views on revelation, as expressed in his *Systematic Theology*, I, 1950, 106 f., suggest influence on his thinking by the American emphasis on the Old Testament heritage.

[21] See his *Kirche und Kultur*, 1924, (*Sammlung gemeinverständlicher Vorträge*, III).

[22] See his *Das Dämonische, Ein Beitrag zur Sinndeutung der Geschichte*, 1926 (same series, 119). This term goes back to Goethe, *Dichtung und Wahrheit*, IV, 20. It is used by Tillich as a symbol of the uncanny, potent, destructive capacity. Goethe saw it in the personality of a man like Napoleon.

[23] Tillich, *Kairos, Zur Geisteslage und Geistesbewegung*, 1926.

[24] Tillich, *Religiöse Verwirklichung*, 1926.

[25] F. Kattenbusch, *Die Deutsche evangelische Theologie seit Schleiermacher* (Part I, 1917); Part II, *Zeitenwende auch in der Theologie*, 1934.

Chapter Twelve

Apologetic of the 'Twenties and 'Thirties

[1] Eissfeldt, "Christentum und Altes Testament", in *Adolf von Harnack zum 70. Geburtstag*, 1921, 29 f. (Reprint from *Kartellzeitung des Eisenacher Kartells*.) Professor at Halle. Cf. n.20.

[2] E. Sellin, *Das Alte Testament und die evangelische Kirche der Gegenwart*, 1921. The author, Professor at the University of Berlin, edited the *Kommentar zum Alten Testament* series, intended as a conservative counterpart to the two great liberal series, the *Göttinger Handkommentar* edited by W. Nowack and the *Kurzer Handcommentar*, edited by K. Marti. The undertaking demonstrated that there was little difference between conservatives and liberals in higher criticism. Sellin's contributions to Old Testament scholarship were many, and he was a pioneer in organizing excavations in Palestine. See below, chapter 17, on his Old Testament Theology. His *Introduction to the Old Testament*, tr. by G. W. Montgomery, 1923, is well known.

[3] F. Baumgärtel, *Die Bedeutung des Alten Testaments für den Christen*, 1925, deserves a résumé here, but may be passed by, as his more recent views will be dealt with later.

[4] R. H. Kennett, "The Contribution of the Old Testament to the Religious Development of Mankind", in *The People and the Book*, ed. A. S. Peake, 1925, 383 f. He was Professor at Cambridge. He wrote some excellent scholarly books and was a keen critic.

[5] G. H. Box, "The Significance of the Old Testament in Relation to the New", *ibid.*, 433 f. Box was Professor in King's College, London. He wrote both in the field of Old Testament and of Judaism.

[6] G. Adam Smith, "The Hebrew Genius as Exhibited in the Old Testament" in *The Legacy of Israel*, ed. I. Abrams, A. A. Bevan, S. Singer, 1927. On Smith cf. above, chapter 9. The topic here dealt with received more detailed treatment by the American scholar (Professor in Hartford and noted for his knowledge of Islam), D. B. Macdonald, *The Hebrew Literary Genius*, 1933, and *The Hebrew Philosophical Genius; A Vindication*, 1936.

[7] F. C. Burkitt, "The Debt of Christianity to Judaism", *The Legacy of Israel*, 69 f. Professor at Cambridge, he contributed notably to the study of early Christian literature, especially the Syriac.

[8] C. G. Montefiore, *ibid.* Cf. also his essay "The Old Testament and Judaism", in *Record and Revelation*, ed. H. W. Robinson, 1938.

[9] A. S. Peake, "The Permanent Value of the Old Testament", in his *The Servant of Yahweh*, 1931. Peake had already discussed the biblical problem in his *The Bible, its Origin, its Significance and its Abiding Worth*, 1913, and *The Nature of Scripture*, 1922. He was Professor in Manchester and wrote some excellent commentaries.

[10] J. Meinhold, *Altes Testament und Evangelisches Christentum*, 1931. The author was Professor at Bonn. He wrote some excellent scholarly books; he had already clashed with ecclesiastical authorities in 1896 by his *Jesus und das Alte Testament*.

[11] J. Hempel, *Das Alte Testament und die Geschichte*, 1930, 73 f. Professor at Göttingen before the late war. Hempel was editor of the *Zeitschrift für alttestamentliche Wissenschaft* and his contributions to Old Testament scholarship are many. He analysed the religious

developments in Israel with a discernment for underlying forces and movements such as was demonstrated in other fields by a man like W. Dilthey. At the same time he is a master of criticism and at home, too, in Palestinian archæology. His *Die althebräische Literaturgeschichte*, 1930, is particularly useful.

[12] Hempel, "The Religious Value of the Old Testament", a lecture given in the U.S. and published there in *The Lutheran Church Quarterly*, 1933, 335 f.

[13] E. Brunner, "Die Bedeutung des Alten Testaments für unseren Glauben", *Zwischen den Zeiten*, 1930, 30 f. The author, second only to Barth among the Dialectic theologians, formerly Professor in Zürich, is now Professor at the International Christian University, Tokyo, Japan. It is needless to go into his general position, on which cf. Wiesner, *Das Offenbarungsproblem in der dialektischen Theologie*, 39 f., or to list here his large output in the field of Systematic theology. E.T. Lutterworth (London), Westminster (Philadelphia).

[14] In his lecture *Die Unentbehrlichkeit des Alten Testaments für die missionierende Kirche*, 1934, he stresses the importance of the Old Testament so sharply as to assert that as certainly as the Church can no longer be the Church without Jesus Christ, so little can it be the Church without the Old Testament.

[15] O. Procksch, "Die kirchliche Bedeutung des Alten Testaments", *Neue Kirchliche Zeitschrift*, 1931, 295 f. Professor in Greifswald, Procksch had conservative leanings. He wrote important books in the Old Testament field. On his posthumously published Theology of the Old Testament see chapter 17, n. 19. On Girgensohn cf. chapter 11, n. 17.

[16] Procksch, "Pneumatische Exegese", *Christentum und Wissenschaft*, I, 1925, 145 f. See also his "Ziele und Grenzen der Exegese", *Neue Kirchliche Zeitschrift*, 1925, 485 f.

[17] J. Hänel, *Das Wort Gottes und das Alte Testament*, 1932. A Professor at Münster, he has contributed some worth-while work to biblical scholarship. In the wake of Otto's ideas he wrote *Die Religion der Heiligkeit*, 1931.

[18] V. Herntrich, *Völkische Religion und Altes Testament*, 1933. He contributed a book on Ezekiel in 1932. Professor in Hamburg.

[19] A. Alt, J. Begrich, G. von Rad, *Führung zum Christentum durch das Alte Testament*, 1934. Alt, Professor at Leipzig, is one of the foremost experts in historical-geographical research concerning ancient Palestine. J. Begrich had high attainments, notably in the study of Hebrew history and in pursuing Gunkel's line of research further; it is a source of regret that he was drafted into the army and killed in the Italian campaign. G. von Rad, Professor at Göttingen, has produced some important works on Pentateuchal criticism. On his views on Old Testament theology, see p. 278 f.

[20] O. Eissfeldt, *Einleitung in das Alte Testament*, 1934. One of the leading Old Testament scholars, with great achievements notably in literary criticism and in the field of Semitic Religion (i.e., the religions

represented by the inscriptions of Phœnicians and other Syrian peoples), therein continuing the labours of W. W. von Baudissin.

[21] Eissfeldt, "Geschichtliches und Übergeschichtliches", *Theologische Studien und Kritiken*, CIX, 1947, 37 f.

[22] R. Press, "Das Alte Testament als Wort Gottes", *Theologische Blätter*, 1934, 224 f. A clergyman, who has written some excellent scholarly articles.

[23] P. Volz, "Das Alte Testament und unsere Predigt", *Luthertum*, 1937, 326 f. Volz was Professor at Tübingen and wrote some important books. His Commentary on Deutero-Isaiah in Sellin's series is particularly noteworthy.

[24] G. R. Berry, "The Old Testament: A Liability or an Asset?" *Colgate Rochester Divinity School Bulletin*, 1930, 8 f. A Professor in that Baptist institution, Berry was quite radical as an Old Testament critic.

[25] J. A. Bewer, "The Christian Minister and the Old Testament", *Journal of Religion*, 1930, 16 f. He was Professor at Union Theological Seminary in New York and combined a critical attitude with deep piety. His *Literature of the Old Testament*, 1922, is the leading *Literaturgeschichte* on this subject in English, and has been widely used for a generation. His *Annotations on the Prophets* in the *Harper's Annotated Bible Series* promise to be very useful for years to come.

[26] "The Authority of the Old Testament", *ibid.*, 1936, 1 f.

[27] W. F. Lofthouse, "The Old Testament and Christianity", in *Record and Revelation*, edited by H. W. Robinson, 1938, 458 f. Formerly Principal of Handsworth College, Birmingham, he has written scholarly papers and contributed a volume to the Clarendon Bible.

[28] H. W. Robinson, "The Philosophy of Revelation", *ibid.*, 303 f. This gives his thought *in nuce*. See also his *Inspiration and Revelation in the Old Testament*, 1946; *Redemption and Revelation*, 1942. He was Principal of Regent's Park College, Oxford. His output was large and not confined to the Old Testament field.

[29] E. G. Kraeling, *The Book of the Ways of God*, 1938, (1939 in the American edition). The author was active both as clergyman and teacher; in the latter capacity he taught Old Testament at Union Theological Seminary and for some years also Semitic Languages at Columbia University. He recently published the oldest find of Aramaic papyri from the Jewish colony at Elephantine, *The Brooklyn Museum Aramaic Papyri*, 1953.

Chapter Thirteen
The Revival of the New Testament Approach

[1] A spokesman of dissatisfaction with biblical exegesis as carried on by Old Testament scholars was the clergyman C. Cramer. His book, *Amos, Versuch einer theologischen Interpretation*, 1930, assails

the emphasis placed on the personalities of the prophets and would understand them and their message entirely from the doctrine of the divine election of Israel. But that, too, is historicism and gives the Old Testament no immediate significance for us. Subsequently he followed Vischer's line. See also his "Hegel oder Herder oder——", *Theologische Blätter*, 1932, 140 f. H. Hellbardt, "Die Auslegung des Alten Testaments als theologische Disziplin", *ibid.*, 1937, 129 f., holds Christ contained in the Old Testament as in consubstantiation. See Eichrodt's criticism of this in "Zur Frage der theologischen Exegese des Alten Testaments", *ibid.*, 1931, 73 f.

[2] W. Vischer, "Das Alte Testament und die Verkündigung", *Theologische Blätter*, 1931, 1 f. See his earlier "Das Alte Testament als Wort Gottes", *Zwischen den Zeiten*, 1927, 379 f. *Die Bedeutung des Alten Testaments für das Christliche Leben*, 2nd edn., 1927.

[3] Vischer, *Das Christuszeugnis des Alten Testaments*. I, *Das Gesetz*, 1934 (E.T. by A. B. Crabtree, *The Witness of the Old Testament to Christ*, 1949). II, *Die Propheten*, 1942. Vol. III is still due.

[4] Separate themes from the Pentateuch were treated in his *Jahweh der Gott Kains*, 1929; "Der Gott Abrahams, Isaaks und Jakobs", *Zwischen den Zeiten*, 1930.

[5] A separate theme from "the Prophets" was treated in "Der Gottesknecht", *Jahrbuch der Theologischen Schule zu Bethel*, 1930.

[6] Separate subjects from "the Writings" were *Esther*, 1937 (in *Theologische Existenz Heute*, no. 48) and *Hiob, ein Zeuge Jesu Christi*, 5th edn., 1942.

[7] R. Abramowski, "Vom Streit um das Alte Testament", *Theologische Rundschau*, 1947, 65 f.

[8] For a critique see G. von Rad, "Das Christuszeugnis des Alten Testaments", *Theologische Blätter*, 1935, 249 f.; also the valuable remarks of Baumgärtel, p. 91 f. of the work mentioned below, note 32 to chapter 17.

Chapter Fourteen

The Old Testament and the Existential Question

[1] Cf. W. Wiesner, *Der Offenbarungsbegriff in der dialektischen Theologie*, 76 f.

[2] E. Grisebach, *Erkenntnis und Glaube*, 1923.

[3] M. Heidegger, *Sein und Zeit*, I, 1927.

[4] F. Gogarten, *Glaube und Wirklichkeit*, 1928. Gogarten was Professor in Breslau.

[5] Gogarten, "Einheit von Evangelium und Volkstum", *Deutsche Theologie*, 1933.

[6] Gogarten, "Ist Volksgesetz Gottesgesetz?" *ibid.*, 1934.

[7] R. Bultmann, "Die Bedeutung des Alten Testaments für den Christlichen Glauben", *Glauben und Verstehen. Gesammelte Aufsätze*, 1933. The author was one of the most radical New Testament

critics; his *Geschichte der Synoptischen Tradition*, 1921, was particularly important. Professor at Marburg, he has recently become
a storm centre of discussion through his "Das Problem der Entmy-
thologisirung der Neutestamentlichen Verkündigung", in his
Offenbarung und Heilsgeschehen, 1941; reprinted in *Kerygma und
Mythos; Diskussionen und Stimmen zum Problem der Entmytho-
gisirung*, ed. H. W. Bartsch, 2nd edn., 2 vols., 1951–52. A good
survey in A. N. Wilder, "Mythology and the New Testament",
Journal of Biblical Literature, LXIX, 1950, 113 f.

[8] Bultmann, "Ursprung und Sinn der Typologie als hermeneutische
Methode", *Theologische Literaturzeitung*, 1950, 205 f.

Chapter Fifteen
The Old Testament as Antithesis to Christianity

[1] E. Hirsch, *Das Alte Testament und die Predigt des Evangeliums*,
1936. The author was Professor in Göttingen prior to the late war.
He has published a great deal—most recently a *Geschichte der
neueren evangelischen Theologie*, 4 vols., 1949–52.

[2] See his *Christliche Freiheit und Politische Bindung*, 1935, 76 f.

[3] I have changed his terminology in the interest of lucidity in
English presentation; he speaks of *lex simplex* and *lex in lege*.

[4] See his *Luthers Deutsche Bibel*, 1928.

[5] His *Kierkegaardstudien*, 2 vols., 1933, show his interest in this
thinker.

[6] *Das vierte Evangelium*, 1936, 320 f.

[7] See above, p. 176.

[8] *Das Alte Testament*, 71 f.

[9] He gives the reference to Kierkegaard as *Papirer* 1/1 A 151
(1854).

[10] *Pap.* 11/1 A 184 (1854).

[11] For a criticism from this angle see G. von Rad, "Gesetz und
Evangelium im alten Testament", *Theologische Blätter*, 1937, 41 f.;
J. Hempel, *Zeitschrift für die alttestamentliche Wissenschaft*, LIV,
1936, 298 f.

Chapter Sixteen
Recent Discussions

[1] W. F. Albright, *From the Stone Age to Christianity*, 1940. The
author, Professor at John Hopkins University in Baltimore, is the
most versatile Orientalist of our time and has played a great role as
a pioneer of truly scientific Palestinian archæology. (See his Pelican
Book, *The Archæology of Palestine*, 1949.) He edits the *Bulletin of
the American Schools of Oriental Research*.

[2] R. H. Pfeiffer, *Introduction to the Old Testament*, 1940, the most
detailed modern work of its kind and bibliographically the most

informative. The author, who teaches at Harvard, is a keen Old Testament critic and has achievements in Assyriology to his credit as well.

[3] H. F. D. Sparks, *The Old Testament in the Christian Church*, 1944. The author is a Professor at Oxford University.

[4] H. H. Rowley, *The Relevance of the Bible*, 1942. The author is a Professor at Manchester University and one of the most learned and productive of Old Testament scholars. He is a prime mover in international co-operation and understanding on the part of men engaged in Old Testament study, and edits the valuable Book List put out annually by the *Society for Old Testament Study*.

[5] See further his *The Rediscovery of the Old Testament*, 1946; *The Relevance of Apocalyptic*, 1944.

[6] *The Authority of the Bible*, 1949 (Joseph Smith Lecture); *The Unity of the Bible*, 1953.

[7] *The Unity of the Bible*, 1953.

[8] R. B. Y. Scott, *The Relevance of the Prophets*, 1944. The author is Professor at McGill University, Montreal.

[9] G. E. Wright, *The Challenge of Israel's Faith*, 1944. See further, chapter 17. The author, noted for his work in Palestinian archæology and geography, is Professor at the McCormick Theological Seminary in Chicago. He edits the *Biblical Archæologist*, a publication of the American Schools of Oriental Research that does much to disseminate knowledge about recent discoveries. Of other pertinent studies by Wright we may mention here his *The Old Testament Against its Environment*, 1950; his lecture *The Old Testament; Impediment or Bulwark of the Christian Faith*, 1945; also his article, "Interpreting the Old Testament", *Theology Today*, III, 1946, 176 f.

[10] M. Burrows, *Outline of Biblical Theology*, 1946 (see further, chapter 17). The author is Professor at Yale; his role in obtaining permission to publish the Dead Sea scrolls and in editing them so promptly deserves particular mention.

[11] A. G. Hebert, *The Authority of the Old Testament*, 1947; *The Throne of David, A Study of the Fulfilment of the Old Testament in Christ and his Church*, 1941. The author was Professor of New Testament at Kelham (Newark).

[12] C. H. Dodd, *The Bible Today*, 1946. The author was Professor at Cambridge and is a New Testament scholar of high rank, with many publications to his credit. He had already written a book on the Biblical problem, *The Authority of the Bible*, 1928, 3rd edn., 1952.

[13] S. A. Cook, *The Rebirth of Christianity*, 1942; see earlier his *The "Truth" of the Bible*, 1938. Professor at Cambridge, he was a master scholar of the school devoted to historical and comparative religious study. His *The Old Testament; A Reinterpretation*, 1936, presents the modern critical view afresh.

[14] I. G. Matthews, *The Religious Pilgrimage of Israel*, 1947. The author was Professor at Crozer Theological Seminary, and has a humanistic approach.

[15] H. Cunliffe Jones, *The Authority of the Biblical Revelation*, 1946. W. J. Phythian Adams, *The People and the Presence*, 1942. G. E. Phillips, *The Old Testament in the World Church*, 1942. C. R. North, *The Old Testament Interpretation of History*, 1946. J. Woods, *The Old Testament in the Church*, 1949. W. A. C. Elmslie, *How Came our Faith*, 1948. W. A. Smart, *Still the Bible Speaks*, 1948. *Biblical Authority To-day*, ed. A. Richardson and W. Schweitzer, 1951.

[16] G. von Rad, "Typologische Auslegung des Alten Testaments"; W. Zimmerli, "Verheissung und Erfüllung", in a discussion of principles for a projected new Commentary series, *Evangelische Theologie*, XII, 1952–53, nos. 1/2. See the critique of both contributions by Baumgärtel in the work to be cited, chapter 17 n. 32, p. 106 f. On typology see J. Daniélou, *Sacramentum futuri; Études sur les origines de la typologie biblique*, 1950.

[17] Two noteworthy studies from the German quarter are K. Elliger, *Die Bedeutung der Geschichte Israels für die Kirche Jesu Christi*, 1948, and H. W. Hertzberg, *Werdende Kirche im Alten Testament*, 1950.

Chapter Seventeen

Toward a Biblical Theology?

[1] On the origin of this discipline see above, p. 56.

[2] B. Stade, "Über die Aufgaben der biblischen Theologie des Alten Testaments", *Zeitschrift für Theologie und Kirche*, III, 1893, 30 f. Reprinted in his *Akademische Abhandlungen*, 2nd edn., 1907, 77 f. Stade was Professor in Giessen, founder of the leading Old Testament journal, the *Zeitschrift für die alttestamentliche Wissenschaft*. See on him Gunkel, "Bernhard Stade", in his *Reden und Aufsätze*.

[3] B. Stade, *Biblische Theologie des Alten Testaments*, I, 1905; Vol. II, *Die Jüdische Religion von der Zeit Esras bis zum Zeitalter Christi*, 1911, was done by A. Bertholet.

[4] E. Kautzsch, *Biblische Theologie des Alten Testaments*, 1911 (As *The Religion of Israel* it appeared in the Extra Volume of Hastings, *Dictionary of the Bible*, 1904, 612 f.). B. Duhm's noteworthy *Theologie der Propheten*, 1875, also used "Theology" in this manner.

[5] *Die Religion in Geschichte und Gegenwart*, 2nd edn., I, 1089 f. art. *Biblische Theologie und Biblische Religionsgeschichte*).

[6] C. Steuernagel, "Alttestamentliche Theologie und alttestamentliche Religionsgeschichte", *Vom Alten Testament; Festschrift Karl Marti*, ed. K. Budde, 1925, 266 f. He was Professor in Breslau.

[7] O. Eissfeldt, "Israelitisch-jüdische Religionsgeschichte und alttestamentliche Theologie", *Zeitschrift für die alttestamentliche Wissenschaft*, XLIV, 1926, 1 f.

[8] W. Eichrodt, "Hat die alttestamentliche Theologie noch selbständige Bedeutung in der alttestamentlichen Wissenschaft?" *ibid.*, XLVII, 1929, 83 f.

[9] W. Staerk, "Religionsgeschichte und Religionsphilosophie in ihrer Bedeutung für die biblische Theologie des Alten Testaments", *Zeitschrift für Theologie und Kirche*, N.F., IV, 1923, 289 f.

[10] G. van der Leeuw, *Phänomenologie der Religion*, 1935.

[11] F. Baumgärtel, *Die Eigenart der alttestamentlichen Frömmigkeit*, 1932.

[12] J. Lindblom, "Zur Frage der Eigenart der alttestamentlichen Religion", in *Werden und Wesen des Alten Testaments*, ed. P. Volz, F. Stummer, J. Hempel, 1936, 128 f.

[13] A. Weiser, "Die Theologische Aufgabe der alttestamentlichen Wissenschaft", *ibid.*, 207 f.

[14] Weiser, "Vom Verständnis des Alten Testaments", *Zeitschrift für die alttestamentliche Wissenschaft*, LXI, 1945–48, 17 f.

[15] Mention should be made of E. Koenig, *Theologie des Alten Testaments*, 1922, a work of conservative character with too much space expended on rebuttal of loose statements or extreme views of other scholars. He also wrote a *Geschichte der alttestamentlichen Religion*, 1912. On him see chapter 9, n. 1.

[16] E. Sellin, *Theologie des Alten Testaments*, 2 vols., 1933. On him see chapter 12, n. 2.

[17] L. Köhler, *Theologie des Alten Testaments*, 1936 (3rd edn., 1953). E.T. in preparation, Lutterworth Press, 1955. Professor in Zürich. His new Hebrew Dictionary (with Aramaic supplement by W. Baumgartner), providing both English and German renderings, will prove a useful tool for students and scholars.

[18] W. Eichrodt, *Theologie des Alten Testaments*, 3 vols., 1933–38. The author is Professor in Basel. He has written numerous papers bearing on the theological theme, beginning with *Ist die altisraelitische Nationalreligion Offenbarungsreligion?* 1925. See now his *Man in the Old Testament*, tr. by K. and R. Gregor Smith, 1951.

[19] O. Procksch, *Theologie des Alten Testaments*, 1950. On him cf. chapter 12, n. 15. His paper "Geschichte als Glaubensinhalt", *Neue Kirchliche Zeitschrift*, 1925, 485 f. also merits attention.

[20] M. Burrows, *An Outline of Biblical Theology*, 1946. See above, p. 260 f.

[21] G. Bertram, "Die Aufgabe einer Theologie beider Testamente", *Kirche im Angriff*, XII, 1936, 416 f. He is Professor in Jena.

[22] O. J. Baab, *Theology of the Old Testament*, 1949. The author is Professor at the Garrett Biblical Institute, Evanston, Ill., U.S.A. Cf. also his article "Old Testament Theology: its Possibility and Methodology", in *The Study of the Bible Today and Tomorrow* ed. by H. R. Willoughby, 1947, 401 f.

[23] Mention should be made here of N. H. Snaith, *The Distinctive Ideas of the Old Testament*, 1950. H. W. Robinson's discussion, "The Characteristic Doctrines", in *Record and Revelation*, 321 f., should likewise not be overlooked. His other essay in that volume was outlined above, p. 216.

[24] R. C. Dentan, *Preface to Old Testament Theology*, 1950. He is

Professor at the Berkeley Divinity School in New Haven, Conn., U.S.A.

[25] N. W. Porteous, "Old Testament Theology", in *The Old Testament and Modern Study*, ed. H. H. Rowley, 1951, 311 f. He is Professor at the University of Edinburgh.

[26] G. von Rad, "Grundprobleme einer biblischen Theologie des alten Testaments", *Theologische Literaturzeitung*, 1943, 226 f. In connection with the idea of history emphasized by von Rad, cf. M. Noth, *Geschichte und Gotteswort im Alten Testament*, 1950 (E.T. in Bulletin of the John Rylands Library, March, 1950). The author is one of the leading Old Testament scholars of our time. The paper shows from the historical side how difficult is the theological task.

[27] von Rad, "Das Problem des alttestamentlichen Schöpfungsglaubens", *Werden und Wesen des Alten Testaments*, 138 f. The study referred to is *Das formgeschichtliche Problem des Hexateuchs*, 1938.

[28] G. E. Wright, *The Challenge of Israel's Faith* (see chapter 16, n. 9).

[29] Wright, *God who Acts; Biblical Theology as Recital*, 1952.

[30] C. H. Dodd, *The Apostolic Preaching and its Developments*, 1936.

[31] H. H. Rowley, "The Unity of the Old Testament", *Bulletin of the John Rylands Library*, XXIX, 1946, No. 2; *The Unity of the Bible*, 1953 (cf. above chapter 16, n. 4).

[32] F. Baumgärtel, *Verheissung. Zur Frage des evangelischen Verständnisses des Alten Testaments*, 1952. Also his related paper "Das alttestamentliche Geschehen als heilsgeschichtliches Geschehen", in *Geschichte und Altes Testament, Albrecht Alt zum 70 Geburtstag*, 1953, 13 f. For his antithesis to von Rad see his "Der Dissensus im Verständnis des Alten Testaments", *Evangelische Theologie*, 1954, 298 f. This scholar is Professor at Erlangen and wrote a valuable study on Job. Cf. also n. 11 above.

[33] We may note in passing that the Systematic theological discussion of H. Richard Niebuhr, *The Meaning of Revelation*, 1941, also stresses "internal history", "where value does not mean strength as in external history, but quality, and time is not quantitative but organic and social, so that what is past is not gone but abides in us as our memory and what is future is not non-existent but already present in us as our potentiality".

[34] F. Baumgärtel, "Erwägungen zur Darstellung der Theologie des Alten Testaments", *Theologische Literaturzeitung*, 1951, 258 f.

[35] H. Stephan, *Geschichte der evangelischen Theologie seit dem Deutschen Idealismus*, 1938, 328.

INDEX

SUBJECTS

Subjects cont.

Subjects cont.

Subjects cont.

NAMES*

*Except those of Antiquity, which are in the Index of Subjects.

Names cont.

Names cont.

SCRIPTURE PASSAGES

Scripture passages cont.